T0331941

Labour Markets in Low-Income Countries

Labour Markets in Low-Income Countries

Challenges and Opportunities

DAVID LAM

and

AHMED ELSAYED

OXFORD
UNIVERSITY PRESS

OXFORD
UNIVERSITY PRESS

Great Clarendon Street, Oxford, OX2 6DP,
United Kingdom

Oxford University Press is a department of the University of Oxford.
It furthers the University's objective of excellence in research, scholarship,
and education by publishing worldwide. Oxford is a registered trade mark of
Oxford University Press in the UK and in certain other countries

© David Lam and Ahmed Elsayed, 2022

The moral rights of the authors have been asserted

Impression: 1

Published in the United States of America by Oxford University Press
198 Madison Avenue, New York, NY 10016, United States of America

British Library Cataloguing in Publication Data

Data available

Library of Congress Control Number: 2021939919

ISBN 978–0–19–289710–7

DOI: 10.1093/oso/9780192897107.001.0001

Printed and bound by
CPI Group (UK) Ltd, Croydon, CR0 4YY

Links to third-party websites are provided by Oxford in good faith and
for information only. Oxford disclaims any responsibility for the materials
contained in any third party website referenced in this work.

Preface

This volume draws on the expertise of dedicated international researchers who have collaborated with the IZA – Institute of Labor Economics and the UK Foreign, Commonwealth and Development Office (FCDO, formerly the Department for International Development) to enhance our knowledge on how labour markets in low-income countries can contribute to fostering economic and social prosperity. Summarizing the main results from selected research projects under the umbrella of the Growth and Labour Markets in Low-Income Countries Programme (GLM|LIC) on behalf of the FCDO, this book also derives important lessons from the projects for labour market programmes and policies. We wish to thank all colleagues engaged in this ambitious project who have provided us with insightful studies on a broad variety of topics.

A wealth of promising new studies are yet to come as the IZA/FCDO initiative proceeds. To further underscore the eminent role of women in low-income countries' economies, the project has been renamed Gender, Growth, and Labour Markets in Low-Income Countries Programme (G^{2}LM|LIC). Providing additional insights on gender issues and the effects of the unprecedented COVID-19 pandemic on societal outcomes in the developing world, this new research shall be presented in a second volume of this important research programme.

This book would not have been possible without the untiring advice and support by our teams at IZA and FCDO. We are particularly indebted to Holger Hinte at IZA, who played a substantial role in organizing the content of the volume, writing the chapters, and distilling the key takeaways for the reader. He was supported by Mark Fallak and Götz Siedler in preparing and condensing the material for each chapter. Abigail Collins-Carey, Raka Datta, and Lionel Antonio Muñoz Rosas provided valuable comments on earlier drafts of the book. The views expressed in this volume are those of the authors and do not necessarily represent the opinions of FCDO or IZA.

Many wonderful colleagues have contributed to the success of the GLM|LIC initiative since its beginning in 2011 through consultancy, project coordination, administration, and event management. We would like to thank (in alphabetical order) Marco Caliendo, Martin T. Clemens, Peter Feinson, Corrado Giulietti, Viola Hartmann, Sven Kleinert, Benedetta Musillo, Maryam Naghsh Nejad, Janneke Pieters, John Piper, Hilmar Schneider, Dominik Spitza, Lydia Simons, Dawn Wood, and Klaus F. Zimmermann. We look forward to continuing this important joint venture and are grateful for the funding provided by the UK government.

The findings and insights presented here underscore that investing in development research can yield an important stimulus for sustainable development policies.

David Lam and Ahmed Elsayed
June 2021

Contents

List of Figures and Tables

Figures

Tables

1

Labour Markets in Low-Income Countries

Introduction and Demographic Background

Jobs are the key to economic growth and poverty reduction. The dramatic declines in poverty in the developing world in the last fifty years (World Bank 2020), a period in which world population increased by 4 billion (UNDESA 2019a), could not have occurred without rapid job creation. Whether the job is working as a subsistence farmer, engineer, schoolteacher, security guard, garment worker, government worker, or market vendor, earnings from labour provide support to most families in the world and determine whether they are able to meet their basic needs.

Employment and job creation are key components in achieving economic growth and sustainable development, particularly in low-income countries (LICs). Despite the importance of studying labour markets in LICs, and investigating which policies are more successful, the evidence remained, until recently, rather limited. Against this backdrop, the joint IZA/FCDO (German IZA – Institute of Labor Economics and the Foreign, Commonwealth, and Development Office) Growth and Labour Markets in Low-Income Countries (GLM|LIC) programme was established in 2011 after identifying an important research gap on labour markets and growth in LICs. The GLM|LIC programme has taken important steps to close this gap. The programme supported forty-three research projects until 2018. In addition to academic papers, the programme also produced policy briefs and synthesis papers that cover several aspects related to the challenges facing labour markets of these countries and the policies that are successful in addressing these challenges.

Starting from 2019, the focus of the programme is mainly on gender issues. Building on the success of GLM|LIC, a new programme, 'Gender, Growth and Labour Markets in Low-Income Countries' (G²LM|LIC), marks the extension of the successful IZA/FCDO cooperation and aims to foster research that guides future gender and labour market policies.

This book provides an in-depth discussion of the Growth and Labour Markets in Low-Income Countries Programme research findings and the policy lessons learned from its projects implemented across a diverse set of low-income countries. The book concentrates on giving the reader a clear picture of the structure

Labour Markets in Low-Income Countries. David Lam and Ahmed Elsayed, Oxford University Press.
© David Lam and Ahmed Elsayed (2022). DOI: 10.1093/oso/9780192897107.003.0001

of the labour markets in LICs, discusses the different policies, and investigates to what extent, and under what conditions, they could be successful.

1.1 Demographic Background of the Employment Challenge

Any discussion of labour markets in LICs must take into account the dramatic demographic changes that have affected the growth and composition of the working-age population around the world in recent decades. As shown in Lam, Leibbrandt, and Allen (2019), over 1 billion people will be added to the working-age population of the world between 2020 and 2050. About 70% of the additional working-age population will be in sub-Saharan Africa, a dramatic change from previous decades, when Asia accounted for most of the growth of the world's working-age population. This rapid growth of the working-age population will need to be met by equally rapid job creation if countries are to avoid rising unemployment.

Figure 1.1 shows the size of the working-age population (defined as ages 15–64, following standard international definitions) for the world and various regions from 1950 to 2100, based on the United Nations Population Division's estimates from 1950 to 2019 and projections from 2020 to 2100 (UNDESA 2019b). The figure shows the rapid growth of the working-age population that has occurred in recent decades. The working-age population of the world grew at an annual rate of over 2% per year in the 1970s and 1980s, doubling between 1970 and 2005—an addition of 2.1 billion in just thirty-five years. As discussed in Lee (2003), Lam (2011), and Lam, Leibbrandt, and Allen (2019), this period of rapid population growth was historically unprecedented. It was primarily the result of rapid declines in infant and child mortality in developing countries, which resulted in rapid population growth and young populations. Asia experienced very rapid growth of its working-age population, adding almost 1 billion people in just twenty-five years between 1970 and 1995. Growth at this speed requires 3.3 million new jobs every month merely to keep up with the expansion of the working-age population.

As seen in Figure 1.1, Eastern/Southeastern Asia (dominated by China) had one of the fastest-growing working-age populations in the world in the 1970s and 1980s, with growth reaching almost 3% per year. Due to rapid declines in birth rates, this rate of growth has fallen dramatically and is projected to become negative by 2027. Central/Southern Asia (dominated by India), with somewhat later and slower fertility decline, now has a faster-growing working-age population than Eastern/Southeastern Asia and is projected to overtake Eastern/Southeastern Asia in the size of the working-age population around 2040.

As seen in Figure 1.2, which shows each region's share of the global working-age population, Eastern/Southeastern Asia had well over a third of the world's

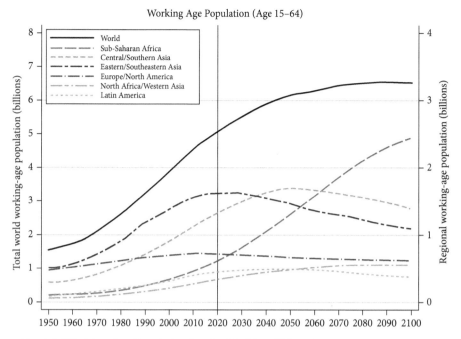

Fig. 1.1 Working-Age Population for the World and Major Regions, 1950–2100

Notes: Based on United Nations World Population Prospects 2019 Revision. Population estimates from 1950 to 2019. Medium variant population projections from 2020 to 2100. Regions are UN Sustainable Development Goal regions. For details see United Nations (2019b) and Lam, Leibbrandt, and Allen (2019).

working-age population in the 1990s, but its share has been falling and will continue to fall throughout the century. Sub-Saharan Africa, by contrast, accounted for less than 10% of the world's working-age population until around 2010, but its share will be rising rapidly in the coming decades. By 2050 it will have over 20% of the world's working-age population, projected to reach almost 40% in 2100. Sub-Saharan Africa's working-age population is projected to increase by 700 million between 2020 and 2050, more than doubling from 600 million to 1.3 billion.

Figure 1.3 shows the projected growth of the working-age population between 2020 and 2030 and between 2040 and 2050 in individual countries in sub-Saharan Africa, South Asia, and a group of comparison countries and regions. Note that most of the people included in these projections were already born in 2020, making the projections relatively insensitive to assumptions about fertility decline, the biggest source of uncertainty in demographic projections for this century (Lam, Leibbrandt, and Allen 2019). Niger, the country with the largest increase, will have a roughly 50% increase in its working-age population between 2020 and 2030. This is an increase of 5.8 million individuals, requiring the creation of almost

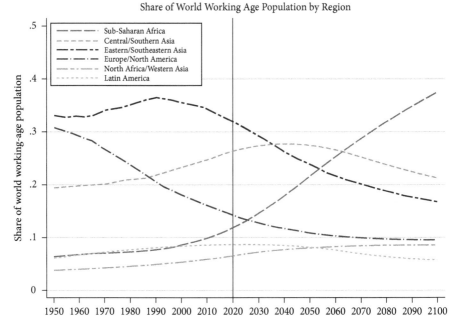

Fig. 1.2 Share of Global Working-Age Population by Region, 1950–2100

Notes: Based on United Nations World Population Prospects 2019 Revision. Population estimates from 1950 to 2019. Medium variant population projections from 2020 to 2100. Regions are UN Sustainable Development Goal regions. For details see United Nations (2019b) and Lam, Leibbrandt and Allen (2019).

50,000 new jobs per month in order to keep up with the growth of the working-age population. The percentage growth between 2040 and 2050 will be smaller, 43%, the delayed effect of modest declines in fertility in recent years, but the absolute increase between 2040 and 2050 will be higher—11.2 million working-age people. The general pattern in Figure 1.3 is that the growth rate of the working-age population will fall in every country and region shown between the 2020–30 decade and the 2040–50 decade. Growth rates will still be high in most African countries, however, with sub-Saharan Africa as a whole projected to have a 25% increase in its working-age population between 2040 and 2050, down from 34% between 2020 and 2030.

For sub-Saharan Africa as a whole, the working-age population will increase by 34% between 2020 and 2030—an addition of 205 million people. It will require 1.7 million jobs per month to keep up with this growth of the working-age population. Between 2040 and 2050, the working-age population will increase by 265 million, requiring 2.2 million jobs per month. Sub-Saharan Africa is projected to hit the milestone of needing 2 million jobs per month by 2037, with the number not falling below 2 million per month until 2075 based on UN projections. While

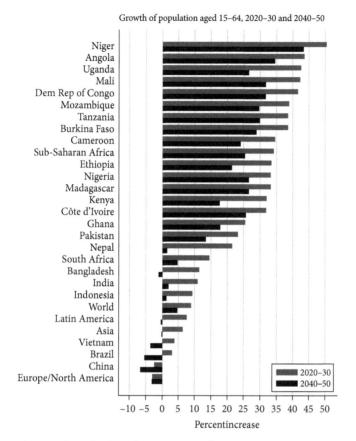

Growth of population aged 15–64, 2020–30 and 2040–50

Percentincrease

Fig. 1.3 Growth of Working-Age Population, 2020–30 and 2040–50, Selected Countries and Regions

Notes: Based on United Nations World Population Prospects 2019 Revision. Population estimates from 1950 to 2019. Medium variant population projections from 2020 to 2100. For details see United Nations (2019b) and Lam, Leibbrandt, and Allen (2019).

these numbers are staggering, it is important to keep in mind that the working-age population of Eastern/Southeastern Asia increased by more than 2 million per month from 1980 to 1990, reaching a high of 2.2 million per month. The growth rate of the working-age population of Eastern/Southeastern Asia reached about 2.9% per year in the 1980s. This is very similar to the 3% annual growth rate experienced by sub-Saharan Africa today, with the growth rate projected to decline slowly in coming decades. In other words, the demographic challenge facing sub-Saharan Africa's labour market is similar in both percentage growth and the absolute number of jobs required as that faced by Asia in the 1980s and 1990s. An important difference, however, is that Africa will experience these high rates of growth for a longer period time, with annual growth in sub-Saharan Africa not projected to drop below 2.5% per year until after 2040.

One of the striking features of Figure 1.1 and Figure 1.3 is that sub-Saharan Africa will soon be the only major region with significant growth of its working-age population. China's working-age population is already shrinking, with the rate of decline increasing in coming decades. India's working-age population will only increase by 11% between 2020 and 2030, and by 2% between 2040 and 2050. The working-age population in Latin America is growing very slowly and will soon begin to decline.

This is a major change in the demography of the global labour force. The growth rate of the world's working-age population is falling steadily, with the location of the growth shifting rapidly from Asia to Africa. Sub-Saharan Africa is already accounting for the greatest part of the growth of the global labour force. Between 2020 and 2030 the world will add 448 million people to its working-age population. Sub-Saharan Africa will add 206 million, 46% of the total. From 2040 to 2050, sub-Saharan Africa's growth will be equal to 100% of the growth in the world's working-age population, with modest positive growth in some other regions offset by declines in Asia and most other regions.

The reason that Africa continues to have a rapidly growing working-age population, while growth rates have declined in most other regions, is that Africa has had much slower declines in fertility rates (Bongarts and Casterline 2013; Bongaarts 2017; Casterline 2017). As shown in Lam, Leibbrandt, and Allen (2019), variation in the pace of fertility decline is the primary explanation for variations in the rate of growth of the working-age population across countries. Note that the growth rates of the working-age population shown in Figure 1.3 will not be significantly affected by assumptions about fertility. Even for 2050, most of the working-age population has already been born. Faster (or slower) fertility decline will affect 15–29-year-olds in 2050, but will not affect older groups. While assumptions about mortality will affect these projections, mortality rates are low in the working ages, and reasonable variations in those rates will have only modest impact on the growth of the working-age populations.

A related point is that sub-Saharan Africa will soon be the only major region with a falling dependency rate—the ratio of the number of dependent children and elderly divided by the number of working-age adults (Lam, Leibbrandt, and Allen 2019). The early stages of fertility decline have the effect of shifting the population away from a child-dominated population towards a concentration in working ages. This has been called the 'demographic dividend' or 'demographic bonus', creating a situation in which the share of the population in working ages increases and dependency rates decline (Lee and Mason 2006; Canning, Raja, and Yazbeck 2015). Eventually the growth of the working-age population is overcome by the growth of the elderly population, shifting from the favourable demography of the demographic dividend to an age structure in which the elderly are the fastest-growing group and the dependency ratio begins to increase. As shown in Lam, Leibbrandt, and Allen (2019), most regions outside of Africa, including Asia and Latin America, already have rising dependency ratios because of the rapid growth of their elderly population. Sub-Saharan Africa, by contrast, has dependency ratios that are falling and will continue to fall for most of the century.

The demography of the labour force creates both challenges and opportunities for sub-Saharan Africa. On the one hand, generating 2 million jobs per month in the coming decades will be a daunting task. Even this rate of job creation would only hold constant the proportion of the working-age population that is employed. Reducing unemployment rates would require even faster job creation. At the same time, being the only region with a growing working-age population may create opportunities for international investment, job creation, and economic growth.

How labour markets function will play a critical role in determining whether low-income countries in Africa and other regions can meet this job creation challenge. Can Africa reproduce the Asian success story of producing jobs fast enough to keep up with almost 3% growth of the working-age population? How effectively will rapidly growing youth cohorts be absorbed into the labour force? Will education and skills be developed that allow young people to find good jobs that produce economic growth and poverty reduction? Will the labour force be able to efficiently match workers to the jobs that are being created? What roles will rural–urban and international migration play in meeting the employment challenge? Will women, who are rapidly equalling or surpassing men in education across the developing world, be effectively and equitably absorbed into the labour force? What kinds of programmes and policies will help ensure that countries are successful in all these elements? This book explores these and other issues that are central to the role of labour markets in driving economic growth and poverty reduction in the coming decades.

1.2 The GLM|LIC Programme

With the demographic challenges discussed in section 1.1, employment growth will need to be extremely robust in the coming decades in LICs, especially those in sub-Saharan Africa. This will require labour markets that are dynamic and efficient, able to absorb millions of additional workers each month. Recognizing the importance of the labour market in meeting these demographic challenges, driving economic growth, and speeding the pace of poverty reduction, the programme on Growth and Labour Markets in Low-Income Countries was created as a partnership between the United Kingdom's Department for International Development (now part of the FCDO) and the German IZA – Institute of Labor Economics in 2011. The core goal of this joint initiative is to improve worldwide knowledge on labour market issues in LICs and provide a solid basis for capacity building and development of future labour market policies. The GLM|LIC programme has already taken significant steps to close the research gap on labour markets and growth in LICs. The programme has contributed to the growing interest in understanding labour markets in the poorest countries by producing high-quality research outputs and policy documents, as well as through interactions with various stakeholders and impacts on programs and policies.

Calls for proposals were widely disseminated around the world. Between 2011 and 2018, 230 proposals were submitted over four rounds, with forty-three projects selected. Proposals were reviewed through an initial round of peer review by anonymous reviewers with appropriate expertise. Input from those reviews was used by a distinguished International Advisory Committee to recommend proposals for funding. Reviewers set a very high standard for rigorous evaluation of labour market policies and programmes. Many of the projects used a randomized controlled trial (RCT) design, evaluating treatment effects on participating and non-participating individuals. The use of RCTs has become increasingly common in development economics, with the importance of its contributions indicated by the awarding of the Nobel Prize in Economics in 2019 to three economists who have been instrumental in advancing its use—Abhijit Banerjee, Esther Duflo, and Michael Kremer. By the time the GLM|LIC programme began, standards regarding research design, statistical power, and rigorous econometric techniques had been well established among development economists carrying our RCTs. Similar high standards were applied to projects using other approaches, such as the use of national labour market surveys or longitudinal household surveys collected by the projects.

The projects supported by GLM|LIC cover a wide range of countries. Twenty-five low-income countries were represented in research projects, along with a number of projects that had a broad cross-country focus. The programme also focused on including researchers from developing countries in the research teams. Three research projects of GLM|LIC are run by research teams based in LICs.

Annual research and policy conferences and workshops are an important component of the Growth and Labour Markets in Low-Income Countries Programme. Conferences and workshops were held in a wide range of countries, including Bangladesh, Côte d'Ivoire, Ethiopia, France, India, Kenya, Mozambique, Nepal, Peru, Uganda, the UK, the USA, and Zambia. Moreover, the programme organized a number of training programmes that aimed at enhancing the research ability of southern researchers in Delhi (2012), Nairobi (2013), Dhaka (2015), Lusaka (2016), Abidjan (2017), and Addis Ababa (2018).

Starting from mid-2019, a new phase of the programme began with a focus is mainly on gender issues. The new programme 'Growth, Gender and Labour Markets in Low-Income Countries' (G^{2}LM|LIC) marks the extension of the successful IZA/FCDO cooperation and aims to foster research that guides future gender and labour market policies. The programme aims particularly to enhance equality of opportunity for women in the labour market.

1.3 Volume Overview

The following chapters analyse some of the most important issues affecting labour markets in low-income countries. The chapters build heavily on the new research evidence that has been provided by the GLM|LIC programme.

Chapter 2 examines barriers to labour market clearing and investigates how to make it easier for firms and workers to find each other in LICs. The chapter builds on findings of several GLM|LIC projects that mainly use RCTs to study the role of different constraints: (1) the distance from residential areas to job hubs constraint, and (2) asymmetric information in local labour markets constraint. The results highlight the importance of job-search constraints as mechanisms for exclusion of the most disadvantaged. They also show that when they are well targeted, low-cost interventions can have large impacts, improving both efficiency and equity in the labour market. A GLM|LIC project in Ethiopia found positive effects of low-cost programmes designed to help reduce search costs and improve matching, including a skills certification programme and transportation vouchers.

Chapter 2 also discusses evidence on the impact of improving firms' knowledge about workers' characteristics using an RCT design from Uganda where firms were randomly given information on non-cognitive skills of young job seekers. The chapter also discusses the demand for, and cost of, labour in Africa, building on a GLM|LIC synthesis paper that uses data from Ghana to analyse firms' demand for labour. The chapter also looks at the effect of intra-firm wage disparities on productivity and absenteeism based on a novel RCT in India.

Chapter 3 looks at skills training, one of most common labour market programmes run by governments and NGOs to enable individuals achieve better labour market outcomes. Despite the growing number of training programmes in LICs, many of these programmes go without any rigorous evaluation. Randomized controlled trials can be highly informative about the effectiveness and efficiency of these programmes. Considerable evidence suggests that these programmes are often not very effective, especially considering cost. GLM|LIC research includes new innovations in this area from a number of countries, including Kenya, Liberia, Bangladesh, Pakistan, Togo, Madagascar, and Senegal. The innovations include, for example, combining training with cash transfers that aim to relax credit constraints and adding behavioural interventions such as behavioural transformation programmes. Some of the interventions also investigate the role of non-cognitive skills. The outcomes studied go beyond the regular labour market outcomes of employment and wages and include other social outcomes such as risk or violence. The chapter summarizes the findings of these RCTs and discusses the lessons learned about what types of trainings and the (geographic and cultural) contexts in which these programmes would work. Some additional GLM|LIC projects involving training programmes targeted at women are discussed in Chapter 8, which focuses on gender dimensions of labour markets in LICs.

Chapter 4 discusses challenges in rural labour markets in LICs, a fundamental issue given that small-scale farming remains the primary source of income for a majority of the population in LICs. A GLM|LIC project using labour force survey data from Kenya, Tanzania, and Zambia confirms that the rural sector still dominates employment in those countries, accounting for 60% of employment in Kenya and Zambia, and almost 75% in Tanzania. GLM|LIC projects spanning a number of African countries show that labour markets in rural areas often do not work efficiently, leaving many distortions in the supply of labour. The chapter also discusses topics related to credit constraints, harvest cycles, and the challenge of smoothing consumption over time. A GLM|LIC project that uses nationally representative data sets from Ethiopia, Malawi, Tanzania, and Uganda finds evidence that there may be an excess supply of labour in rural areas, but with substantial heterogeneity across cultivation phases, genders, and agro-ecological zones. An innovative GLM|LIC RCT in Zambia finds evidence that credit constraints influence the decision of many poor farm households to work in the off-farm wage labour market rather than work on their own farms during the lean season before the harvest. This suggests that improved access to credit could increase farm productivity, help maintain food consumption across the agricultural cycle, and reduce poverty.

Chapter 4 also addresses the important question of whether Public Works Programmes (PWPs) are effective. PWPs are very important in many LICs, receiving large amounts of money from governments and international agencies. These programmes are designed with a number of goals in mind, including employment creation, poverty reduction, and infrastructure development. A GLM|LIC project using a randomized design to study the large-scale Malawi Social Action Fund found that the programme was not successful in its goal of improving food security. Another project focuses on India's massive National Rural Employment Generating Scheme (NREGS), analysing the impact of making payments directly to women rather than to their husbands, which is discussed in Chapter 8.

Chapter 5 deals with migration, including rural–urban migration and international migration. A survey of international migration done for GLM|LIC notes that international migration flows, while large and important, are smaller than they were in the late nineteenth and early twentieth centuries. Today's migration patterns are quite different, however, with heavy South–North migration movements that are linked to large remittance flows and other connections that connect low-income countries to the international economy. The chapter looks at the impact of credit and information constraints and discusses evidence on how responsive rural labour markets are to labour demand shocks. An innovative GLM|LIC 'big data' project uses mobile phone records in Rwanda to track seasonal labour migration, demonstrating the responsiveness of internal migration to regional wage differences. Mobile phones also feature in a GLM|LIC project that uses an RCT designed to analyse the impact of mobile banking on remittances between rural and urban areas in Mozambique. A GLM|LIC project using historical data from Malawi analyses the impact of remittances from South African mines to Malawi, demonstrating the large impact international remittances can have on labour markets and entrepreneurial activity in sending countries.

Chapter 5 also looks at forced migration, an important form of migration in many LICs. The impact of forced migration and its effect on education, skills, and employment are analysed using evidence from a GLM|LIC project looking at the labour market impacts of forced migration in the case of the Rwandan genocide, which resulted in 1 million refugees entering Tanzania. Using data before and after the forced-migration shock, the project shows that greater exposure to the refugee shock resulted in Tanzanians having a lower likelihood of working outside the household as employees. Several GLM|LIC projects focusing on women's labour market migration are discussed in Chapter 8.

Chapter 6 deals with formality, informality, and regulations. The chapter discusses issues related to sectoral transformation, economic growth, and employment and builds on findings from GLM|LIC projects that address these topics across several countries, including Bangladesh, India, Vietnam, and Zimbabwe. The topic of informality is of particular importance because it accounts for the majority of employment in many LICs, yet its role in the process of economic growth and its links with the formal sector remain poorly understood. GLM|LIC studies in both Bangladesh and Vietnam show that the informal sector can play an important role in economic development and may not always be simply the 'last resort' of workers who are unable to secure formal jobs. The Vietnam study shows that rapid economic growth was associated with rapid growth of the formal sector, with younger cohorts driving the transition. Vietnam's success story is in stark contrast with the poor economic performance of Zimbabwe in recent decades. Focusing on formal and informal manufacturing firms in Zimbabwe, a GLM|LIC study using longitudinal firm data found evidence of considerable allocative inefficiencies in firms, dampening growth in the formal manufacturing sector and causing the sector to grow even more slowly than the overall economy.

Chapter 6 also looks at the question of whether labour costs are too high in Africa and at the possible role of labour market regulation. A GLM|LIC study finds evidence that countries in sub-Saharan Africa tend to have a high ratio of labour costs to GDP per capita relative to similar countries outside Africa and explores the possible mechanisms at work. Although the proportion of workers in the formal sector is still small in LICs, the number of formal workers is on the rise, increasing the importance of labour market regulations. Chapter 6 discusses two important types of regulation—social insurance mandates and minimum wages—based on evidence from new research projects. A GLM|LIC project in Ethiopia evaluated the impact of a recent pension reform on employment, wages, and other labour market outcomes. The study found a decline in employment in smaller firms, a shift of low-skilled labour into informality, and a shift of larger firms towards higher-skilled workers. A GLM|LIC analysis of minimum wages across sub-Saharan Africa found that the minimum wage relative to the mean wage is higher in Africa than in middle-income countries, though there are large variations across countries in the extent of coverage, the nature of minimum wage policies, and the extent of compliance.

Chapter 7 focuses on children and youth, a critical topic given the young age structures in many LICs. Drawing on a GLM|LIC synthesis paper, the chapter analyses trends in child labour across LICs and discusses the links between child labour and economic growth. Widespread child employment can dampen future economic growth through its negative impact on child development and depress current growth by reducing unskilled wages and discouraging the adoption of skill-intensive technologies. Child employment also appears to be a result, as well as a cause, of slow economic growth. Rising incomes are associated with a greater demand for children's education and leisure and with improvements in the family's ability to buffer economic shocks without child labour. All these factors lead to declines in the economic activity of children when income levels are on the rise. The chapter also discusses the challenges to youth employment in LICs, particularly in Africa. While the large cohort of youth entering Africa's labour force is better educated than previous cohorts, jobs remain elusive in the formal wage sector, given the limited success in African economies in structural transformation from low-productivity agriculture to higher-productivity non-agricultural sectors.

Chapter 8 focuses on the gender dimensions of labour markets in LICs. Achieving gender equality and empowering all women and girls is one of the Sustainable Development Goals (SDGs), and gender inequality in the labour market has been a central theme of the GLM|LIC programme from the outset. This chapter presents results from a number of GLM|LIC projects that focus on gender dimensions of labour markets. As discussed in a survey of trends in women's labour market activity commissioned by GLM|LIC, labour force participation rates of women remain low in many low-income countries. While women's employment rates tended to increase with economic development and falling fertility rates in Latin America and some other regions, there has been little or no increase in South Asian countries, with the notable exception of Bangladesh. A variety of factors appear to be at work, including rising incomes of husbands, social norms, and the sectoral composition of economic growth.

A GLM|LIC project analysing the impact of globalization on fertility and women's employment found that trade liberalization tends to reduce fertility in countries with a comparative advantage in sectors with high proportions of women but found little effect on women's labour force participation rates. A

GLM|LIC project in Kyrgyzstan and Tajikistan analysed the extent to which public transfer programmes and migrant remittances had a negative impact on women's employment. Longitudinal survey data in Kyrgyzstan found low rates of female labour force participation, with some evidence that transfer programmes reduced employment, while longitudinal survey data from Tajikistan found no significant effect of migration and remittances on female labour force participation.

Chapter 8 also looks at the impact of training and employment programmes targeted at women. As discussed in Chapter 3, training programmes are popular among governments and non-governmental organizations (NGOs), but the small proportion of programmes in LICs that have been rigorously evaluated have often had disappointing results. GLM|LIC has supported novel training programmes with rigorous evaluation and a number of innovative features, including projects specifically targeted to women. An example of a programme with positive results is the Empowerment and Livelihood for Adolescents programme in Uganda, in which vocational and life skills training was found to increase women's employment while reducing teen pregnancy and early marriage. A GLM|LIC project designed to encourage micro-franchising among young women in Nairobi slums showed promising short-term results but had disappointing long-term outcomes, perhaps indicating that micro-franchising may not be the economic activity for these young women.

Chapter 8 also describes GLM|LIC research demonstrating that women's employment is affected by their control over finances and access to safe transportation. A GLM|LIC project focusing on India's National Rural Employment Guarantee Scheme, the largest public works programme in the world, found that women increased their labour force participation when they were given the combination of bank account, direct deposit of their earnings into the account, and basic financial instruction. The results suggest that women's empowerment through control over finances may increase employment and improve other outcomes. A GLM|LIC project in Lahore, Pakistan, is analysing the impact on women's employment of improved transportation options, with demand assessments indicating that both men and women are more supportive of women working when women-only transport is available.

Finally, Chapter 9 focuses on the lessons of GLM|LIC research for labour market policies and programmes. The chapter addresses the question of what type of programmes works, and under which conditions. Lessons from projects that had disappointing results are, in many ways, as informative as lessons from projects that had positive results. The chapter recaps key points from Chapters 2 to 8 regarding labour market interventions including training programmes, public works programmes, and programmes designed to reduce labour market frictions due to imperfect information, transport costs, and barriers to access. The chapter discusses the lessons from GLM|LIC projects about the ways in which social norms may limit economic activity of women, including examples of how women's labour force activity can be increased by removing restrictions on women's physical mobility and giving women greater control over their own finances. The chapter also discusses some of the important lessons from GLM|LIC projects about the importance of rigorous programme evaluation, especially evaluation that allows long-term follow-up of programme participants. The chapter concludes with brief overviews of the final round of projects supported by the GLM|LIC programme.

References

Bongaarts, J., 2017. Africa's Unique Fertility Transition. *Population and Development Review*, 43(S1): 39–58.

Bongaarts, J., and Casterline, J., 2013. Fertility Transition: Is Sub-Saharan Africa Different? *Population and Development Review*, 38 (s1): 153–68.

Canning, D., Raja, S., and Yazbeck, A. S., 2015. *Africa's Demographic Transition: Dividend or Disaster?* Washington, DC: World Bank Publications.

Casterline, J. B., 2017. Prospects for Fertility Decline in Africa. *Population and Development Review*, 43: 3–18.

Lam, D., 2011. How the World Survived the Population Bomb: Lessons from Fifty Years of Extraordinary Demographic History. *Demography*, 48(4): 1231–62.

Lam, D., Leibbrandt, M., and Allen, J., 2019. The Demography of the Labor Force in Sub-Saharan Africa: Challenges and Opportunities, GLM|LIC Synthesis Paper No. 10.

Lee, R., 2003. The Demographic Transition: Three Centuries of Fundamental Change. *Journal of Economic Perspectives*, 17 (4): 167–90.

Lee, R., and Mason, A., 2006. What Is the Demographic Dividend? *Finance and Development*, 43(3): 16–17.

UNDESA (United Nations, Department of Economic and Social Affairs, Population Division), 2019a. World Population Prospects 2019: Highlights (ST/ESA/SER.A/423).

UNDESA (United Nations, Department of Economic and Social Affairs, Population Division), 2019b. World Population Prospects 2019: Summary of Methodological Updates Introduced in the 2019 Revision. New York: United Nations.

World Bank, 2020. Poverty and Shared Prosperity 2020: Reversals of Fortune. Washington, DC: World Bank. doi:10.1596/978-1-4648-1602-4.

2

Barriers to Labour Market Efficiency
in Low-Income Countries

A major challenge in the labour markets of many developing countries is the difficulty of finding jobs due to a lack of information on where to find them or how to apply and signal relevant skills. Large disparities in information often exist between rural and urban areas with respect to the visibility of job openings and both access to and knowledge of application procedures.

A lack of available information on workers' hard and soft skills can particularly affect young workers with less work experience and lower ability to signal their skills. Other obstacles include a lack of financial resources to cover application costs, and mobility constraints due to transport infrastructure deficits. Psychological costs can particularly affect the job searches of women if social norms are against female labour and pose a risk of harassment. These barriers can lead to inefficient matching of labour supply and labour demand and restrict economic growth.

Similar barriers exist on the other side of the market: identifying the best candidates can mean high search and screening costs for firms, when applications are incomplete or simply missing. These costs can prevent firms from gaining sufficient knowledge of the supply side in general, and of individual workers' characteristics in particular. This may affect firms' hiring behaviour, wage setting, and staff development. Smaller firms may also have limited knowledge or ability to select the best applicants, or to engage recruitment agencies.

Technological deficits and absence from sectoral recruitment platforms can prevent firms and job seekers matching efficiently through smooth (virtual) job ads and application processing. Barriers can also restrict small firm expansion if capital markets are inefficient and the capital is more expensive for smaller businesses to access. At the other end of the scale, a lack of information may cause larger firms to use a more capital-intensive production technology, thus reducing their demand for labour.

Lastly, barriers to market clearing may enlarge the informal labour market; if workers and firms cannot match efficiently, job seekers may search for job opportunities outside the formal labour market, which in turn can hamper economic growth. In this respect, low attendance may severely constrain firms if workers

Labour Markets in Low-Income Countries. David Lam and Ahmed Elsayed, Oxford University Press.
© David Lam and Ahmed Elsayed (2022). DOI: 10.1093/oso/9780192897107.003.0002

decide voluntarily to take up informal work on a day-to-day basis or are hindered by transport inefficiencies.

Therefore, examining the barriers to market clearing and job matching in low-income countries is not only of theoretical interest—it also serves to better understand the basic needs labour markets have if they are to function well. Active labour market policies and other policy interventions aiming to fight poverty and enhance poor households' welfare risk failure if these fundamental market relations are dysfunctional.

The Growth and Labour Markets in Low-Income Countries Programme has addressed these issues in a number of research projects that enrich our picture of market-clearance barriers and strategies to overcome them. The available studies evaluate existing interventions to improve labour market efficiency and equity in several LICs. Their main findings are summarized in this chapter.

2.1 The Impact of Information Frictions in Incomplete Labour Markets

Constraints on information are among the most prevalent barriers to market clearing in low-income economies. If firms are not able to get relevant information about the skills of job applicants due to incomplete or missing applications, this will necessarily affect their personnel strategies. In the absence of conclusive applications, skill certifications, or otherwise clear signals about workers' abilities, firms are forced to base their hiring decisions on job referrals and previous work experience.

If (young) workers lack these signals, they are at high risk of being pushed outside the formal market. A lack of opportunity or ability to signal their general qualifications and job-specific skills will inevitably affect not just their actual application chances, but eventually their search behaviour, their choice between formality and informality, their mobility patterns, and their education decisions. **There is therefore a substantial danger of information barriers around workers' skill profiles restricting the efficient allocation of resources.**

There are also information frictions in the opposite direction. Potential job applicants, especially new entrants to the labour market, may have difficulty learning about available jobs, discovering about the process of applying for jobs, and may face high costs searching for jobs.

GLM|LIC research projects illustrate how overcoming informational constraints, in terms of workers' hard (i.e., specific and technical) and soft skills (i.e., those dealing more with personality traits, e.g., communication, time management, team work, etc.) does not necessarily require costly policy interventions. Supported by GLM|LIC, a set of studies evaluated two job-search support and skills-signalling programmes, as well as the outcomes of job fairs for urban youth in urban Ethiopia (Addis Ababa). Its aim was to identify ways to help young workers in large low-income cities find and secure jobs (Abebe et al. 2017, 2020a, 2020b). Young workers at the entry level are faced with special challenges in accessing firms that often base their selection criteria on work experience or written applications, while many young people in large cities do not even know about job openings due to less extensive personal networks, spatial distance, and other information barriers. As a result, many young people leave large cities to be precariously self-employed in nearby peripheral or rural areas.

A number of studies have shed some light on obstacles—such as job search costs and information deficits—that prevent young urban job seekers from signalling their skills to the market (see, for example, Card et al. 2011; Pallais 2014). Yet little is known so far about overcoming such barriers under the special conditions of low-income urban societies facing high population growth rates and high youth unemployment (see, for example, Kluve 2016; McKenzie 2017). More intensified research in the field would be highly relevant in order to evaluate and modify existing policy strategies in this context. This may also contribute to addressing poverty traps and weakening crime and emigration incentives, and thus deserves full policy attention.

So far, research has been mostly focused on programmes that aim to connect rural workers to jobs in developing countries' urban areas. Here, search support and information have been evaluated as a useful and effective strategy to reduce search frictions (see, for example, Bryan, Chowdhury, and Mobarak 2014; Jensen 2012). Do such strategies also work in congested urban centres with widespread informality and precarious employment? There is also the growing research consensus that traditional active labour market policies based on an overall 'average' do little to influence whether participants take up a job or not. Can better targeting help to overcome this deficit?

Franklin (2018) showed that a transport subsidy offer had at least positive short-term effects on young job seekers in Ethiopia's capital Addis Ababa. Building on these findings, Abebe et al. (2017, 2020a) used a randomized sample of more than 3,000 young inhabitants of the same city to study the effect of direct transport subsidies, as well as the results of a workshop designed to assess and certify cognitive abilities and improve their job application skills. These analyses are the first to simultaneously quantify the relative importance of two different types of frictions and compare the effects of two active labour market interventions.

According to the studies, both of these rather simple and cheap treatments substantially increased the short-term chances of a worker taking up a new or better job under the specific, highly challenging conditions of a rapidly expanding urban labour market. The studies further show that **job application training may induce sustainable effects on formal employment, job duration and work satisfaction**, while the impact of transport subsidies seems to dissipate over time.

The experimental interventions were aimed at reducing spatial and informational barriers to improve employment for the most disadvantaged groups in the labour market. The transport subsidy was designed to induce more frequent visits to urban centre job vacancy boards by reimbursing the costs. Baseline survey data revealed that those living 10 km closer to the urban centre screened city job boards almost seven times more per year and applied for permanent jobs more often.

The application training aimed to improve workers' ability to signal their skills. Better signalling ability is among the most effective factors in enhancing the employability of lower-educated workers, enabling them to overcome unemployment and poorly paid temporary, casual or self-employment.

Such poorly paid roles are widespread in Addis Ababa, as in many growing cities in low-income countries: roughly 65% of the young people surveyed in the studies were employed, but only 25% had a formal contract, and less than 20% were permanently employed. The vast majority of this group is living on informal, insecure, or precarious employment, mostly lacking written contracts, regular working weeks, and social security, while about 20% are unemployed.

Abebe et al. (2017, 2020a) conducted two follow-up surveys eight months and four years after treatment to explore changes in workers' individual job search and employment situations. Attrition was rather low, with more than 90% of participants taking part in the first follow-up and over 85% remaining after four years.

The transport subsidy treatment: Given that job searching is costly, forcing job seekers in LICs to either rely on social networks or to travel to find information on local job openings, the programme offered a modest daily transport subsidy to the participants (up to three times per week and lasting a median of sixteen weeks between September 2014 and January 2015 for each recipient). Recipients were required to pay for the first journey themselves and collect the daily subsidy at a disbursement office in Addis Ababa, close to a central bus station and in the neighbourhood of major job vacancy boards that represent one of the most popular job search methods. Around 50% of the participants randomly selected into the transport subsidy treatment group made use of the subsidy at least once; 81% of them did so at least once again and intensified their travelling in search of jobs. Overall, 74% took the subsidy at least once a week during the entire study period, resulting in an average total of sixteen subsidy-collections. The marginal costs of the intervention per individual were below 20 USD, based on a per-day subsidy of around 1 USD that roughly equalled 10% of the overall median spending all participants had for themselves in a week.

The job application treatment: The training workshop was designed in close cooperation with the School of Commerce at Addis Ababa University—an institution offering personnel selection services which are widely accepted and trusted among many medium and large firms in the city. In addition, a number of qualitative interviews with firm managers were conducted to better tailor the content of tests administered to the participants. During the first one-day session, job seekers took tests to assess their cognitive abilities as well as a work-sample test (for example, taking minutes during a meeting, working on tasks under time pressure). The resulting certificates could be personally collected later at the School of Commerce. The second workshop day was dedicated to making effective job applications, focusing on CV and application letter writing, and preparing for job interviews. Out of the group of randomly identified participants, 61% attended the workshop (September–October 2014) while 80% of the workshop participants picked up their certificates. However, not all certified participants made use of the certificate: only 42% of those who collected the certificate and sent their applications to one or more positions reported including the certificates and receiving a positive reaction from firms. Marginal costs for each participant were around 18 USD.

2.1.1 Significant Short-Term Effects on Job Quality, but not on Overall Employment

Abebe et al. (2017, 2020a) applied rigorous evaluation methods to assess the effectiveness of both treatments in the short and long term. It should be noted that neither the transport subsidies nor the training workshop had a significant short-term impact on employment probability, work hours, earnings, or job satisfaction. The modest average increases in employment probability, by 3.8 percentage points for transport subsidy recipients, and by 2 percentage points for workshop participants, are both statistically insignificant. These results align with other recent studies in finding that conventional strategies of active labour market programmes in developing countries often fail to establish more than very modest effects on overall employment (see Groh et al. 2012; Jensen 2012; McKenzie and Woodruff 2014; Crépon and van den Berg 2016).

However, the conclusion is not that the interventions did not fulfil their purpose; they were not intended to increase *overall* employment, but rather to foster *formal* and *permanent* employment, especially for disadvantaged groups. In this regard, the interventions led to noticeable improvements within a couple of months: the analyses show impressively large positive effects on the probability of finding a stable permanent or formal job (with a written contract), and a remarkable increase in employment rates and earnings among the most disadvantaged job seekers. Both the transport support and the workshop gave workers the incentive and momentum to look for work more frequently and more efficiently in the short term.

What were the short-term outcomes of the project?

1. **The job application workshop did not affect the probability of searching for a job or the number of applications sent out to potential employers.**

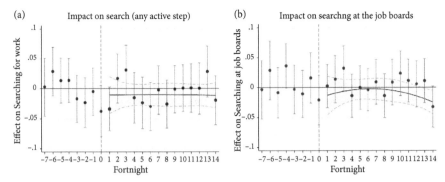

Fig. 2.1 Impact of the Application Workshop on Search Behaviour (a) impact on search (any active step) (b) impact on searching at the job boards

Note: The green dotted line indicates the fortnight when the treatment begins.
Source: Abebe et al. (2020a)

Prevailing financial constraints not targeted by the workshop prevented participants from searching with more intensity (see Figure 2.1).

2. **Training of job application skills had a large effect on job quality through increased search efficacy and certification of skills.** Eight months after the workshop, participants were almost 60% more likely to work in a permanent job, and roughly 30% were more likely to have a job in the formal labour market. In the control group, 17% had a formal job; this value was 5 percentage points higher in the treatment group. That is, workshop participation did not intensify job search but it did make job search more successful.

3. **This job quality effect is concentrated among low-educated workers.** High-school graduates without further education received an offer of a permanent job every 4.6 applications—hence they were far more successful than control group individuals, who received a job offer for every 10.5 applications. The workshop apparently elevated the quality of applications and hence the likelihood of success.

4. **The transport subsidy treatment had similar short-run effects on a lower level.** Making use of the transport subsidies stimulated the probability of permanent employment, as well as formal employment, by around 30%. This can be explained by the fact that most formal and permanent jobs are announced on the job boards, which were screened more frequently by transport subsidy recipients.

5. **Receiving transport subsidies reduced the urgent need to work for a daily living and thus induced more intensive job search activities.** While subsidized, the programme participants were 12.5% more likely to engage in any job search activity and showed a 9 percentage-point higher probability to search for a job at the vacancy boards compared with the control group,

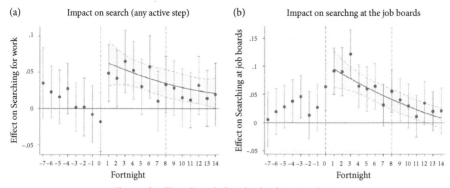

Fig. 2.2 Impact of the Transport Subsidy on Search Behaviour

Note: The green dotted line indicates the fortnight when the treatment begins.
Source: Abebe et al. (2020a)

representing an increase of about 30%. This effect decreased at a steady rate after stopping the transport subsidy programme (see Figure 2.2).

6. **As a result of workshop participation, younger and less experienced workers partially caught up with older workers**. The gap in permanent employment between young and older workers fell by roughly 20%.

7. **Both treatments were cost-efficient at rather low costs per participant**. An approximate calculation reveals rather modest costs of, on average, about 365 USD for each job seeker helped into a formal job by transport subsidies, and 344 USD for placed workshop participants. The estimated costs for helping a worker into a permanent job through workshop attendance are about 264 USD. According to the authors, these figures are equivalent to 2.7–3.7 times mean wage monthly earnings.

8. **Disadvantaged groups benefited most from both treatments**. The short-term effect on job quality was largest among participants who had not yet actively searched for a job, had no earlier work experience, or only low savings. While better-educated programme participants hardly benefited at all, the impact on lower-qualified workers (high school) and women was very strong. The probabilities of women finding permanent and formal work both increased by 35% when they received transport subsidies; attending the workshop raised their chance of finding permanent employment by 45% and the likelihood of securing a formal contract by 35%. At the same time individuals with no education beyond a high-school diploma saw their probability of finding permanent employment increase by 10 percentage points after workshop participation, and by 5 percentage points after using financial transport support. In other words, the workshop tripled the chances of a permanent job for this group while the transport subsidy doubled it.

The probability of being formally employed increased by above 30% for the low-qualified.

9. **Indirect effects of the treatment approach may occur** in so far as changing the search behaviour of non-participants with the same characteristics living in clusters assigned to the programme, when the proportion of treated job seekers is low in a cluster (these effects may turn negative as the proportion increases).

Abebe et al. (2017) further investigated a variation of effects depending on the distance of participants from the town centre. In cities like Addis Ababa employment opportunities decreased with the spatial distance from the city centre, resulting in a high prevalence of self-employment in the periphery. The programme—the transport subsidy in particular—proved to address this problem. Upon receiving the transport treatment, respondents who reside far from the centre were less likely to be self-employed and become as likely to be self-employed as individuals who lived close. These results can be viewed as suggestive evidence that spatial barriers influence the occupational structure of urban labour markets and that enhancing mobility can help unravelling such spatial patterns.

2.1.2 Do the Positive Effects of Application Training Last?

Expanding the findings of their first study, Abebe et al. (2020a) investigated the longer-term impact of both treatments over a period of four years. The signalling effects of workshop participation not only persisted but extended to a positive impact on workers' earnings and job satisfaction. The transport subsidy was meanwhile limited to short-term effects and had no significant impact in the longer term. Both the inability to signal skills and the cost of job searching presented temporary barriers to formal employment, but only the signalling constraints had a lasting impact on labour market outcomes.

1. **Employment duration and utilization of workers' skills increased over time.** Job duration was 10% longer for workshop participants, while they were 8 percentage points more likely to be in jobs suited to their skills four years after treatment.

2. **The positive impact on workers and firms persists over time**. Match quality increased through workers' better search focus and firms' better targeting of job offers.

3. **This higher match quality translated into higher earnings**. Four years after workshop participation workers earned 25% more than individuals in the control group, indicating a clear advantage from learning how to apply for a job and how to signal skills to the market. Over time, permanent and

formal employment were increasingly correlated. These earnings effects are mainly due to higher productivity and wages, rather than driven by selection into a specific employment. In other words, learning how to signal skills led to better job match quality.

4. **Lower-educated workers experienced larger effects on job quality and earnings** than higher-qualified workers. The intervention thus reduces the earnings gap between lower- and higher-educated workers, illustrating the gains improved signalling has on labour market outcomes.

5. **The long-term earnings effects far outstrip the costs of the treatment.** Hence scaling up is a policy option.

6. **Job satisfaction increased by 7 percentage points on average**, hinting at better job quality of workshop participants.

7. **Rates of formal and permanent employment aligned** between workshop participants and control group, showing some catch-up effect among the control group over time.

8. **The initial effects of transport subsidies on job quality eroded over time** with no statistically significant difference to the control group in terms of permanent and formal employment.

Abebe et al. (2020a) argued that, given the strongly dissipating effects of the transport subsidy, the financial cost of job search do not seem to constrain efficient job searching and job quality over the long term. This conclusion might well be doubted, even if the treatment did by definition not contribute to increasing firms' screening abilities and did not affect match quality. In fact, the subsidy was very limited in scope and still achieved a significant short-term impact on job-search behaviour. Extending it over a longer period could actually lead to different outcomes in the longer run than those observed in the experiment. Furthermore, the findings implicitly reveal that combining different treatments—application training, job search subsidies, and other interventions—might result in synergistic effects.

This begs the question of whether scaling up application training would increase the positive effects, and overall welfare, through more efficient matching in the labour market. Based on the empirical evidence, Abebe et al. (2020a) rightly stated that the share of lower-educated workers who would face the risk of being pushed aside in a labour market more reliant on skills certification or signalling would be rather small, given the frequency of job opportunities for lower-educated workers. Inflation of applications should not be a concern either, as the experimental findings clearly indicate that job search intensity does not change significantly.

Lastly, the research results on job duration contradict the concern that over-selling skills could lead to reduced match quality in the event that firms have limited ability to screen candidates. Statutory probation periods—as required by law in Ethiopia—could further reduce this risk. The core finding that experimental workers obtained more permanent and more formal jobs in the short term and observed higher earnings in the long term, should give policymakers reason to pursue this promising and cost-efficient approach.

2.1.3 Are Job Fairs a Useful Tool for Addressing Matching Constraints in Incomplete Labour Markets?

One potential accompanying approach for addressing informational barriers with respect to workers' skills has been examined by Abebe et al. (2020b). In randomizing participation in job fairs among 1,000 young educated job seekers and some 250 representatives of large firms, this study complements the findings provided by Abebe et al. (2017, 2020a).

For the experiment, two job fairs were organized in Addis Ababa, Ethiopia, in 2014 and 2015. To facilitate interaction and to distinguish treatment effects, job seekers participating in the first fair were given concrete recommendations on which firms would suit them best. To prepare for the second job fair, job seekers also received a complete list of job vacancies among all firms represented at the fair. In addition, firms received a list of job candidates' skills profiles, allowing them to indicate their selection of favourites. Detailed surveys were conducted prior to the first fair and some months after the second.

Take-up rates of 60% among job seekers and roughly 70% among firms were low compared to the workshop and subsidy treatments described above. Despite a high interaction rate—75% of workers had at least one interview with a firm representative—the overall employment impact was disappointing: a total of fourteen hires from seventy-six job offers made to forty-five job seekers, presumably due to a mismatch of expectations. More jobs (fifty-five) were offered to low-skilled workers. Firms stated that a lack of work experience was a key constraint to offering more jobs to high-skilled job seekers at the fairs.

Nonetheless, the experiment revealed some positive indirect learning effects with regard to workers' and firms' expectations and search behaviour. At the time of the endline survey, both firms and workers were found to have adjusted and increased their search efforts. Workers also revised their wage expectations. It was mainly low-skilled workers, reducing the minimum wage they were willing to accept, who visited the job vacancy boards more often and experienced a substantial increase in their probability of taking up a formal job. The study once more illustrates that a mismatch of expectations on both sides of the market may be a severe constraint that must be addressed to increase the effectiveness of active labour market policies in low-income countries.

In summary, Abebe et al. (2017, 2020a, 2020b) provided convincing evidence that spatial and informational barriers are highly relevant factors determining employment outcomes in rapidly growing urban regions of LICs, thereby confirming and building on findings in Franklin (2018). Overcoming these obstacles may primarily benefit the most disadvantaged groups in city societies: women, youth, and people with lower qualifications. Taking part in a job application workshop enables disadvantaged participants to better signal their abilities and find a job. Using modest transport subsidies to overcome distance barriers meanwhile helps to increase mobility as well as formal employment, and helps reduce self-employment levels, at least in the short-term. Improving workers' ability to signal their skills should then be seen as a key tool for addressing inequality in the labour market.

Furthermore, the results underline the high value and cost efficiency of intervening at the entry-level of workers. Such programmes are likely to have indirect treatment effects (though this is not yet thoroughly evaluated) of accelerating job matching, due to increased job applications, and reducing job turnover due to stronger qualification signals. Active labour market policies should pay explicit attention to such simple interventions that reduce skill information and matching frictions and could work in many developing countries.

The outcomes of the job fair and job application treatments emphasize the point: information barriers are hampering market clearing. **If valuable skills go unseen by firms, this disadvantages the most vulnerable groups in the labour market**. At the same time, the findings reveal how policy interventions could tackle these constraints, for example by supporting skills certification, implementing suitable information channels, or facilitating the acquisition of work experience and firm contacts for workers by certifying internships.

To investigate this topic further, GLM|LIC supported a research project on the role of informational barriers in the low-income economy of Uganda (Bassi and Nansamba 2020). The authors conducted a large field experiment in an urban setting, revealing that both sides of the market react positively to the provision of additional information about skills in the absence of certifying institutions, and that the probability of a job offer increases with the level of certified soft skills. The analysis concludes that introducing a mandatory certification policy on soft skills might offer a policy strategy to tackle information frictions, but at a significant risk of welfare losses for the lowest-skilled workers.

The field experiment was conducted in 2015 and addressed two important aspects of informational constraints in incomplete labour markets: (1) a *matching component* randomly selected potential employees for job interviews with a firm, to address the deficits in information on each other; (2) a *signalling component* provided certification of applicants' soft skills, in terms of work ethics and interpersonal skills, to measure the impact of disclosing additional information not yet available to both workers and employers.

The impact of the signalling approach is, by and large, in line with research findings on the positive effect on hiring probabilities and welfare among higher-performing workers (see Pallais 2014), that results from the certification of skills on job search activities, employment, and earnings (see Carranza et al. 2020), as well as the disclosure of additional information on workers' abilities in an online labour market. Reference letters—as another form of signalling—may have positive employment outcomes for youth and female workers (see Abel, Burger, and Piraino 2020). Collectively, matching frictions—further constrained by informational barriers—are particularly relevant in developing countries (see Donovan, Lu, and Schoellman 2018).

To begin with, it should be noted that the target group of Bassi and Nansamba (2020) were not unemployed disadvantaged young people but instead medium-skilled vocational training graduates. To allow this entry-level group to suffer information frictions in the labour market poses an even larger risk of wasting human capital by impeding job matching. Conversely, a successful signalling intervention should result in larger employment returns compared with other groups.

The set of soft skills measured and certified during the experiment was based on the preferences firm owners stated in the baseline survey, and included the following five characteristics: attendance, communication skills, creativity, trustworthiness, and willingness to help others (see Figure 2.3—pro-sociality and discipline were excluded for attention constraints). Notably, attendance was explicitly classified by firm managers as a soft skill that they find difficult to observe yet value highly. This hints at significant levels of absenteeism—a frequent phenomenon in the developing world (see Chaudhury et al. 2006).

Each skill was graded on an A–E scale—mirroring the Ugandan educational grading system—by the trainees' teachers and authors' assessment based on a questionnaire (creativity), and a trust game with real money (trustworthiness). This innovative experimental setting allowed the authors to examine reactions on both sides of the market, and to assess whether: (1) managers alter their recruitment behaviour, and (2) whether workers' employment opportunities change based on the provision of soft skills certificates.

In cooperation with the non-profit organization BRAC Uganda—a key player in development and micro-finance programmes in many developing countries—the research team selected almost 1,100 eligible small and medium firms in seventeen urban areas in Uganda. Each operated in one of six selected sectors (carpentry, catering, hairdressing, motor mechanics, tailoring, and welding) with at least two employees. The researchers also selected more than 1,000 eligible young workers who had completed their vocational training in one of the six sectors. The selected sectors represent a large share of the Ugandan labour market, with most vocational training institutes (VTI) offering related courses. The focus on young workers is motivated by the higher likelihood of information frictions among this group, and also the high—and growing—share of the youth labour force in Uganda.

Most firms in the study sample were formally registered, employed at least four workers, and required market experience of at least five years. Those who

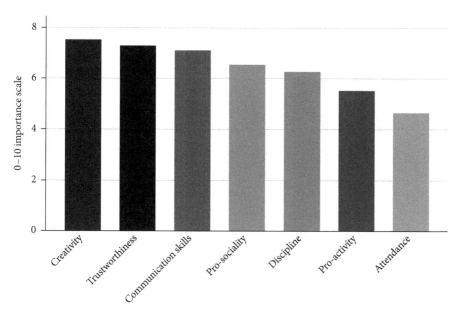

Fig. 2.3 Information on Applicants' Soft Skills Valued Most Among Firms in Uganda

Note: Data from baseline survey of 422 firms interested in being matched. Firm owners were asked to rate on a 0–10 scale (not important at all/extremely important), how important it would be for them to be provided with additional information on different soft skills of job candidates during recruitment. Figure depicts mean importance given to each skill.
Source: Bassi and Nansamba (2020)

completed a baseline survey were invited to participate in a BRAC programme that facilitated job interviews with 'fresh' VTI graduates, without being told of the detailed nature of the experiment. Of the survey sample, 422 firms agreed to participate. The authors' indicator variables show that smaller firms in male-dominated sectors such as welding, motor mechanics, and carpentry were more likely to participate, indicating a larger demand for labour in these sectors.

Firm owners mostly acted as personnel and hiring managers. Managers with higher cognitive ability (tested as part of the survey) headed more profitable firms, according to the authors. On the whole, they declared a substantial interest in the non-cognitive skills of potential employees, despite believing them difficult to observe, and relatively scarce. They ranked soft skills second after practical skills, viewing them as more relevant than numeracy and literacy from the firm's perspective. Difficulties in assessing job applicants' soft skills were reported as more important than general problems with finding employees or evaluating their practical skills. In contrast, firm managers reported low expectations of the likelihood of finding employees with solid soft skills, while judging worker theft the most important firm constraint, above a lack of access to capital or a lack of demand (see Figures 2.4 and 2.5).

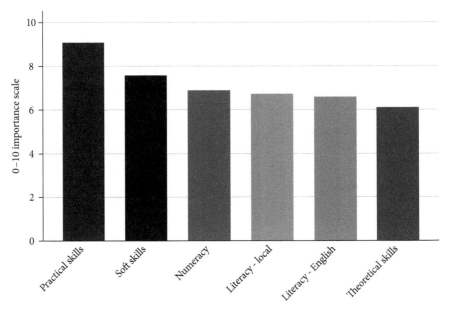

Fig. 2.4 Returns to Various Skills as Perceived by Firm Owners in Uganda

Note: Data from baseline survey of 422 firms interested in being matched. Firm owners were asked to rate on a 0–10 scale (not important at all/extremely important) the importance of workers' skills for their businesses. Figure depicts mean importance given to each skill. Column 'Soft Skills' reports the average value of five skills.

Source: Bassi and Nansamba (2020)

Importantly, more than one-third of employees—among all firms in the baseline survey—were hired through an informal channel without any formal assessment or referral (see Figure 2.6). Typically, job offers are made at the end of the job interview, reflecting the risk of additional costs for the firm if it later proves difficult to contact applicants due to inadequate communication technologies.

Eligible vocational training graduates had a median age of 20 with eleven years of education prior to a two-year programme of vocational training (with hairdressing and motor mechanics being most popular). Of them, 60% planned to search for a formal sector job in a smaller business, 10% already had a job offer, and 25% had some previous work experience. Vocational training in Uganda does not usually include soft skill components and is limited in terms of job placement activities. There are no private institutions offering soft skills assessment and certification.

All trainees were informed that BRAC would arrange job interviews and measure cognitive and non-cognitive skills, before offering these measurements to potential employers. Of the trainees, 787 confirmed their interest, and took part in a cognitive test and questionnaire to measure their soft skills. The authors'

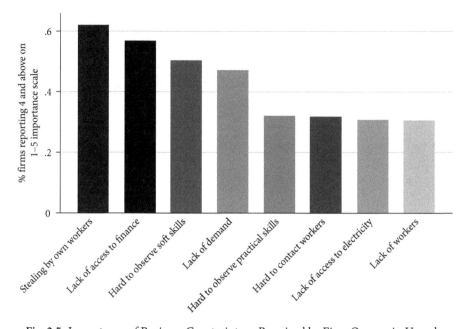

Fig. 2.5 Importance of Business Constraints as Perceived by Firm Owners in Uganda

Note: Data from baseline survey of 422 firms interested in being matched. Firm owners were asked to rate on a 1–5 scale (not important at all/extremely important) the importance of these potential constraints workers' skills for their businesses. Figure reports percentage of firm owners that answered 4 or above on the scale for each constraint.

Source: Bassi and Nansamba (2020)

statistical analysis shows that trainees with a higher level of non-cognitive skills, as captured in the experiment, were more likely to remain in the sample, which reveals some self-selection of participants. Trainees with very low levels of soft skills were the least likely to be interested in the experiment, while workers with higher levels of soft skills apparently expected greater returns from signalling their soft skills to potential employers. More generally, this indicates the role of self-selection of potential workers as a primary driver determining the outcomes of labour policy programmes (see Hardy and McCasland 2017).

With this setting, Bassi and Nansamba (2020) allocated workers and firms to sectoral and regional 'submarkets', and randomly separated treatment and control groups within each of these. Grouped firms and workers were then randomly matched again for over 1,200 face-to-face job interviews, where 50% of the trainees and firms corresponded to the control group. In the end, 515 (42%) job interviews took place, with 32% of workers not attending due to their loss of interest and 30% of the firms withdrawing themselves also due to lost interest. The final survey sample remained balanced, though; the study found no evidence of out-selection of a specific group of firms and/or workers.

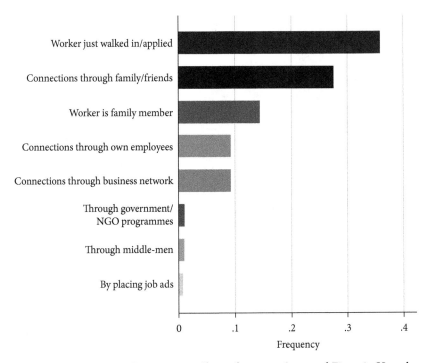

Fig. 2.6 Most Frequent Recruitment Channels among Surveyed Firms in Uganda
Note: Frequency of recruitment channels for the workers employed at baseline in the sample of
firms included in the matching–signalling experimental intervention.
Source: Bassi and Nansamba (2020)

Both the treatment and control groups took part in the matching module of
the experiment, while only workers and firms in the treatment groups received
signalling about workers' soft skills, in the form of an 'official' signed certificate
stating the degree in each of the five workers' soft skills.

A random half of all job interviews took place without workers and firms being given any prior information on soft skills scores. Instead participating trainees
received a placebo document only confirming programme participation. For the
other half of interviews, a detailed soft skills certificate was given and explained to
each participating trainee on the day of interview by BRAC staff members. BRAC
staff also showed the transcript to the employer at the start of the interview (which
then proceeded unobserved). The original document remained with the workers
for further use. Its high value among workers is underlined by the fact that control group participants reported a willingness to pay 44% of their average monthly
earnings to receive one.

To examine the impact of the signalling experiment, firm owners were surveyed
again six months after treatment, while workers took part in two follow-up surveys
after twelve and twenty-six months.

2.1.4 Does Signalling Skills Positively Affect Job Matching, Employment, and Welfare Outcomes?

The outcomes of this experiment are enlightening in that they underline the importance of removing informational barriers on both sides of the market that restrict efficient job matching:

1. **On the demand side, signalling of skills increased belief in workers' abilities.** Firm owners with higher cognitive abilities, as noted by a further survey on their abilities undergone by the researchers, reported that access to soft skills information helped them to view applicants more positively, and above their expectations. Controlling for manager heterogeneity confirms that this effect is not limited to the highest-score experimental workers but applies also to average workers. As downward revisions of beliefs in the abilities of the lowest-certified applicants were limited, the signalling intervention provided, on the whole, positive information to higher-ability managers. This revision of beliefs can have positive side effects in the recruitment process, even if the certified applicant did not get a job offer, or if they rejected it. Low-ability firm managers, however, revised their beliefs to a far lower extent.

2. **The cognitive and managerial ability of firm managers appears to be closely related to the size of informational barriers.** Higher-ability managers already: employed more skilled workers prior to the experiment; showed a strong tendency to update their belief in workers' skills and responsiveness following the signalling experiment; and were 13 percentage points more likely to hire a worker after the job interview. Low-ability firm owners, by and large, did not change their hiring behaviour in response to information disclosure; on average their workforce was less educated than the experimental trainee. This finding indicates a strong need for additional training in managerial skills among firm owners.

3. **On the supply side, the signalling intervention led high-scoring trainees to revise their belief in their employability and search behaviour upwards.** In the two years following the treatment, they reported: 7% higher expected earnings; 5% higher expected employment likelihood; a higher willingness to bargain for job contracts and wages; fewer problems to signal their skills to potential employers; and a stronger orientation towards larger firms and the public sector. At the same time, they were 15% less likely to be casually working. That is, while search intensity did not increase on average, the direction of job search changed significantly.

    This change in beliefs and behaviour was apparently not based on learning their soft skills, but on the value of the certificates in signalling such skills. Awareness of soft skills scores remained high in the two-year survey. Over

90% of all participants reported they still had the certificate two years after treatment, while 74% stated they were using it in job search activities. In a divergence from traditional firm-based job test schemes that do not disclose results to job applicants, the experiment denied firms an informational advantage by signalling test scores to both sides of the market. This allowed applicants to reach out to other job opportunities as well.

4. **The level of managerial abilities of firm owners seems to be closely related to the role firms can play in reducing or retaining informational barriers in the labour market.** If managers do not respond to signalling, the outcomes for workers are doubtful. This finding hints at the need for better training in managerial skills.

5. **The signalling treatment led to a higher probability of acquiring additional human capital.** While low-scoring workers benefited most from a rise in wage employment, high-scoring workers were roughly 4 percentage points more likely to have invested in additional education or training compared to the control group. This indicates a complementary dynamic between the certifying and acquiring of skills.

6. **Positive assortative matching was increased through the certificates.** Hiring intensity among the participating firms did not change on average, but higher-ability managers were more likely to employ workers with certificates. This was based on the managers' better judgement of qualifications and the positive self-selection of applicants in recognizing their soft skills.

7. **The certificates did not affect overall employment but did induce a change in the allocation of workers to firms.** While higher-scoring workers were more likely to be employed in firms with higher-ability managers, their employment likelihood in lower-ability firms was reduced given that the applicants significantly increased the minimum wage they were willing to accept. Employment gains reported by job applicants in the follow-up surveys stemmed from workers having found jobs in other firms (see Figure 2.7). Overall, workers were no more likely to be wage workers or self-employed at the time of the follow-up surveys, nor did the treatment affect the number of hours worked in the last job. Fewer than fifty workers were hired as a result of the treatment, while even fewer were still employed at the matched firm two years after treatment.

8. **The research did not find any impact of the signalling treatment on self-employment probability**, suggesting that skills certification makes its impact by proving skills to potential employers, rather than by increasing self-confidence, risk behaviour, and entrepreneurship willingness among workers.

9. **Average earnings increased due to the transition of workers to more productive jobs.** According to the authors' statistical analysis, the certification treatment led to an 11% rise in monthly earnings relative to the control

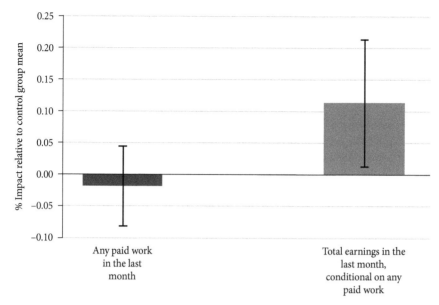

Fig. 2.7 Impacts of Soft Skills Certificates on Paid Employment and Earnings in Uganda

Note: Estimated impacts averaged over two years post-intervention (percentage increase over the control mean). The black bars correspond to 95% confidence intervals.
Source: Bassi, Nansamba, and Rasul (2018)

group average (see Figure 2.7). This can be explained by workers successfully searching for better job opportunities in the post-intervention period, by engaging in further education and retreating from casual work. On the demand side, the availability of soft skills information, and the fact that higher-ability firm owners with more productive businesses respond stronger to the certification, may induce higher wages for certified applicants. This finding confirms the role of beliefs and behaviour, and the importance of tackling informational barriers in terms of workers' unobserved skills.

2.1.5 Is Mandatory or Voluntary Country-Wide Certification of Skills a Realistic Policy Option?

Given that the outcomes of the skills certification programme described above were overall rather positive, and at a low cost of 19 USD per worker, the study assumes cost-effectiveness of the intervention even under a conservative scenario. Self-reported advantages in worker screening through the certificate, extension of job interview duration, and an upward revision of the ideal size of the firm's workforce among higher-ability managers, provide some indication of potentially lasting effects on firms' recruiting behaviour. Thus, to discuss upscaling a certificate intervention or even adopting mandatory soft skills certification appears plausible initially. However, Bassi and Nansamba (2020) have advised caution, as the impact on overall welfare may be ambiguous.

The additional information provided by the certificate allows firms to identify more appropriate workers but can also make hiring them more expensive as they become aware of alternative options. The certificate appears to incentivize high-scoring workers to find a job on their own initiative or gain further education, and to help lower-scoring workers get hired. In fact, the most significant gains of the signalling programme in terms of job offers and hires were found in the middle of the skills distribution: high-scoring workers did not enjoy a substantial increase in job offers, yet they faced large incentives to change their search and education behaviour, while lowest-scoring workers partially self-selected out of the programme.

If these groups were included in a voluntary or mandatory scheme, undesired effects would presumably occur. Both schemes would have similar effects with respect to 'outing' low-scoring workers. Not being able to provide a certificate would give a negative signal to firm managers, independently of voluntary or mandatory requirements. Firm managers showing a high interest in certain soft skills would sift out the workers with the lowest-certified additional skills, thus decreasing their job opportunities and potentially pushing them into the informal job sector.

Hence mandatory or voluntary skills certification may induce a better allocation of labour, produce net welfare gains, and increase inequality among workers at the same time. Policies aimed at overcoming information barriers in the recruitment process need to take account of the trade-off between (1) a better allocation of resources based on additional information, and (2) the risk of disadvantaging or even stigmatizing workers.

On the other hand, as Bassi and Nansamba (2020) argued, upscaling a certification programme may be the best answer to this trade-off between efficiency and equity. The study revealed positive effects on human capital formation among participating workers that could be enhanced, if the certification programme served as a systematic incentive to increase education, independently of the programme.

Upscaling a skills certification scheme would imply the provision of independent, reputable certification institutions. The authors rightly note that it would need significant effort to establish the credibility of new institutions, while entrusting vocational training institutes with this task could affect enrolment decisions among low-skilled trainees in the event that their expectations on their soft skills as signalled by a certificate are too low.

The low take-up rate in the experimental setting, in terms of hires resulting from job matching, deserves further research as it aligns with other research confirming rather weak responses to matching treatments (see for example Alfonsi et al. 2017 for a youth employment experiment in Uganda). While low take-up should not be viewed as an indicator of low treatment relevance, it remains uncertain whether upscaling would substantially increase employment outcomes.

Apart from that, the results of this GLM|LIC research project underline that **information barriers at the point of recruitment can help to explain the limited success of policies aimed at job matching in developing economies** (see for example Groh et al. 2015; Beam 2016; Alfonsi et al. 2017; Abebe et al. 2020a). Distributing skills information to both sides of the job market, and positive self-selection of applicants, can help to better target such policies and to facilitate job market screening by firms. As a secondary measure, supporting training in managerial skills and the setting up of firm-based assessment modules for soft skills could further enhance the efficiency of this approach.

2.2 What Constrains Labour Demand for Firms in Sub-Saharan Africa?

Barriers to market efficiency may result from imbalances in the distribution of labour between small and larger firms in low-income countries. If labour supply is more driven to smaller businesses with less productivity and lower wages, or to small-scale self-employment, total economic growth and workers' welfare may be negatively impacted, especially given population growth in the developing world.

Whether such a trend towards small firms can be observed in Ghana's manufacturing sector has been examined in a research project supported by GLM|LIC. Teal (2017) explored rich census and panel data to identify employment expansion patterns among small and large firms, finding that the latter are capital intensive and thus fail to expand employment, whereas small firms experience high returns on labour with very low capital intensity. As a result of financing constraints and small firms offering only lower wages, transitioning to informal self-employment instead of formal wage work is a widespread alternative.

The authors base their analysis on the 1962, 1987, 2003, and 2014 census data for Ghana's urban manufacturing sector. Descriptive figures—including an estimate for self-employed enterprises with employees—show that the number of large firms (one hundred or more employees) increased 2.5 times from 1962 to 2014. For medium-size firms (ten to ninety-nine workers) the increase was 3.3 times, while the number of small firms (fewer than ten employees) increased 5.6 times over the same period. The shares of total sectoral employment reveal a different picture: the employment share of small firms doubled from 32% to 64%, while the shares of medium-size and large firms fell sharply, from 30% to 15%, and from 37% to 20%, respectively. Although small firm growth slowed between 2003 and 2014, it is this segment that clearly dominates the manufacturing sector in urban Ghana (see Figures 2.8 and 2.9). More than 95% of all manufacturing firms in the data sample have fewer than ten employees; the average size was three employees in 2003.

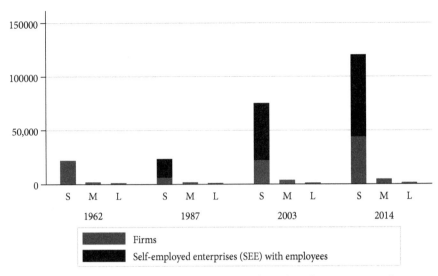

Fig. 2.8 Number of Manufacturing Firms and Self-Employed Enterprises with Employees in Urban Ghana

Note: See Teal (2017), p. 5, table 1 for detailed information on data sources. Small firms (S) with 1–9, medium firms (M) with 11–99, large firms (L) with 100, self-employed enterprises (SEE) with 1–4 employees.
Source: Teal (2017)

Notably, the figures for small firms include household-based self-employment enterprises with up to four employees. Trends in this segment appear to be the most important driver in terms of both small firm and total sector expansion. The number of self-employed businesses more than tripled from 1987 to 2003; a faster growth rate than regular firms during this period. Self-employed enterprises represented 63% of all small firms with up to nine employees in 2014, and 72% of firms with four or fewer employees. Among all firms in the sector, 63% were self-employed enterprises that same year. The share in sectoral employment of self-employed firms meanwhile increased to 36% in 2014.

This hints at the core role of self-employment in urban manufacturing in Ghana, but it stands in strong contrast to another striking figure: even when self-employment is taken into account, large firms are dominating in terms of value added, with a share of 63% among the largest 1% of manufacturing firms.

The study aimed to understand why significant employment growth in Ghana's manufacturing sector is due to small firms and household-based enterprises, which may not yield an optimal allocation of resources. It did so by merging 1991–2003 panel data on workers' and firms' characteristics and modelling the relationship between firm size and labour productivity per worker. The findings hint at the presence of market distortions leading to a sub-optimal allocation of labour:

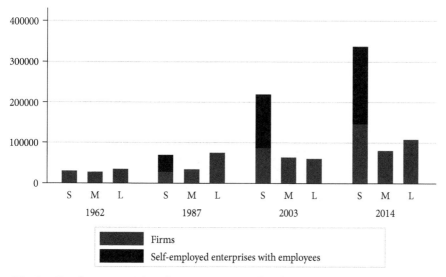

Fig. 2.9 Employment in Manufacturing Firms and Self-Employed Enterprises with Employees in Urban Ghana

Note: See Teal (2017), p. 5, table 1 for detailed information on data sources. Small firms (S) with 1–9, medium firms (M) with 11–99, large firms (L) with 100, self-employed enterprises (SEE) with 1–4 employees.
Source: Teal (2017)

1. **There is a clear positive link between labour productivity and firm size.** Larger firms utilize more capital-intensive production technologies, have lower capital costs, observe higher productivity, and thus pay higher wages. Conversely, the growing presence of small firms in Ghana's urban manufacturing sector indicates that the average productivity of firms has fallen.
2. **The negative link between profit rate (profits relative to the value of capital stocks) and firm size is equally evident.** Smaller firms in the sample have a far higher profit rate. This seems due to larger firms facing lower capital costs along with productivity growth.
3. **Profits per employee and median real annual earnings are three times larger for large firms than for small firms.** Firm size is a driver of both trends (see Figures 2.10 and 2.11). Larger firms choose higher-skilled workers and benefit from the product of their unobserved and unpaid skills.
4. However, on average, **larger and more productive firms did not grow in terms of employment.** Older firms are not larger, when controlling for productivity. **This points to the existence of significant barriers to market clearing and the expansion of larger businesses that may restrict overall economic growth.**

What can explain the puzzling result that employment has rebalanced in favour of enterprises with low productivity and relatively low wages? In the case of Ghana's

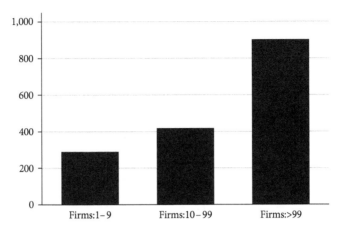

Fig. 2.10 Median Real Annual Profits per Employee in Ghana's Manufacturing Sector

Note: See Teal (2017), p. 5, table 1 for detailed information on data sources. Constant USD prices.
Source: Teal (2017)

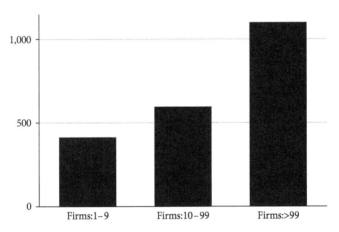

Fig. 2.11 Median Real Annual Earnings per Employee in Ghana's Manufacturing Sector

Note: See Teal (2017), p. 5, table 1 for detailed information on data sources. Constant USD prices.
Source: Teal (2017)

urban manufacturing industry, Teal (2017) concluded that the lack of employment growth in larger firms is closely related to the intensive formation of small firms. Put more technically, the high returns to physical capital investment in small firms raise the opportunity costs of additional labour to larger businesses. As a worker is faced with the opportunity to open up a small-sized enterprise and be self-employed, while rendering comparatively high returns to the wage that could be earned in a larger firm, the latter are confronted with an upward-sloping supply curve of labour, where hiring an additional worker becomes very costly. This 'blockage' to the employment growth of larger and older firms thus acts as a further incentive to establish small firms or additional household-based self-employment.

The study found little evidence that efficiency wages or rent capture of actual workers in larger firms had increased their wages above those available elsewhere, thus hampering the expansion of other firms. Instead, the author suggested another major barrier to employment expansion was posed by the higher profit of small firms and self-employed businesses. Profit per worker for small firms (with an average of three employees, in the study sample) may be substantially above the median wage in all but the largest firms. The study calculated the returns to small firms' capital to be roughly 900 USD as compared to median wages in the same firms of 500 USD. In such a scenario, forming a small firm or becoming an entrepreneur may be more attractive to workers than wage work. This aligns with Blattman and Dercon's (2016) finding that self-employment is viewed as a realistic alternative to wage jobs among entry-level job applicants in Ethiopia.

Relieving financial constraints would certainly help to disrupt these relationships. Better access to credit markets would lower the average capital cost for smaller firms, thus setting them on the road to productivity growth. At the same time, the increase in smaller firm wages would facilitate employment growth in larger, more productive firms.

Yet, as Teal (2017) remarked, the inefficiencies of capital markets in low-income economies make small-firm labour and self-employment a persistently attractive option. In the case of urban manufacturing in Ghana, the GLM|LIC study showed that simple economic modelling needs to be carefully amended to better capture the ambiguous outcomes of barriers to market clearing.

2.3 Does Wage Disparity Interfere with Market Clearing?

As discussed earlier in this chapter, attendance is—from the firm's perspective—among the most valued of workers' 'soft skills' in vulnerable low-income labour markets, where worker absenteeism appears to be widespread (see Chaudhury et al. 2006; Bassi and Nansamba 2020). **High absenteeism produces uncertainty and productivity losses in the formal labour market**. At the same time, given that paying wages in cash on a daily or weekly basis is quite common in many countries lacking reliable banking infrastructure, absenteeism may well be a sign that absent workers take up other casual and informal job opportunities instead. In this respect, increasing attendance in regular jobs could contribute to reducing market imbalances and increasing labour productivity in the formal sector.

Supported by GLM|LIC, a study by Breza, Kaur, and Shamdasani (2018) on workers' relative-pay concerns showed that workers' productivity and attendance are related to perceived wage inequality or unfairness. In a number of behavioural experiments with manufacturing employees in India, the authors found that **productivity drops and attendance substantially decreases if co-workers perceive their pay to be less than that of their peers**. This is particularly the case when differences in productivity are difficult to observe.

Productivity differentials were meanwhile difficult to observe. Pay inequality can then even interfere with social cohesion among workers—this may come at a high cost, particularly in developing economies where many economic activities are rooted in social connections.

To test the effects of different settings of relative pay on attendance, output and cohesion, the research team partnered with local contractors in the semi-rural periphery of Bhubaneswar—the capital and largest city of Odisha state, in Eastern India. Most workers in this region are engaged in agricultural work and are thus dependent on the seasonality of labour in this sector. That is, they are usually forced to search for jobs during the lean season (see Chapter 4 in this volume). These jobs, if available, are mostly short-term contract employment in industrial sectors such as construction and manufacturing, However, unemployment is quite common among agricultural workers in the lean season.

The experiment employed 378 adult male workers for thirty-five days in three low-skill manufacturing sites producing rope, brooms, floor mats, and other items (only one product per unit). Work was supervised and measured by hired 'managers', before local contractors sold the output on the local market. During the employment period, the experimental job was the main source of earnings for the workers' households—on average they had been unemployed for fifteen of the thirty days prior to the experiment. Workers received a flat daily wage for each day of attendance, at the same level as other short-term daily pay outside the experiment. All participants had previous experience with flat daily pay, as it is the typical pay structure for short-term contracts in the area. Almost half of the participants had previously worked under piece rates (whereby workers are paid for each item they produce).

For each round of the experiment, fifteen to thirty workers were selected from different villages and randomly assigned to the different product units with three workers per unit. Units were physically separated from each other to ensure a closed reference group. Workers' tasks remained unchanged for the entire employment period and were strictly individual, with no joint production at any time.

Payment conditions were announced on the first working day: during the fourteen days of training all workers received the same daily wage. There were no minimum output requirements, but workers were strictly fired for absences of three subsequent days or disruptive behaviour. Workers were told they would

Table 2.1 Experimental Wage Design to Assess Workers' Attendance, Output and Cohesion Behaviour in India

Worker Rank	Pay Disparity	Compressed Low	Compressed Medium	Compressed High
Low Productivity	W_{Low}	W_{Low}	W_{Medium}	W_{High}
Medium productivity	W_{Medium}	W_{Low}	W_{Medium}	W_{High}
High productivity	W_{High}	W_{Low}	W_{Medium}	W_{High}

Note: Randomization design; key comparison groups are marked with a box.
Source: Breza, Kaur, and Shamdasani (2018)

receive feedback on their productivity, and that daily pay in the subsequent period of twenty days would be be subject to a one-time pay rise, depending on the productivity ranking of each worker within their unit. After the initial training period all workers were randomized into one of four wage treatments, including unequal wages for all three co-workers according to their productivity rank, as well as three different levels of compressed wages (see Table 2.1).

Importantly, while workers were privately told of their wage increases by their managers, learning about co-workers' wages depended entirely on self-disclosure. The effect of absences on productivity was not shared with the workers (one day's absence was ignored, the second was recorded as zero production; no participants had three subsequent days of absence). Each worker was presented with their individual wage calendar on each day of attendance, as a reminder of their wage evolution. With wages raising by 4, 8, or 12%, all groups of workers were then paid above the level of external employment options.

The effect of increased wages on output and attendances was directly measured, whereas the extent of conflict or social cohesion was examined through a set of cooperative games on the final day of employment ('fun farewell') and by a separate survey on trust among co-workers, perceived wage fairness, and worker happiness. The final survey revealed a very high level of worker learning within their production unit: over 90% of workers with identical wages, and over 75% of workers with differential pay, correctly reported the wages of their co-workers. In contrast, less than 8% knew wage levels in other production units, showing that comparison took place mainly within units.

Attendance and Productivity of Workers Responds to Wage Schemes
What are the main outcomes of this experiment on workers' output and attendance?

1. **The study reveals that output of workers in units with differential pay decreased significantly**, relative to workers of the same rank and absolute wage

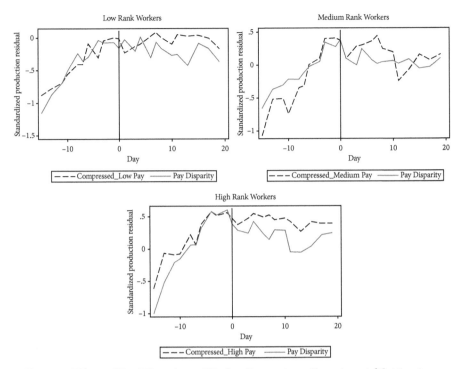

Fig. 2.12 Effects of Pay Disparity on Worker Output in an Experimental Setting in India

Note: Y-axis shows residuals of standardised output after removing individual fixed effects in the pre-period. Each plot compares workers of the same rank who earn the same wage, but are in compressed vs. pay disparity production units. Day 0 marks the beginning of the wage separation treatment.

Source: Breza, Kaur, and Shamdasani (2018)

level in the three groups with low, medium, and high compressed wages. After experiencing similar upward trends in productivity due to learning, workers with differential wages performed worse than workers with compressed wages across all productivity levels, and reduced their output by 22% on average (see Figure 2.12). Quality of production did not change significantly.

2. **This decline in output was mainly driven by a substantial decline in attendance, which accounted for more than half of the slowdown.** The attendance of a worker who was paid less than both of their co-workers was 12 percentage points lower. Remarkably, earning a higher wage than unit peers did not change the picture: median wage workers in pay disparity groups reduced attendance by 13 percentage points, while high-wage workers observed a slightly lower decline of 10 percentage points. This decline for all ranks is from a base of 94% attendance among workers in units with

compressed wages. That is, while the experimental design clearly served as an incentive for high attendance, it was in decline from the very moment pay inequality was introduced (which was disclosed among co-workers within a few days).

3. **While workers receiving lower wages than their peers reduce both their work effort and attendance, the negative impact on the productivity of higher-earning workers is entirely through attendance.** The study did not find evidence of reduced output during the days when workers in medium and high-wage pay disparity groups were present. This indicates that factors such as resentment at work may induce workers' absence. The negative effects of pay inequality on attendance strengthen over time.

4. **The high levels of absenteeism are only partially caused by workers choosing other short-term jobs on days of absence.** According to a survey, workers who applied for the experiment but were not hired took up casual work on less than 25% of days. Applying this rate to workers taking part in the experiment suggests that they waived 9% of their wages (and hence gave up more than the experimental wage premium over and above external options) in order to avoid a job with pay inequality schemes in place. Even when assuming that workers find other work every day they are absent, the foregone earnings amount to 7% of the respective earnings of workers outside the experiment. It should be noted, though, that the experiment did not capture potential welfare losses and excludes home production.

5. **Wage disparity is not in itself problematic, but perceived wage fairness is a driver of attendance.** The study did not find evidence that aversion to inequity affects output and attendance when different levels of productivity within a unit were large and easy to observe for workers. In contrast, perceptions of wage unfairness caused all experimental workers to reduce attendance and even forego earnings, regardless of whether they were paid more or less than co-workers.

6. **If wage disparity is not justified from a worker's perspective, cooperation within the production unit and reported happiness is reduced.** While higher-paid workers in pay disparity units considered their earnings fair, on average, being forced to work under disparity conditions apparently decreased their work satisfaction, attendance, and willingness to cooperate. This hints at an increase in resentment and reduced social cohesion in the work environment, stemming from discontent among lower-paid co-workers (which was confirmed by play games that showed better results for workers matched to external instead of unit partners).

7. **In an imperfect labour environment, dissatisfaction with wage inequality may induce distrust and perceptions of employer favouritism,** if the reasons for disparity of earnings are not obvious. Workers' relative-pay

concerns could thus affect wage scheme decisions in firms and give employers a reason to focus on wage compression instead of productivity-oriented wages.

Together, these findings illustrate the complex interrelationships between firms' wage structures, work satisfaction, output, and attendance. Given the high prevalence of flat-cash pay for daily and casual labour in low-income countries, and the importance of social networks for gaining access to jobs, insurance, and credit, it is not surprising that wage compression is prevalent in developing economies. **The social cost of wage disparity may outweigh its benefits in many settings.**

However, wage compression brings its own cost and distorts market clearing by depressing high-skilled workers' wages below the market-clearing level, while lifting low-skilled workers' earnings above this level. As a result, involuntary unemployment or informal labour among the low-skilled will increase, while labour supply of the high-skilled will decrease (see Akerlof and Yellen 1990).

Breza, Kaur, and Shamdasani (2018) suggested a threefold approach to tackle this problem and grow worker support for wage disparity schemes. Potential tools could include structuring organizations in team-oriented ways. This approach could match workers to reference groups more effectively, raising the work morale by increasing output transparency, and establish wage differentials for certain visible subgroups (for example, to foster gender equality). Yet many firms will not have the ability to implement demanding wage schemes (which would need systematic productivity screening) in a vulnerable economic environment. Supporting firms to reconsider their wage structures may thus be a useful policy strategy.

2.4 Tackling the Mobility Constraint: Do Transport Subsidies and Gendered Public Transport Help?

Barriers to market clearing in LICs are multifaceted and may also occur on a very practical level. For instance, the cost, availability and reliability of public transportation may present a severe barrier to job and education attendance. Excess labour supply in rural areas can persist, if travelling to urban areas with (potentially) better job opportunities is hampered by deficient transport infrastructure and prohibitively high costs. This may depress living conditions of rural workers during the lean season (see Chapter 4 in this volume). Furthermore, transport barriers can deter temporary labour migration, or even act as a driver of gender inequality.

While the benefits of better public transport infrastructure and punctuality are self-explanatory, the impact of transportation costs and the positive outcomes of relieving this barrier have been shown by recent research. Franklin (2018) and the above mentioned GLM|LIC studies by Abebe et al. (2020a), while Abebe et al.

(2017) examined the effects of temporary transport subsidy interventions on job search activities and employment in Ethiopia.

The latter studies highlight the temporary activation effect of transport subsidies among low-skilled young workers and women (see Chapter 3 in this volume). In a randomized experiment, a modest subsidy incentivized job seekers to look for job openings more frequently, with more focus, and with greater success. In this respect the transport subsidy had a dual effect: it allowed workers to use public transport more intensively to search for a job closer to the urban centre, and screen job vacancy boards there. Search activities and the probability of formal employment both increased by roughly 30% on average, compared to control group participants. The transport subsidy did not raise the absolute number of applications, but it allowed participants to search for jobs more efficiently and to focus on higher-quality work. At the same time the subsidy apparently helped reduce the need to engage in subsistence labour instead of looking for a better job or engaging in additional education.

However, these positive outcomes did not last. In the experimental setting, with a transport subsidy offer in place for a maximum period of twenty weeks, a survey among participating workers four years after treatment revealed that the positive effect had completely dissipated. Nevertheless, this is not to say that continuous transport subsidies could not result in more sustainable outcomes, while they still remain a relatively cheap intervention.

The findings provided by Abebe et al. (2017) also shed light on the relationship between the proximity to job markets and the prevalence of informal self-employment. The transport subsidy reduced self-employment among job seekers living further from the nearest urban centre.

Hence supporting mobility through better public transport infrastructure and subsidies for workers may help to overcome geographical barriers to market clearing. Conversely, these results indicate that financial constraints limit the intensity and ambition of job search activities among lower-qualified men and women, thus aggravating social inequality and leading to informal work. Relieving these constraints may thus represent a cost-efficient tool for improving the equity of opportunities in developing labour markets.

Notably, female participants experienced the strongest increase in employment probability. This finding hints at explicit deficits in female labour mobility that could be addressed by the subsidies—at least in the absence of strong social norms against working women.

In fact, transport barriers in developing countries may take a different direction that reaches beyond the scope of financial support. **Primarily in South Asia, prevalent social norms severely interfere with free mobility and economic activities of women outside their households** (see Chapter 8 in this volume). Using public transport unaccompanied by men is often stigmatized, and women risk sexual harassment and violence when travelling alone. As a result, female immobility rates are extremely high (see Adeel and Yeh 2018 for Pakistan)—a severe barrier to an autonomous role for women in the labour market, and to their training enrolment, employment prospects, and social status.

Against this demanding background, GLM|LIC supports research exploring the impact of gendered transport modes (women's compartments in trains and buses or women-only transport) on women's socio-economic outcomes (see Sajjad et al. 2018 and Chapter 8 of this volume for first results). This topic is highly relevant from a gender perspective but has not captured much research attention until today.

Collectively, mobility constraints—whether they stem from a lack of financial resources, deficient and unreliable public transport infrastructure, or social norms—must not be underestimated with respect to labour markets in low-income countries. Improving labour mobility at the local and regional level may contribute substantially to raising employment opportunities among disadvantaged groups.

Key Takeaways From This Chapter

- Inefficient matching of labour supply and demand impedes growth and development in LICs.
- Job search support and improved skills signalling can reduce information frictions in both directions.
- Job application training and transport subsidies are cost-effective programmes to help disadvantaged workers find stable, formal employment in urban labour markets.
- Active labour market policies must also address the mismatch of expectations among job seekers and employers.
- Certification of hard and soft skills can reduce information barriers, though at the risk of disadvantaging or even stigmatizing workers.
- Barriers to market clearing may impede total economic growth and workers' welfare by driving labour supply to smaller businesses with lower productivity and wages.
- Relieving financial constraints and improving access to credit markets would lower smaller firms' average capital cost and facilitate productivity growth.
- Supporting firms to implement wage structures with higher perceived fairness of pay could reduce absenteeism and increase worker output.
- Improving mobility through better public transport infrastructure and subsidies for workers may help to overcome geographical barriers to market clearing, especially for women.

References

Abebe, G., Caria, S., Fafchamps, M., Falco, P., Franklin, S., and Quinn, S., 2017. Anonymity or Distance? Job Search and Labour Market Exclusion in a Growing African City. GLM|LIC Working Paper No. 34.

Abebe, G., Caria, S., Fafchamps, M., Falco, P., Franklin, S., and Quinn, S., 2020a. Anonymity or Distance? Job Search and Labour Market Exclusion in a Growing African City. *Review of Economic Studies*, 88(3): 1279–1310.

Abebe, G., Caria, S., Fafchamps, M., Falco, P., Franklin, S., Quinn, S., and Shilpi, F., 2020b. Matching Firms and Young Jobseekers through a Job Fair: A Field Experiment in Africa. Working Paper. Available from: https://web.stanford.edu/~fafchamp/JobFair.pdf

Abel, M., Burger, R., and Piraino, P., 2020. The Value of Reference Letters: Experimental Evidence from South Africa. *American Economic Journal: Applied Economics* 12(3): 40–71.

Adeel, M., and Yeh, A. G. O., 2018. Gendered Immobility: Influence of Social Roles and Local Context on Mobility Decisions in Pakistan. *Transportation Planning and Technology*, 41(6): 660–78.

Akerlof, G. A., and Yellen, J. L., 1990. The Fair Wage-Effort Hypothesis and Unemployment. *Quarterly Journal of Economics*, 105(2): 255–83.

Alfonsi, L., Bandiera, O., Bassi, V., Burgess, R., Rasul, I., Sulaiman, M., Vitali, A., 2017. Tackling Youth Unemployment: Evidence from a Labour Market Experiment in Uganda. STICERD - Development Economics Papers, eopp64.

Bassi, V., and Nansamba A., 2020. Screening and Signaling Non-Cognitive Skills: Experimental Evidence from Uganda. USC-INET Research Paper No. 19–08.

Bassi, V., Nansamba, A., and Rasul, I., 2018. The Labor Market Impacts of Soft Skills Certificates. GLM|LIC Policy Brief No. 21.

Beam, E. A., 2016. Do Job Fairs Matter? Experimental Evidence on the Impact of Job-Fair Attendance. *Journal of Development Economics*, 120: 32–40.

Blattman, C. J., and Dercon, S., 2016. Occupational Choice in Early Industrializing Societies: Experimental Evidence on the Income and Health Effects of Industrial and Entrepreneurial Work. IZA Discussion Paper No. 10255.

Breza, E., Kaur, S., and Shamdasani, Y., 2018. The Morale Effects of Pay Inequality. *Quarterly Journal of Economics*, 133(2): 611–63.

Bryan, G., Chowdhury; S., and Mobarak, A. M., 2014. Underinvestment in a Profitable Technology: The Case of Seasonal Migration in Bangladesh. *Econometrica*, 82(5): 1671–1748.

Card, D., Ibarrarán, P., Regalia, F., Rosas-Shady, D., and Soares, Y., 2011. The Labor Market Impacts of Youth Training in the Dominican Republic. *Journal of Labor Economics*, 49(2): 267–300.

Carranza, E., Garlick, R., Orkin, K., and Rankin, N., 2020. Job Search and Hiring with Two-sided Limited Information about Workseekers Skills. CSAE Working Paper WPS/2020-10.

Chaudhury, N., Hammer, J., Kremer, M., Muralidharan, K., and Rogers, F. H., 2006. Missing in Action: Teacher and Health Worker Absence in Developing Countries. *Journal of Economic Perspectives*, 20,(1): 91–116.

Crépon, B., and van den Berg, G., 2016. Active Labor Market Policies. Annual Review of Economics, 8(1): 521–46.

Donovan, K., Lu, J., and Schoellman, T., 2018. Labor Market Flows and Development. Meeting Papers 976, Society for Economic Dynamics.

Franklin, S., 2018. Location, Search Costs and Youth Unemployment: Experimental Evidence from Transport Subsidies. *Economic Journal*, 128(614): 2353–79.

Groh, M., Krishnan, N., McKenzie, D., and Vishwanath, T., 2012. Soft Skills or Hard Cash? The Impact of Training and Wage Subsidy Programs on Female Youth Employment in Jordan. World Bank Policy Research Working Paper No. 6141.

Groh, M., McKenzie, D., Shammout, N., and Vishwanath, T., 2015. Testing the Importance of Search Frictions and Matching through a Randomized Experiment in Jordan. *IZA Journal of Labor Economics*, 4(7).

Hardy, M., and McCasland, J., 2017. Are Small Firms Labor Constrained? Experimental Evidence From Ghana. PEDL Research Papers.

Jensen, R., 2012. Do Labor Market Opportunities Affect Young Women's Work and Family Decisions? Experimental Evidence from India. *Quarterly Journal of Economics*, 127(2): 753–92.

Kluve, J., 2016. A Review of the Effectiveness of Active Labour Market Programmes with a Focus on Latin America and the Caribbean. ILO Research Department Working Paper No. 9.

McKenzie, D., 2017. How Effective are Active Labor Market Policies in Developing Countries? A Critical Review of Recent Evidence. World Bank Policy Research Working Paper No. 8011.

McKenzie, D., and Woodruff, C., 2014. What Are We Learning from Business Training and Entrepreneurship Evaluations around the Developing World? World Bank Research Observer 29(1): 48–82.

Pallais, A. 2014. Inefficient Hiring in Entry-Level Labor Markets. *American Economic Review*, 104(11): 3565–99.

Sajjad, F., Anjum, G. A., Field, E., and Vyborny, K., 2018. Overcoming Barriers to Women's Mobility: Improving Women's Access to Public Transport in Pakistan. GLM|LIC Policy Brief No. 24.

Teal, F., 2017. What Constrains the Demand for Labour in Firms in Sub-Saharan Africa? Some Evidence from Ghana. GLM|LIC Synthesis Paper No. 6.

3

The Role of Employability Training and Behavioural Change

A major challenge that faces young people in developing countries is their lack of relevant skills needed by employers. Governments and NGOs design initiatives to enable individuals in developing countries to bridge their skills gap and achieve better labour market outcomes. Among the most common tools are training programmes that stimulate the acquisition of qualifications and associated skills. Despite the growing number of such training programmes in low-income countries, many lack any rigorous evaluation with respect to their targeting and effectiveness. Considerable evidence suggests, however, that these programmes are often not very effective or cost efficient.

Given the severe constraints in LICs that prevent individuals from entering the labour market, taking up good jobs, or achieving positive outcomes as entrepreneurs, a better understanding and focusing of skills training programmes is critical to any growth strategy. Apart from efforts to enhance vocational and on-the-job training, as well as entrepreneurial abilities, skills training must address the basics: if informational barriers and behavioural issues are not solved first, vulnerable and incomplete labour markets may not be able to fully benefit from traditional skills training schemes. With the youth labour force on the rise in most LICs, a key responsibility for governments is to create favourable conditions for skills acquisition and job matching.

Supported by GLM|LIC, several research projects shed new light on this topic by evaluating innovative employability training as well as preparatory interventions to rehabilitate disadvantaged groups. This chapter presents the core findings—with a focus on the impact of signalling interventions—and draws some policy conclusions.

3.1 How Should Training Programmes Be Designed for Workers?

Today, skills training is at the heart of most development aid strategies worldwide. The United Nations Development Programme identifies skills training as a highly relevant measure in the pursuit of sustainable economic growth

Labour Markets in Low-Income Countries. David Lam and Ahmed Elsayed, Oxford University Press.
© David Lam and Ahmed Elsayed (2022). DOI: 10.1093/oso/9780192897107.003.0003

(United Nations Development Programme 2016). Empirical evidence on the impact of training on the people in low-income regions is scarce but growing. Meanwhile, several studies—see Attanasio, Kugler, and Meghir (2011) for a good example—have proven the relevance of skills training as a means to succeed in the labour market. Research has frequently evaluated the impact of randomized training programmes that offer training to some individuals, while excluding others, by studying the different, similar, or identical effects on both groups.

By using this method of randomized controlled trials (RCT), economists aim to identify the effectiveness of a given programme for a treatment group when compared with similar control groups sharing the same characteristics. As Attanasio, Kugler, and Meghir (2011) have shown in the case of Colombia, such programmes may generate much larger net gains in lower-/middle-income countries than those found in high-income countries: the effect of additional skills should be stronger for treatment groups with lower qualifications or those who lack access to formal education. A training programme for disadvantaged young people was proven to significantly raise earnings and employment for young women, mainly in formal-sector jobs, in Colombia after 2005.

Nonetheless, not every training intervention is likely to work, depending on the country or regional context and the treatment concept. Brooks, Donovan, and Johnson (2018) demonstrated that inexperienced female microenterprise owners in a Kenyan slum substantially benefited from informal mentorship by an experienced entrepreneur in the same community, while a formal business education intervention showed no effect on profits despite changes in business practice. As Groh et al. (2012) have pointed out in evaluating a programme to help female community college graduates in Jordan to find a job, soft-skills training failed to result in a positive average impact on employment, while wage subsidies generated short-term effects only.

These findings emphasize that missing information and mis-shaped information channels are a barrier to profitability and sustainable economic success. The type of information matters: it seems access to localized, specific knowledge (or implementing an alumni model, for example Lafortune, Rothstein, and Schanzenbach 2018), may stimulate economic success; abstract, general information from the classroom does not necessarily work in the same direction.

The body of evaluation literature focusing on training efforts in developing countries is growing continuously, but most of the training programmes in the developing world have not been thoroughly evaluated. According to McKenzie and Woodruff (2014) and McKenzie et al. (2020), who discussed a number of existing business training and entrepreneurship evaluations at the level of small firms in developing countries, these studies are often of limited use and do not allow for generalized conclusions due to small sample sizes, short measurement periods, and survey attrition. Hence, evaluation results seldom clearly reveal whether a strong or modest effect is due to training or is more likely the result of other circumstances. One of the few findings to be distilled from the existing business training evaluations over a short time horizon is that training effects on existing firms and their probability of survival seem to be rather modest, while stronger training effects are seen with respect to entrepreneurs launching new firms more quickly.

Evaluation studies would be incomplete if they failed to consider potential hidden and secondary effects that are not easy to measure yet could influence the overall evaluation effect—positively or negatively. **Skills training and other programmes may result in behavioural and societal changes that should not be underestimated.** Some programmes may not only affect the group of eligible households but also reach beyond. That is, research limiting its focus to the direct effect of the treatment could very well underestimate the true positive impact. For instance, as Angelucci and De Giorgi (2009) have noted, cash transfer programmes at the local level may also indirectly affect ineligible groups living in the same target region who receive loans or reduce their savings. In such a scenario a full evalua-tion set needs to analyse the effects on the entire local economy, rather than being limited to selected treatment and control groups from the same community.

However, the opposite may apply: the treatment effect could be far less positive or even turn negative if undesirable side effects such as free-rider behaviour or windfall effects result from an imprecise definition of treatment groups. At the same time, positive effects may shrink or disappear when it comes to scaling. Field experiments on skills training showing a clear positive impact may lift hopes for larger-scale effects that could be deceptive, depending on the nature of the treatment (see Berge et al. 2012). Effects of training programmes may also be over-estimated because the programmes simply change which individuals are getting jobs, without any increase in overall employment. For example, a skills programme that gives participants a credential may cause those in the programme to be prefer-entially hired by employers, even though they did not actually acquire additional skills and without any overall positive impact on employment or productivity.

Last, but not least, the evaluation of skills training should consider whether its effects could be changed by combining direct interventions aimed at qualification with treatments such as cash transfers or other behavioural incentives. Weak re-sults from an existing skills training programme do not necessarily rule out more positive results being achieved when the programme is combined with additional treatments.

Given this picture of training programmes, policymakers often face substantial uncertainty on how to design (or redesign) skills training programmes in low-income countries, which may lead to undesirable cost inefficiencies under budget constraints.

The Growth and Labour Markets in Low-Income Countries Programme ex-plicitly aims to overcome these deficits by adding careful RCT evaluations of promising training innovations in low-income countries, thus enriching the body

of relevant research findings. Novel GLM|LIC studies provide in-depth evalua-
tions of a number of training interventions across several countries, including
Kenya, Liberia, Bangladesh, Pakistan, Togo, Madagascar, and Senegal. The innovations include, for example, combining training courses with cash transfers and
behavioural interventions aimed at reshaping attitudes that deter people from education. Some of the interventions also investigate the role of non-cognitive skills.

The outcomes studied often go beyond the regular labour market outcomes of
employment and wages, and include other social outcomes such as risk attitudes
or violence. In the following subsections, we summarize the findings of some ex-
emplary evaluations and discuss the lessons learned about the types of training
and the contexts (geographic and cultural) in which these programmes are likely
to work.

3.1.1 Personal Initiative Training vs Traditional Training

One promising approach in skills training has been to incorporate insights from
other fields like behavioural economics, marketing science, and psychology. These
approaches may replace the need for traditional business training or complement
at the margin their effects.

A GLM|LIC-funded project (Compos et al. 2017, 2018, 2020) investigated the
importance of alternative skills by comparing two types of training: traditional
managerial training, and a psychology-based personal initiative training programme. The traditional business training focused on four core topics: accounting
and financial management, marketing, human resource management, and formalization, while the personal initiative training focused on teaching self-starting
behaviour, innovation, identifying and exploiting new opportunities, goal-setting,
planning, and feedback cycles.

The authors conducted a randomized controlled trial with 1,500 microenterprises in Lomé, Togo, 53% of them female entrepreneurs, to compare the impacts
of standard business training to personal initiative training. The microenterprises came from a variety of industries (27% manufacturing, 48% commerce,
25% services). The 1,500 microentrepreneurs were randomly assigned into three
groups, each of 500 firms: a control group, a traditional business training treatment
group, and a personal initiative training treatment group. Both training courses
were held for a total of thirty-six hours in three half-day sessions per week in April
2014, followed by a trainer visiting the businesses individually once a month over
the following four months to reinforce the concepts. Four rounds of follow-up surveys were collected between September 2014 and September 2016, enabling the
tracking of business outcomes for over two years after the training.

The personal initiative had very large effects on innovation and capital investment, but also on business practices learnt in traditional programmes, including
record keeping and HR management. The evaluation showed that entrepreneurs

who took the personal initiative training saw their profits rise by an average of 30% relative to the control group (40% for female entrepreneurs), compared with a statistically insignificant 11% effect for traditional training (5% for female entrepreneurs). The training is cost effective, paying for itself within one year.

The traditional business training led microentrepreneurs to increase their use of standard business practices, such as accounting, marketing, and stock control. However, even without explicitly teaching these practices, microentrepreneurs who received personal initiative training adopted almost as many of these practices as those in the traditional business training programme.

In addition to higher profits and increased use of standard business practices, business owners who received personal initiative training were more innovative, introduced more new products to their businesses, and were more likely to diversify into a new product line than those in traditional training. After personal initiative training, business owners borrowed more and made larger investments. Personal initiative training was particularly effective for female-owned businesses (Compos et al. 2018), for whom traditional training has often been ineffective. Women who received personal initiative training saw their profits increase by 40% compared with the control group and as against a 5% impact for traditional business training. Personal initiative training increased error competence (ability to recover from errors) and entrepreneurial passion, which led to strengthened business success of female entrepreneurs. While both the traditional business training and the personal initiative training cost around 750 USD per participant (a cost subsidized by the study), the personal initiative approach paid for itself within one year given the increase in participants' monthly profits following the training.

This study's findings make a strong case for the role of psychology in supporting profit growth for women entrepreneurs by helping them to develop an entrepreneurial mindset. Based on these promising results, the personal initiative training has been implemented in programmes in several other countries including Ethiopia and Mexico, where it was combined with a traditional business training programme and is being developed in other locations such as Mauritania, Mozambique, and the Democratic Republic of Congo. Research underway in these contexts will reveal whether this training can develop more successful entrepreneurs in other settings as well and will inform if other target groups such as rural communities can benefit from this training.

3.1.2 Demand for Professional Training Interferes with Practical Constraints

Two studies supported by GLM|LIC evaluated training programmes within the ready-made garments (RMG) industry in Bangladesh—a major, rapidly growing sector in the country's emerging economy with over 4 million employees and a share of over 80% of total export earnings (Bangladesh Bureau of Statistics, 2021, p. 98).

Given the high economic—and social—relevance of the Bangladeshi garments industry, skills training at the firm and individual level is an obvious strategy to fight poverty and labour shortages at the same time. But which approach is the more promising and efficient? What does the evaluation of firm-level training reveal when compared to a policy aimed at helping jobless individuals overcome extreme poverty by gaining the qualifications to obtain jobs in the garments industry? While Macchiavello, Rabbani, and Woodruff (2015) analysed the market for training services using a demand experiment with garment factories, Shonchoy, Raihan, and Fujii (2017) studied a local NGO's training programme components aimed at workers.

Promoting managerial skills could help overcome deficits with respect to productivity and poor labour relations in low-income countries' core industrial sectors. This consideration led Macchiavello, Rabbani, and Wodruff (2015) to study the demand for professional training of line supervisors in the garments market in Bangladesh, which has around 3,000 exporting factories. According to the authors, a regular market for training services is almost non-existent so far—less than 10% of supervisors completed any job-related formal training.

In cooperation with local training centres, the German Technical Cooperation Agency (GIZ), and a local marketing service provider, three six-day external training modules were developed and offered to a sample of almost 300 exporting firms, 135 of which were finally reached. All potential customers, most of them human resource (HR) managers, were approached via phone and offered training courses at discount prices. Detailed information about the initiative was offered through a bilingual brochure and a descriptive video. The experiment allowed firms to choose and buy training session slots at randomly varied prices (60–100% of the full training costs) and to test the programme and training quality and convenience via free slots in a chosen module. The modules consisted of training in productions planning, quality enhancing, and human resources practices around leadership and social compliance.

A high number of firm managers—120—requested further information on the programme, with a higher probability of a request for additional details on processing and quality enhancement training (independent from pricing information), while interest in further HR training information declined when price information was given. The marketing experiment proved a lower, more price-sensitive potential demand for HR and social compliance training, with the exception of larger, quality-orientated firms.

However, at the next, more concrete stage—the offer of a free slot test—the initial high response rate declined to just eighty-six firm decision-makers who responded to a phone call. Of these, only sixteen (less than 6% of the whole sample) ultimately accepted a free training slot. The study found the treatment options and prices had no effect on the probability of taking up a free slot.

The experiment further revealed the reasons for rejecting the training offer:

- 25% of the firm representatives refused the offer due to high production pressure.
- 20% said their firms could not spare active supervisors for six days.
- 15% doubted the effectiveness of the training.
- 15% refused to send their employees to external training.
- 10% were afraid to lose their employees to other firms after completion of the training.

Remarkably, only two factories cited their own training initiatives as a reason not to ask for further information or a free test slot.

These results clearly show that **even professionally organized and firm-tailored training programmes aimed at strengthening productivity and better workplace conditions may be directed into a vacuum and miss their targets.** In the case of the Bangladeshi garments industry, high production pressures resulting from severe competition, just-in-time processing, and fast-track deliveries apparently make firms hesitant to train up their lower-level managers. As the study shows, pricing is not a core factor in decisions, indicating that a market solution for training courses without long-term subsidies could nevertheless work. Future research might demonstrate that certified measures—training programmes that have proven their firm-orientated effectiveness—could overcome existing obstacles.

3.1.3 Targeting Worker Skills Training to Firms' Demands and the Low-Educated

If firm-level skills training faces substantial barriers, what about directing training programmes at workers instead? A GLM|LIC study by Shonchoy, Raihan, and Fujii (2017) employed RCT techniques to explore which components of a selected training programme of a local NGO in north-eastern Bangladesh helped individuals to take and keep jobs in the ready-made garments industry or manufacturing sector, and thus reduce their families' extreme poverty. The programme was located in one of the poorest regions of Bangladesh—one that has not been a major location for garment factories. The authors collected detailed information about a total of 2,215 eligible participants' households, before randomly assigning each participant to one of four treatment groups or a control group, then surveying them six, twelve, and eighteen months after the training.

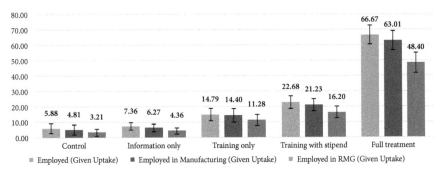

Fig. 3.1 Employment Rate in First Follow-up Survey (six months)
Source: Shonchoy, Raihan, and Fujii (2017), survey data

The free-of-cost training included different components for each treatment group: group i received a day-long job-related information session; group ii was given one month of residential skills training; group iii received the month of residential skills training along with a stipend to finance the costs resulting from joining the training programme (migration from another region and foregone income); while group iv received the same as group iii plus four weeks of on-the-job training during a paid internship in a factory (full treatment). The study evaluated the outcomes for each treatment in terms of job take-up, success, and continuation, and assessed the effects on the families' socio-economic conditions. Interestingly, the study did not suffer from a high attrition rate—on average, across all surveys, just 5% of participants did not respond.

The training programme experienced a take-up rate of overall 66.5% with a low drop-out rate of roughly 5% (due, for example, to seasonal labour demand or non-economic factors). Six months after the treatment, the survey showed an overall employment rate of 21.8%—driven by very high rates for those who passed a full treatment including on-the-job-training (group iv) (see Figure 3.1). Almost 50% of this group were employed in the RMG industry, compared with 4.4% for the group that only received information (group i), 11.3% for those that received one month of residential skills training (group ii) and 16.2% for those that received the training and a stipend. At the same time, just 3.2% of the control group managed to find employment without any training.

Unsurprisingly, the employment rates fell over time: one year after training, the overall employment in any sector fell to 12.2% (overall), while for the RMG sector it fell to 10.5% (full treatment), 6.6% (training with stipend), and about 4% for the other groups including the control group. These numbers are still remarkably high and underline the effectiveness of the programme. Training and accompanying support definitely made a difference, since employment in the manufacturing sector also remained significantly above the control group level (see Figure 3.2).

Fig. 3.2 Employment Rate in Second Follow-up Survey (twelve months)
Source: Shonchoy, Raihan, and Fujii (2017), survey data

In general, the study shows how useful skills training initiatives may be when orientated towards industry demands and well targeted towards the poor. However, mere information strategies hardly show any sustainable effect, whereas **combining skills training with on-the-job learning and/or stipends reveals substantial and lasting effects on employment and socio-economic status.** These findings include a clear policy message for LICs' emerging industry sectors: skills training offered to individuals should facilitate networking between participants and factories to secure the largest positive effects.

3.2 Using Training to Address Risky Behaviour in Times of Social Instability

Skills training may represent a chance to escape a vicious circle of low qualification, unemployment or precarious income, and crime, that is present—especially for young men—in many LICs, hindering economic growth and fostering social instability. In the worst cases, fragile societies mobilize this disadvantaged group for rioting or rebellion. Policy strategies for cognitive abilities training thus need rehabilitation efforts to first lay the groundwork for shaping values, behaviour, and non-cognitive abilities. Blattman, Jamison, and Sheridan (2017) undertook a field experiment in Liberia to evaluate whether adulthood non-cognitive investments and interventions can influence and change behaviour, a topic with little empirical evidence so far (see Heckman and Kautz 2014).

The authors recruited 999 high-risk men (from a sample of around 1,500) aged 18 to 35 in Liberia's capital Monrovia, mostly involved in dealing and consuming drugs, and in theft and violence. Given the country's recent history—two civil wars, combat, and displacement of the population's majority—the selected group had spent several years in chaos, without functioning social and labour market structures. At an average age of 25, most members of the target group worked in low-skill and illicit labour market segments with an average monthly income of 68 USD, for roughly fifty hours per week. More than one-third were formerly engaged in armed groups.

The interventions programme took a dual approach. One quarter of the participants were randomly assigned to an eight-week cognitive behaviour therapy (CBT) addressing anger, impulsivity, depression, and other behavioural barriers. The CBT group therapy, 'STYL' (the Sustainable Transformation of Youth in Liberia), was developed by the local community organization NEPI (Network for Empowerment & Progressive Initiative) and conducted by former street youth, ex-criminals, and ex-combatants. The programme aimed to foster patience, self-control, and a non-criminal attitude as a community member, by giving guidance that focused on reflection and willingness to change, goal-setting, and cooperation.

The workshop sessions were held three times per week for three to four hours, engaging around twenty participants in role-playing, experience exchange, and stimulation of behavioural change regarding social norms. Homework lessons included visits by advisors as well as a focus on goal identification and planning of steps towards resocialization and employment. An extended literature has shown that social identity can be changed through therapies targeted at reshaping preferences and values (see for example Akerlof and Kranton 2000; Almlund et al. 2011). But does it also work for the most disadvantaged in a fragile low-income society?

To test this, another random group received an unconditional cash offer of 200 USD (equalling three months' wages) via a lottery run in partnership with a non-profit organization that distributed the cash. A second group received CBT and cash. The last group of participants received no support and thus served as the control group. On average, both treatments amount to around 530 USD per participant. The survey included pre-interviews, with follow-up interviews a few weeks and a full year after the programme. Two-thirds of the participants (among them the most likely higher-risk individuals) attended most or all therapy sessions, with 98% collecting the cash grant.

The experimental findings clearly indicate that **a targeted intervention may deter high-risk individuals from their former risky behaviour** as a first, but potentially decisive, step on the way to focused skills training later on. They signal as well, though, that undertaking such a strategy—which seems inevitable for developing societies shaken by violence—will need patience and continuous focused interventions.

As a result of receiving therapy followed by a cash grant, participants changed their *anti-social* behaviour (violence, crime, and related behaviour). Compared to the control group, drug-dealing and theft shrunk by a third within weeks. One year later, the participants reported a lower likelihood of exhibiting aggressive and hostile behaviour, thus revealing a lasting programme effect. The likelihood of carrying a weapon and engaging in criminal activities even fell by half. While the control group reported stealing to be an almost weekly activity, on average, the recipients of therapy and cash showed substantially lower rates. It seems **the behavioural therapy succeeded in generating non-cognitive changes with respect to self-control, time preferences and values. The cash, meanwhile, strengthened, stabilized, and prolonged this effect by sending reinforcing signals and allowing for some saving and activity changes, at least for a limited period**.

For those not receiving the cash support, the therapy effects diminished step by step over the course of the study year. An isolated cash intervention resulted in a similar, rather transient, effect in encouraging individuals away from illicit behaviour. Although the study did not find evidence that the cash was wasted, its effect on enhancing chances of reducing criminal activity was limited (although stealing was considerably reduced), again due to high-risk levels in the absence of functioning security provided by the state in the neighbourhoods targeted individuals lived.

The study is an important addition to existing research, in transferring results that have so far only been shown for rehabilitation programmes in developed countries such as the USA (see Heller et al. 2017) to the framework of low-income countries. **Reducing anti-social behaviour within a high-risk treatment group by up to around 50% looks to also be an achievable policy goal for developing societies that aim to lay the foundations for efficient skills training programmes**.

In an ongoing GLM|LIC project Hicks et al. (2011) compare and contrast the relative efficacy of providing vocational training and small business start-up grants in Kenya. The project builds on an earlier randomized evaluation of a vocational training voucher programme in Kenya that included nearly 2,200 youths. In the previous programme, a randomly selected half of programme participants were awarded a voucher that covered the cost of vocational training. The project will support the analysis of the near-term impacts of vocational training, including an evaluation of the differential returns between private and public training and the impacts of training in the informal sector. Furthermore, the project will support an additional intervention which will randomly select half of the voucher winners and half of the non-winners to receive an unconditional cash grant that is sufficient to purchase toolkits or provide seed capital for their entrepreneurial ventures.

The randomized cross-cutting design of this project will enable the researchers to simultaneously estimate the impacts of vocational training, start-up grants, and the combination of both interventions. The use of randomization in treatment assignment will circumvent concerns about selection bias and confounding factors. Furthermore, detailed longitudinal data (the Kenya Life Panel Survey) covering nearly fifteen years is available on all programme participants, which will enable the exploration of heterogeneous treatment effects on different sub-populations in the sample. This panel data will also allow the researchers to closely examine the dynamics and patterns of youth employment outcomes. In addition to providing rigorous evidence on the near-term and medium- to long-term returns to vocational training for African youth, a key contribution of this project will be to provide some of the first experimental evidence on the complementarities between vocational education and financial capital in Africa, by combining randomized interventions with high-quality longitudinal data.

GLM|LIC supported a number of skills training programmes specifically targeted to women. These projects are discussed in Chapter 8, which focuses on gender dimensions of labour markets in LICs. These training programmes included many of the features discussed here, including cash transfers, soft skills, and behavioural interventions.

Overall, the research initiated by GLM|LIC on skills training, skills signalling, and adjacent fields supports the assessment of whether subsidies that facilitate job search and public transport in low-income societies should accompany skills-orientated intervention strategies targeted at disadvantaged groups. The findings show that skills signalling interventions, in particular, offer a cost-efficient means of overcoming information barriers and supporting better job matching, as well as increasing job quality and earnings.

At the same time, internship programmes may be a simple but effective tool when combined with external skills training. This dual treatment, according to GLM|LIC results, may facilitate matching between disadvantaged job seekers—with limited ability to signal their employability—and potential employers in large low-income cities. Rehabilitation strategies may also offer an instrument for reshaping the values of the socially excluded towards employability.

Key Takeaways from this Chapter

- Training programmes do not necessarily increase overall employment as they may improve the prospects of some job seekers at the expense of others.
- Through behavioural and societal changes, positive effects as well as undesirable side effects of skills training may extend beyond eligible households.
- Promoting managerial skills could help increase productivity and improve labour relations in LICs' core industrial sectors.
- Practical constraints in high-pressure work environments make firms hesitant to engage in training their employees.
- Skills training offered to individuals generate larger positive effects when networking between participants and factories is facilitated.
- Behavioural therapy combined with cash grants has proven successful at reducing high-risk individuals' anti-social behaviours, thus paving the way for efficient skills training.

References

Akerlof, G. A., and Kranton, R. E., 2000. Economics and Identity. *Quarterly Journal of Economics*, 65: 715–53.

Almlund, M., Duckworth, A. L., Heckman, J., and Kautz, T., 2011. Personality Psychology and Economics. In E. Hanushek, S. Machin, and L. Woessman, eds., *Handbook of the Economics of Education*. Amsterdam: Elsevier, 1–181.

Angelucci, M., and De Giorgi, G., 2009. Indirect Effects of an Aid Program: How Do Cash Transfers Affect Ineligibles' Consumption? *American Economic Review*, 99, 486–508.

Attanasio, O., Kugler, A., and Meghir, C., 2011. Subsidizing Vocational Training for Disadvantaged Youth in Colombia: Evidence from a Randomized Trial. *American Economic Journal: Applied Economics*, 3, 188–220.

Bangladesh Bureau of Statistics, 2021. Statistical Year Book Bangladesh 2020. Available from: http://bbs.portal.gov.bd/sites/default/files/files/bbs.portal.gov.bd/page/b2db8758_8497_412c_a9ec_6bb299f8b3ab/2021-05-14-05-49-4eb195f4d4984822389711e9be6832bb.pdf.

Berge, L. I. O., Bjorvatn, K., Juniwaty, K. S., and Tungodden, B., 2012. Business Training in Tanzania: From Research-driven Experiment to Local Implementation. *Journal of African Economies*, 21: 808–27.

Blattman, C., Jamison, J. C., and Sheridan, M., 2017. Reducing Crime and Violence: Experimental Evidence from Cognitive Behavioral Therapy in Liberia. *American Economic Review*, 107, 1165–1206.

Brooks, W., Donovan, K., and Johnson, T. R., 2018. Mentors or Teachers? Microenterprise Training in Kenya. *American Economic Journal: Applied Economics*, 10, 196–221.

Campos, F., Frese, M., Goldstein, M., Iacovone, L., Johnson, H. C., McKenzie, D., and Mensmann, M., 2017. Teaching Personal Initiative Beats Traditional Training in Boosting Small Business in West Africa. *Science*, 357(6357): 1287–90.

Campos, F., Frese, M., Goldstein, M., Iacovone, L., Johnson, H. C., McKenzie, D., and Mensmann, M., 2018. Is Personal Initiative Training a Substitute or Complement to the Existing Human Capital of Women? Results from a Randomized Trial in Togo. *American Economics Association Papers and Proceedings*, 108: 256–61.

Campos, F., Frese, M., Goldstein, M., Iacovone, L., Johnson, H. C., McKenzie, D., and Mensmann, M., 2020. Personal Initiative Training Leads to Remarkable Growth of Women-Owned Small Businesses in Togo, G²LM|LIC Policy Brief No. 32.

Groh, M., Krishnan, N., McKenzie, D., and Vishwanath, T., 2012. Soft Skills or Hard Cash? The Impact of Training and Wage Subsidy Programs on Female Youth Employment in Jordan, Policy Research Working Papers. The World Bank.

Heckman, J. J., and Kautz, T., 2014. Fostering and Measuring Skills: Interventions that Improve Character and Cognition. In J. J. Heckman, J. E. Humphries, and T. Kautz, (eds.), *The Myth of Achievement Tests: The GED and the Role of Character in American Life*. Chicago: University of Chicago Press, 293–317.

Heller, S. B., Shah, A. K., Guryan, J., Ludwig, J., Mullainathan, S., and Pollack, H. A., 2017. Thinking, Fast and Slow? Some Field Experiments to Reduce Crime and Dropout in Chicago. *Quarterly Journal of Economics*, 132: 1–54.

Hicks, J. H., Kremer, M., Mbiti, I., and Miguel, E., 2011. Vocational Education Voucher Delivery and Labor Market Returns: A Randomized Evaluation among Kenyan Youth. Report for Spanish Impact Evaluation Fund (SIEF) Phase II.

Lafortune, J., Rothstein, J., and Schanzenbach, D. W., 2018. School Finance Reform and the Distribution of Student Achievement. *American Economic Journal: Applied Economics*, 10, 1–26.

Macchiavello, R., Rabbani, A., and Woodruff, C., 2015. The Market for Training Services: A Demand Experiment with Bangladeshi Garment Factories. *American Economic Review*, 105: 300–4.

McKenzie, D., and Woodruff, C., 2014. What Are We Learning from Business Training and Entrepreneurship Evaluations around the Developing World? *World Bank Research. Observer*, 29: 48–82.

McKenzie, D., Woodruff, C., Bjorvatn, K., Bruhn, M., Cai, J., Gonzalez-Uribe, J., Quinn, S., Sonobe, T., and Valdivia, M., 2020. Training Entrepreneurs. *VoxDevLit*, 1(1). Available from: https://voxdev.org/sites/default/files/Training_Entrepreneurs_Issue_1.pdf

Shonchoy, A. S., Raihan, S., and Fujii, T., 2017. Reducing Extreme Poverty through Skill Training for Industry Job Placement. GLM|LIC Policy Brief No 9.

United Nations Development Programme, 2016. Human Development Report 2015: Work for Human Development. Available from: https://doi.org/10.18356/ea1ef3b1-en.

4

Challenges in Rural Labour Markets

Despite some remarkable economic growth in recent years, most low-income countries are still widely agriculture-orientated societies, while facing challenges rooted in the expansion of urban areas and the resulting large gap between rural and urban labour market conditions. Given that small-scale farming remains the primary income source for a majority of the population in developing countries, while extreme poverty is widespread, policies need to be informed by the complex mechanisms that affect the efficiency and prospects of rural labour markets in developing regions.

Economic research may contribute to the understanding the characteristics of rural labour markets in low-income countries. However, collecting data in this sector is rather difficult. Even more importantly, the dependency of rural markets on harvest and lean seasons, climate conditions undergoing substantial change, and natural catastrophes, on the one hand, and—on the other hand—a mostly constrained access to financial resources, credit, or modern banking technologies, pose huge challenges to governments and international development aid policies.

Strategies need to simultaneously address poverty reduction, employment creation, and infrastructure enhancement within the constraints of limited public budgets and relative uncertainty as to which policies induce sustainably positive effects. What are the challenges of correctly measuring labour demand and supply in rural settings? Does facilitating access to credit markets improve the efficiency of labour allocation, and alleviate income inequality among poor households that largely depend on the agricultural calendar and face high risks during the hungry or "lean" season? Under which circumstances do expensive PWPs produce lasting positive outcomes for participating population groups?

Research initiated and supported by the Growth and Labour Markets in Low-Income Countries Programme evaluates existing interventions and discusses new approaches with the aim of expand our knowledge about the fundamental drivers of rural labour market development.

4.1 The High Relevance of the Rural Sector Prevails

Agricultural employment has played a dominant role in the labour markets of most LICs. In many cases, however, the available data on rural labour market

Labour Markets in Low-Income Countries. David Lam and Ahmed Elsayed, Oxford University Press.
© David Lam and Ahmed Elsayed (2022). DOI: 10.1093/oso/9780192897107.003.0004

structures and the labour force attachment of selected groups is rather incomplete, for example lacking completed time-series or reliable surveys. This may lead to research which either underestimates or overestimates policy effects, or which may be unable to evaluate them at all without additional data. While recent progress in scientific data collection has widened the scope for socio-economic research, there is still a significant lack of comparable cross-country data and more detailed statistics on specific labour market segments.

Modelling labour markets based on imperfect data poses a challenge for economists. Furthermore, existing models going back to the dual sector model (traditional rural vs. modern non-agricultural sector), originally shaped by Lewis (1954), may fail to fully map the actual range of today's labour markets in LICs. According to the basic model, a decrease in agricultural labour demand as an economy industrializes produces an excess labour supply that drives cheap workers into the emerging non-rural sector. However, as the excess supply in the rural sector dissipates, the non-agricultural segment must pay higher wages—thus stimulating further movement of labour supply from the rural sector. This mechanism will, overall, enhance economic development in disadvantaged regions, according to this theory.

Despite offering an enhancement of this simple model (for example, the important contribution by Fields (2006), current economic modelling does not necessarily capture the complete status quo of low-income labour markets, a study by Bhorat et al. (2017) argued. Supported by GLM|LIC, the authors undertook a thorough analysis of the de facto segmentation of the sub-Saharan labour markets of Kenya, Tanzania, and Zambia, based on an evaluation of existing survey data. Their findings underline that a better understanding of these segments will help to target policy interventions and increase cost efficiency. The study presented a detailed comparative view across the three countries, illustrating differences in terms of labour market segmentation. This reveals interesting insights into the heterogeneity of economic development that need to be considered when identifying effective policy options.

For instance, the extents of urbanisation and poverty seem to be positively correlated: the most urbanized country of the three, Zambia, has the highest poverty headcount. This suggests that the change in labour supply depicted in the classic model does not necessarily lead to a rise in occupational quality, but instead to precarious employment or even unemployment. Contrary to common thinking, further decomposition reveals that unemployment in sub-Saharan Africa, as traditionally measured (that is, individuals reporting that they were not working but were actively looking for work in the previous week or month), is not a negligible factor. It reaches a substantial level in most urban areas while being relatively low in rural regions. Youth unemployment is meanwhile mostly concentrated in urban areas.

Only Kenya showed a substantially higher level of urban unemployment for females than males. There it was more than double the male rate, yet was comparable to the male rate in Zambia and Tanzania. Rural–urban labour migration can collide with constrained labour demand and inflexible urban wages resulting in a lack of appropriate urban jobs.

Other factors in which the three countries differ include the ratio of employment to the size of the rural population. The survey data analysed by Bhorat et al. (2017) show that a large rural sector with a high level of agricultural employment correlates with high labour-force participation and low unemployment. This was the case in Tanzania, where unemployment was clearly below the sub-Saharan average, while Kenya and Zambia showed a different pattern, with roughly 15% points lower employment in agriculture and a 5 percentage point higher unemployment rate.

The most reasonable explanation seems to be the existence of an extended subsistence sector in rural Tanzania. The agricultural sectors in Kenya and Zambia, by contrast, are comparatively less traditional but more industrialized and commercialized, and do not offer subsistence jobs to the same extent in the absence of urban job opportunities.

There may also be other influencing factors, such as different preferences for avoiding subsistence labour, access to social transfers, or scarcity of available rural land. This aligns with the fact that almost 90% of Tanzanians employed in agriculture are self-employed, while in Zambia (76%) and Kenya (66%) the percentage is significantly lower.

Consequently, labour force participation rates of the low educated are higher in Tanzania than in Zambia and Kenya. At the same time, Zambia and Kenya reveal a substantial lack of job opportunities for the better educated, resulting in higher unemployment. This finding contradicts the assumption of prevailing labour market models that, in general, suggest a higher likelihood of the better skilled to be employed. Thus, **better skilled workers may face a higher unemployment risk**. Clearly, the shortfall in skilled jobs may be traced back to an underdeveloped manufacturing and secondary sector in many African countries.

Against this analytical background, Bhorat et al. (2017) identified six core segments that reflected the heterogeneity of labour markets in sub-Saharan countries, reporting the relative employment shares of each segment (see Figure 4.1). Besides the traditional segments of rural agriculture and non-agricultural urban private-sector employment, the segmentation depicts urban agriculture as well as both urban and rural non-agricultural work in the public sector.

The shares presented here show that the rural sector still dominates the region, accounting for roughly 60% of the overall employment in Zambia and Kenya, and almost 75% in Tanzania. But agricultural employment was not limited to rural sectors; in Tanzania, agricultural jobs in urban areas accounted for a remarkable

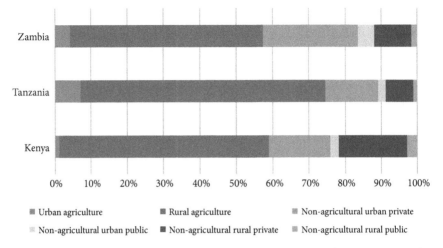

Fig. 4.1 Employment Shares of Labour Market Segments in Zambia, Tanzania, and Kenya

Note: Labour Force Survey data for Zambia (2012) and Tanzania (2006); Integrated Household Budget Survey data for Kenya (2005/2006); no consistent comparable data available at the time of the study. *Source:* Bhorat et al. (2017)

7% of the total employment. Furthermore, rural non-agricultural employment in the private sector had reached a level (about 19% in Kenya, as the less urbanized country, 10% in Zambia, 8% in Tanzania) that should no longer be overlooked by economic modelling. Within this segment, more than 40% of Kenyan workers were employees; in Tanzania and Zambia the level was just half this. In contrast, the urban non-agricultural private sector showed high rates of self-employment (above 62% in Tanzania, 52% in Zambia, 35% in Kenya). Undoubtedly this reflects a substantial urban informal sector which also needs to be captured by modelling.

In Zambia and Kenya, 60% of total employment was in the primary sector, which consisted almost entirely of agriculture with a lesser role for mining. In Tanzania the corresponding figure was 80%. **Across all three countries, secondary-sector employment (mainly manufacturing and construction) made up less than 10% of the total.** This is important, as policies traditionally focus on manufacturing as the key to economic growth in sub-Saharan Africa.

The tertiary sector accounted for roughly one-third of employment in Zambia and Kenya, and 16% in Tanzania. Wholesale and retail trade in the informal economy made up a large portion of this sector, while the share of public-sector employment was below 4% in Tanzania, and 7% in Kenya and Zambia. Given the high share of agricultural employment, it is no surprise that the majority of the labour force across the three countries were employed in low-skill occupations. In

Zambia, the most urbanised country, 65% were in low-skill occupations. In Kenya and Tanzania, the shares were 76% and 80%, respectively.

Turning to wages in the defined labour market segments, the study draws a rather clear picture: those employed in the rural non-agricultural private or public segment earned consistently higher wages than those offered in the rural agricultural segment in Kenya and Tanzania. To be publicly employed in non-agricultural segments in Kenya may bring double the income of rural segment employment (around 45% more in Tanzania and Zambia), while private non-agricultural employment promised a wage approximately 55% higher in Kenya and 66% higher in Tanzania. Similar wage advantages resulted from urban agricultural employment. The wage impacts of education differed as well, if compared across the six labour market sections. An additional year of schooling induced higher average wage returns in the urban private segments than the rural agriculture segment.

Together, these data evaluations show the plausibility of a more detailed segmentation of low-income countries' labour markets, which confirms the absolute domination of the rural sector while highlighting its heterogeneity and link to urban labour. Most importantly, **the existence of a substantial segment of non-agricultural labour in rural areas needs to be taken into account, as it represents a substantial share of employees as well as the self-employed.** Dual sector-oriented assessments fall short of the mark in view of an increasing market heterogeneity that deserves the full attention of multifaceted economic models. To distinguish between private and public segments seems to be instructive, as they exhibit a different demand for skills. Furthermore, **unemployment should not be ruled out when studying rural labour markets—the findings hint at rather high unemployment in the absence of an extended subsistence agriculture sector, and persistently high unemployment among urban young people, even when well educated.**

Lastly, the study called for the collection of more solid data sets for future research. The cross-country analysis was limited, in so far as surveys of the heterogeneous labour market structures in developing countries often suffer from some weaknesses with respect to question precision, sample representativeness, plausibility of responses, and missing variables that might explain outcomes in depth. With respect to studying labour market outcomes across countries, a few deficits hamper analysis, including a lack of harmonization and detailed information on the formal or informal nature of employment. Refining economic modelling in the field of development economics needs to rely on stable data foundations if it is to facilitate sound evidence-based policy advice. Enhancing the data availability for economic research is a topic that merits additional efforts. Nevertheless, letting the data shape the baseline assumptions of economic modelling in the case of low-income economies appears to be an inspiring research strategy.

4.1.1 Heterogeneous Rural Sectors Call for Asymmetric Economic Modelling

Another approach has been taken by Dillon, Brummund, and Mwabu (2017, 2019). Their 2017 study, supported by GLM|LIC, aimed to shed new light on the incompleteness of rural labour markets in East Africa, and the asymmetric responses of agricultural labour to changes in household composition (see also Chapter 3 in this book). It built on classic separation model tests for complete and competitive markets in rural areas (fundamentally based on Benjamin 1992) by controlling whether excess demand or supply of labour exists and whether wage adjustment brings both sides of the market into equilibrium.

Detecting market asymmetries and potential market failures is highly relevant when tailoring policy responses to challenges in rural regions. In well-functioning markets, the amount of labour used on a farm should not depend on how many workers belong to a household, since labour utilization should be based purely on equating the marginal product of labour to the market wage. The family's labour supply decision should be separate from their labour demand decision, as long as labour can easily move between on-farm and off-farm work and additional labour can be hired from the labour market. When labour markets are incomplete or missing, however, households cannot increase their working hours and are restricted to relying on their own farming work (non-separation). This creates a clear connection between the number of workers in a household and the intensity of farming.

Using panel data, the study shows that a variation of the separation test can sometimes provide insights into the state of rural labour markets. If at one point in time households face a binding constraint on the number of hours it can work in the market, this could lead to a situation of non-separation, with household members working on the family farm up to a point at which the marginal revenue product of farm labour is below the market wage. If, over time, the situation changes and someone exits the household, this reduction in the household's labour endowment would relieve the binding constraint on market work, and therefore separation becomes possible. This would be the case because farm labour falls only to a level that makes it optimal. However, the opposite is not true: if the household labour endowment increases over time, the constraint continues to bind, and therefore non-separation persists with increase in farm labour. The implication is that in a large sample, a binding labour demand constraint predicts a specific pattern of asymmetric average responses to increases vs. decreases in labour endowments.

The study developed variations of the separation model to test for this asymmetric non-separation and to better predict labour responses and the effect of market failures in rural areas. This setting includes heterogeneity of agricultural seasons, gender composition, and the influence of different agro-ecological zones.

By applying this approach to representative survey data in Ethiopia, Uganda, Tanzania, and Malawi, Dillon, Brummund, and Mwabu (2017) showed that different outcomes across countries cannot be identified from standard survey data without allowing for asymmetries. The lesson is rather clear: generalizations of initial country-specific findings will mislead policies. The multifaceted structures of sub-Saharan labour markets mean the results from one region cannot simply be taken as representative of all settings.

In the context of this chapter, the overall descriptive findings once again highlight the complexity of the rural sector in low-income countries.

1. **Labour supply to the household farm is more variable over the course of the year and larger than labour supply to the market.**
2. **Farm work, in contrast to market work, also includes old household members** beyond classic retirement age. For instance, 80-year-olds work the same average number of farm days as 40-year-olds and work more hours than 20-year-olds.
3. **Labour endowment within households is continuously changing**. Between survey waves, 40–80% of all households (depending on the count of children who age into the labour force) had to adapt to a change in the number of working-age members.
4. Since there is no clear pattern of how variability in household size may be correlated within villages, **it is difficult to predefine source and destination villages for internal migration**.
5. Newly arrived internal migrants spend similar time working on the farm as existing household members.

Empirical findings based on the enhanced separation model—that allows for asymmetric non-separation and variation through the agricultural seasons—show rather similar patterns of excess labour supply (labour demand constraints) in the rural areas of all four countries. But there is substantial heterogeneity across the agricultural calendar, genders, and agro-ecological zones. Longer periods of labour underutilization are followed by intensive farm work. Labour supply constraints seem to be more binding for women than men, in that it is less likely for female farm work to be replaced in the market. Rationing of working hours in the market, for example in the face of inflexible ('sticky') wages preventing job opportunities for the household, leads to non-separation: household members engage in family farm work as long as their labour continues to generate returns (more technically, their marginal revenue product) above the market wage.

Interestingly, the opposite appears to be true for the poorest households in Ethiopia where binding labour supply constraints seem to be present, caused by financial market deficiencies rather than a physical shortage of workers. This hints at specific labour market failures in Ethiopia that need further investigation and would not have been easily detected without asymmetric modelling.

The policy conclusions suggested by Dillon, Brummund, and Mwabu (2017, 2019) require that policies be better tailored to a country's specific conditions. Given the widespread shortfall in non-farm opportunities in rural areas, strategies to avoid strong non-separation in less-intensive phases of the agricultural cycle would be very useful. In non-mechanized agriculture, the over-supply of labour in the lean season is difficult to avoid, since harvesting is still very labour-intensive in many developing countries. More mechanization would reduce labour demand and could, in principle, redirect rural excess labour to the private market.

Initiatives to encourage mechanization would fail, however, if policy interventions did not tackle the issue of how to extend the availability of low-to-medium-skilled jobs in non-farm sectors. The latter seems the better strategy, since mechanization would then be widely adopted in response to shrinking rural labour supply.

4.1.2 Do Rural Households Allocate their Labour Efficiently?

This argument leads to the question of whether rural households in low-income regions are able to allocate their working time optimally between farm and non-farm activities, and which factors may act as barriers to time-allocation efficiency. Recent research on the allocation of labour (see for example Berg 2013; Karlan et al. 2014) has made it clear that estimations of marginal products of labour (the return for an extra hour worked) need to account for market failures in terms of informational or financial constraints, or excessive risks, that are widespread in the labour markets of LICs. In this case, households fail to properly distribute their labour input between the fields of activity and miss opportunities to increase their labour income. To have a clear judgement on this topic is important with regards to strategies aimed at enhancing sector productivity, which could yield positive outcomes if households respond by reallocating their labour supply along these productivity lines.

Supported by GLM|LIC, Brummund and Merfeld (2016) undertook a case study for Malawi which shows one of the lowest rates of non-farm business creation among rural households (see Nagler and Naudé 2014 in the sub-Saharan region. With a share of just 17% in 2014, Malawi ranked far below Ethiopia (30%), Tanzania (41%), Uganda (45%), Nigeria (51%), and Niger (59%). Despite this, Malawi is the only country that contributes comprehensive data on non-farm activities to the World Bank's Living Standards Measurement Study (Integrated Surveys on Agriculture, LSMS-ISA); its 2010 and 2013 data were the basis for the study.

While only data on the number of workers is available for other sub-Saharan countries, the LSMS for Malawi includes information on worker characteristics as well as days and hours worked. The survey reveals that Malawian households that are engaged in non-farm and agricultural activities are older and less educated than all households with non-farm enterprises, but younger and more educated than all households operating farm businesses, to cite only a few characteristics. The authors note, though, that the survey data still include substantial weaknesses (for example, lacking detailed information on other inputs into non-farm production apart from household labour). Therefore errors in the specification of the non-farm production function cannot be ruled out, which may lead to its overestimation.

Even against this background of imperfect data, the results are noteworthy and highlight the range of potential future research in this field. In all four specifications of the applied model, **the financial returns of an extra hour worked are larger in non-farm activities than in agriculture**. Reallocating labour from farm to non-farm enterprises could thus increase overall household income.

These kinds of discrepancies between productivity in farm versus non-farm activities may indicate dysfunctional labour markets and the presence of risks, mainly in agricultural production, that cause household allocation decisions to be less than completely optimal. If agriculture is riskier than any non-farm activity, households will allocate more labour resources to safer non-farm work. As a result, the marginal revenue generated by labour will fall relative to that of labour in agriculture.

Interestingly, however, in the case of households that operate both types of businesses in the same survey wave, the difference in the marginal revenue generated by labour in farm and non-farm work was no longer significant: these households seem to allocate their resources efficiently. Or, put more carefully, there is no evidence that these households are inefficient in allocating their labour.

Conversely, this finding suggests that **simply reconsidering how much time to spend on rural or non-farm work, and switching resources to increase income, will not be a realistic option for many low-income households**. Any income advantage would need to stem from the increased returns the households may generate from both fields of activity. This points to the need to stimulate productivity across sectors to enhance poor households' income prospects. It is certainly not a new debate, but the study provides some evidence that raising productivity will increase the efficiency of labour (re-)allocation in low-income countries.

4.1.3 Measuring Farm Labour Input in Agriculture

A major challenge in the field of agricultural economics is the difficulty to precisely measure labour inputs. This is particularly the case for the small-scale farm sector, which represents the majority of agricultural projects in developing countries. These farms employ mostly family members; thus, there is no wage income in which to anchor recall estimates. Written records are rarely kept and the respondents have to rely on recall to report on past events. To arrive at the total amount of labour allocated by a household to farming, the household must accurately report the plots under cultivation, the specific household members who worked on each plot, the activities performed, and their timing and duration.

Given that farming is a seasonal activity and work patterns are irregular during the season, reporting average time farming after the completion of the season requires remembering distant events and making complicated calculations. Alternatively, reporting hours worked over the last seven days at any single point during the agricultural season will not necessarily be indicative of total labour during the season especially when labour inputs vary considerably across weeks during the season.

A GLM|LIC study by Arthi et al. (2017, 2018) examines this issue. To assess the degree of recall bias in household farm labour, the authors conducted a survey experiment in Mara region, Tanzania, over the long rainy season between January and June 2014. Households were randomly assigned to one of the following three alternative survey designs:

1. Weekly visit (benchmark): weekly face-to-face surveys for the duration of the season.
2. Weekly phone (alternative): weekly phone surveys for the duration of the season.
3. Recall modules (business-as-usual): single face-to-face survey at the end of the agricultural season.

The authors find recall bias in the reporting of family farm labour. Labour data collected on a weekly basis, whether in person or by phone, are similar, albeit sometimes moderately statistically different. There are, however, striking and economically meaningful differences between the weekly and recall data. Respondents in recall modules report working up to about four times as many hours per person per plot, compared with respondents reporting labour on a weekly basis. However, they tend to under-report both the number of household members and plots active in farm cultivation. Evidence suggests that these sources of recall bias are driven not only by failures in memory, but also by the mental burdens of reporting on highly variable agricultural work patterns to provide a typical estimate. All things equal, studies suffering from this bias would understate agricultural labour productivity.

A main result that comes out strongly in this study is encouraging the performance of the phone surveys, which show little difference from the results obtained in the benchmark weekly visit design. The results of this project have implications for the debate on why value added per worker is so much lower in the agricultural sector than in the non-agricultural sector—and how such a difference can be sustained in the long-term. The findings suggest that measurement and data quality may be especially important here. Studies suffering from similar recall bias would overstate how much people work on farms, which, ceteris paribus, leads to underestimates of labour productivity on these farms.

4.2 Seasonality, Limited Access to Financial Markets, and the Challenge of Smoothing Consumption

As touched on in the section 4.1, financial constraints and the absence of formal credit markets are among the most important barriers to further economic development in rural areas, as well as households' ability to allocate their working resources more efficiently. Although growing quickly, the literature has not yet fully covered all aspects of this important topic. GLM|LIC is supporting an innovative, still-ongoing research project to investigate the impact of relaxing seasonal fiscal constraints on rural labour supply, productivity, household income, and private consumption.

The research project, supported by GLM|LIC, by Fink, Jack, and Masiye (2014, 2017, 2020) focused on small-scale farming households in Zambia, as the most common form of agricultural activities in sub-Saharan Africa, and revealed under which circumstances relieving credit constraints may be an efficient measure to allow poor farming families to secure their living. These households face a significant challenge every year. A long dry season and a lack of irrigation allow for only one harvest per year, while ownership of livestock, which could help diversity production, is limited. Crop yields and sales revenues from the May to July harvest season must last for the rest of the year, including the difficult 'lean' or 'hungry' season from January to March. Natural disasters and climate effects may further aggravate these households' living conditions and socio-economic prospects.

Many rural households in Zambia (and the entire sub-Saharan region) are likely to be confronted with increasing food shortages during the lean season, indicating a lack of the liquidity needed to buy additional food (see Figure 4.2). Selling rural land or livestock, if owned, in times of urgent need will not work efficiently due to the likelihood of price erosion during the most challenging seasonal periods and could even further reduce families' medium-term welfare. Changing production plans (for example crop mix) will mostly not provide a short-term solution either and may even result in additional risks, including income loss and increasing vulnerability to external (climate and weather) shocks.

Farming households have, in theory, four options to cover immediate liquidity and consumption needs: rely on their own savings, if they exist; raise short-term bridging credit; migrate for the season in search of employment; or generate income from alternative local farm or non-farm labour. Sustainable savings are frequently absent in poor rural settings, despite cautious household behaviour. Relying on credit is not a viable option for many households because access to banking products is still very limited in many rural areas. Borrowing would also

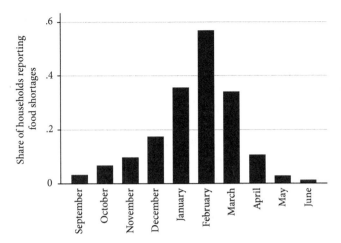

Fig. 4.2 Seasonal Increase of Food Shortages among
Small-Scale Farming Households in Zambia
Source: Fink, Jack, and Masiye (2014), authors' 2012 survey data

require suitable collateral which poor farmers are often unable to provide. The
migration option poses large risks for household members left behind, and uncertain returns on investment that may not offset the absence of a primary (male)
worker.

This leaves many rural households at risk, with the only option being to offer their labour to other farm enterprises or the non-farm market to generate
additional short-term wage income. Independent of their chances of repeatedly
obtaining such jobs in order to avoid running out of savings and food, this strategy has the disadvantage that it requires households to reduce the labour put into
their own farming activities.

These pressures may also induce a seasonal increase in child labour (see Chapter
7 in this volume). As a GLM|LIC study by Galdo, Dammert, and Abebaw (2018)
has discovered through timed surveys in rural Ethiopia, child labour levels vary
substantially through the agricultural seasons, with high rates of 45% to 76% in
the rainy and harvest periods. That is, child labour may serve as a means to enlarge
labour intensity on families' own farms and be viewed by farming households as
insurance to alleviate constraints in the lean season.

If households cannot manage to enlarge their internal labour supply, they face
a high risk of jeopardizing the subsequent success of sowing and harvesting on
their own land. Reducing labour input will most likely result in less harvest output,
which in turn implies fewer resources to invest in the forthcoming season, putting
farming households in even greater danger of staying trapped in a vicious circle.

Regardless, selling their labour appears to be the most common choice of
Zambian households at risk. Similar to the increasing share of families reporting

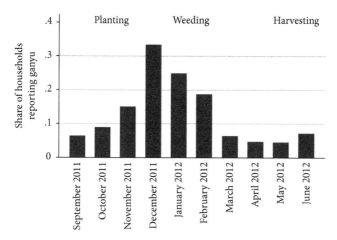

Fig. 4.3 Seasonal Increase of Short-Term Work on Other Farms (*Ganyu*) among Small-Scale Farming Households in Zambia

Source: Fink, Jack, and Masiye (2014), authors' 2012 survey data

food shortages shortly after the harvest season, but on an even higher level, farming households surveyed stated they were increasingly engaged in so-called *ganyu* work (short-term, cash-paid labour on other private farms) over the course of the agricultural year (see Figure 4.3).

These survey findings, presented by Fink, Jack, and Masiye (2014, 2020), are consistent with other studies depicting different levels of consumption across agricultural periods. However, the existing literature has not yet thoroughly established the connection between seasonally varying household income and consumption smoothing.

For example, Chaudhuri and Paxson (2002) noted different findings in an earlier case study on Indonesia based on simulation modelling that suggested a 'buffering behaviour' (p. 9) as a coping strategy for households. Independently of substantial variation in the timing of income flows, the households under study showed similar and rather smooth seasonal consumption patterns. According to the study, this may indicate that precautionary savings (cash and grain) could replace credit markets or the external labour of household members in supporting necessary consumption under the constraints of highly seasonal income. To assume that such a buffering ability to save resources could apply to a significant extent in the sub-Saharan setting—where extreme poverty is widespread—seems questionable but may deserve further research attention.

A study by Dercon and Krishnan (2000) based on data from rural Ethiopia revealed a high variability in poverty and consumption, not only across agricultural seasons but also over years. Consumption levels react to shocks such as natural disasters and crop failure, and families respond to seasonal incentives regarding market prices and changing labour demand. It appears that more households are vulnerable to shocks than previously thought, and their consumption patterns depend largely on the agricultural season.

In a randomized experiment in Mali, Beaman et al. (2014) modified a micro-credit programme to promote agricultural investments via unconditional grants or loans, observing that participating farmers significantly increased their invest-ments and revenues when benefiting from the cash grant, whereas the loan did not show an impact at all. Labour supply effects were not studied.

Karlan et al. (2014) have shown that incomplete insurance affects agricul-tural investment decisions—and will of course also influence other economic behaviour—with the example of Northern Ghana, where farmers were randomly offered either a cash grant, rainfall index insurance, or a combination of both. Access to insurance led to an increase in investments, facilitated the access to additional financial resources, and made farmers more likely to take risks with production. The study concluded that broadening the range of insurance, and tai-loring it to the special needs of farmers while making insurance affordable, may be more important than credit-based inflow of capital in fostering agricultural invest-ment. Although Karlan et al. (2014) did not control for any effects regarding the allocation of labour, it may be assumed that a wider reach of agricultural insurance would impact rural working decisions as well.

Khandker (2012) addressed seasonal food shortages and differences in poverty levels in rural Bangladesh, concluding that these are mainly due to the seasonality of households' income and consumption. Besides encouraging seasonal migra-tion, policy interventions should thus focus on granting targeted loans to reduce negative seasonal effects on poverty.

The impact of such seasonal loan programmes has been analysed by, among others, Bryan, Chowdhury, and Mobarak (2014), with a focus on encouraging longer-distance seasonal labour mobility through grants and credit. These ap-peared to fail in the experimental setting, given risk aversion and limited access to additional credit. The loan incentive did not increase mobility to welfare-maximizing levels. This issue will be investigated further by ongoing GLM|LIC research on seasonal migration and agricultural labour markets in Nepal, which will focus on whether subsidies encouraging temporary labour migration in the lean season positively affects labour supply and demand as well as the seasonal food insecurity. This research project has two goals: (1) to experimentally test whether a seasonal migration subsidy programme adapted to the setting of ru-ral Nepal shows similar promise in addressing seasonal food insecurity there, and (2) to tackle previously unexplored questions on how migration may transform rural, agricultural labour markets by studying the effects of seasonal migration on both rural labour supply and labour demand. This requires a more sophisticated experimental designs that also target the labour demand side, which was never done in Bangladesh.

The optimal timing of financial transfers to enhance rural welfare has been the focus of two recent studies. Bazzi, Sumarto, and Suryahadi (2015) confirmed that delayed transfers matter with respect to household consumption, based on the example of a large-scale unconditional cash transfer programme run in Indonesia.

More interestingly in our context, Burke, Bergquist, and Miguel (2019) analysed the timing and seasonality of microcredits against the empirical evidence that regular seasonal grain price variation does mostly not lead Kenyan small-scale farmers to systematically buy at low prices. The study found that credit constraints prevent farmers from exploiting opportunities for arbitrage. **Timing access to credit products along seasonal lines could therefore enable farmers to buy and sell near the optimal price**, which would in turn increase revenues and household income, and raise microcredit efficiency.

4.2.1 Do Cash or Grain Loans Tackle Lean-Season Constraints?

This instructive finding leads us back to the studies by Fink, Jack, and Masiye (2014, 2020), which ran loan experiments with some 3,000 farming households in 175 rural villages in Eastern Zambia between 2013 and 2015. These were based on an RCT rolled out in January 2014, right at the beginning of the lean season. One group of participants was offered a cash loan of 200 Kwacha (33 USD), representing roughly one-third of the average monthly expenditure of rural households. Another group received an equivalent value of 150 kg of maize (Zambia's staple crop) to cover the basic food needs of a five-person family for a minimum of two months during the hungry season.

Both loans were announced during initial village meetings, to be repaid at the end of the harvest season in July at an interest rate of around 30% over five months (though the actual interest rate for the maize loan depended on grain price fluctuation). This interest rate is far lower than the rates offered by local credit markets, of around 40% on average, as self-reported in the baseline survey. Eligible participants received information about the terms of the loan (but not the duration of the programme) and had to sign a consent form before being given the loan. Repayment dates were notified in advance to the villages; cash or grain was collected at central locations.

The experiment was carried out over two years, with the second loan period starting in January 2015. This allowed the study team to rotate the treatment groups in the second year, so that control group households thus far untreated were assigned to one of the active groups, while some treated households rotated into the control group. Participants who had not fully repaid their loans in the first year were excluded from the programme (the only punishment included in the approach). By applying this experimental strategy, the study aimed to identify the persistence of results and the different impact of repeat and first-time treatments. In addition, timing effects were measured: in the second programme phase, half of the treated villages were told about the loan offers in September, at the beginning of the planting season, the other half were told in January.

Descriptive statistics from the authors' baseline household survey and also administrative data confirm that a detailed assessment of seasonal loan programmes is highly relevant: low cash and grain reserves at the beginning of the lean season were anticipated by 75% of participating farming households. Cash savings in a bank were reported by just 5%, beyond 75% saved money at home, if at all. Average cash savings at the beginning of the planting season were just 80 Kwacha (40% of the cash loan offered during the experiment). Notably, some 60% of the respondents reported saving via grain storage (200 kg on average), but also reported storage losses during the past season at the same rate.

Access to formal cash loans from banks or other public sources was very limited, reported by only 5% of households. Informal loans were low as well, with around 7% using moneylenders and roughly 8% taking money from other households. These informal cash loans came at a fairly high monthly interest rate of around 30% (though less than the reported average rate for non-family/friend loans). Take-up peaked during the planting and harvest season at 40% of households, dropping to 15% during the hungry season. Hardly any households (1%) used alternative loan programmes offered by microcredit institutions or local associations. In-kind input loans of seeds or fertilizers were more common (40% in the baseline survey) than borrowing of cash or food.

Evaluating the data further reveals that working *ganyu* on other rural farms is the most common strategy for coping with food shortages. While seasonal migration is nearly non-existent in rural Zambia, more than half of the survey participants reported favouring *ganyu* over borrowing from their social network (28%), using their savings (22%), or selling livestock and assets (17%). Roughly two-thirds reported having sold their labour supply in the season prior to the experiment, and also anticipated resorting to this in the coming season. *Ganyu* work is usually organized in the local village labour markets, with some farms rotating from a seller to a buyer role during the season. Last but not least, limitations to land access do not seem to constrain households' rural production.

In summary, the experimental design of Fink, Jack, and Masiye (2014, 2020) yields a number of enlightening findings and policy-relevant insights. High acceptance of the loan programme resulted in average take-up rates of 98% and 97% for the cash and grains treatments in both years, with remarkably high rates of full repayment of 95% and 80% (see Figure 4.4). The study explains lower repayment rates in the second year mainly through worsened harvest incomes due to a lack of rainfall in 2015. However, it also finds some behavioural patterns and learning effects: villages where at least one farmer failed to repay in the first year without

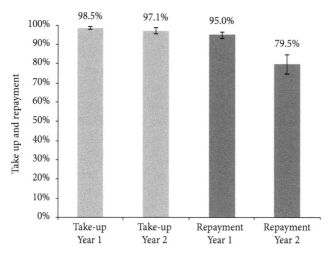

Fig. 4.4 Take-up and Repayment Rates of Cash and Grains Loan

Source: Fink, Jack, and Masiye (2017)

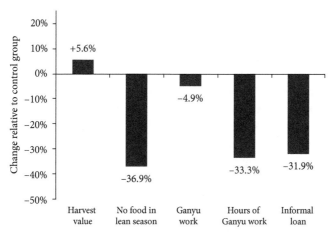

Fig. 4.5 Average Impact of Cash and Grains Loan Relative to Control Group

Source: Fink, Jack, and Masiye (2017)

any consequences besides being excluded from further participation, showed a strong decline in repayment rates of roughly 30 percentage points. Other villages revealed rather low repayment defaults of 6 percentage points.

Beyond these figures, the overall impact of the programme can be considered positive in many respects (see Figure 4.5):

1. **Increased agricultural output and income**. Participating households increased their total output by an average of 8% across both interventions, with a larger, but statistically insignificant effect resulting from the cash loan (11%) than the grain loan (5.6%). This may be partly due to behavioural effects with regards to early notification of programme extension at the start of the planting season. Even with a conservative view, an output increase of at least 5%—corresponding to about ten days of additional labour earnings—underlines the effectiveness of the stimulus in increasing families' labour income.

2. **Increased household consumption**. The loan programmes resulted in a significant reduction in food insecurity. For both loan types, participating households were roughly 37% less likely to face food shortages, and extended the frequency and quality of their daily meals, while the loans did not affect consumption in the harvest season. Thus, the treatment helped to reduce seasonal variation in consumption.

3. **Increased labour on own farms**. Eligible households were 10% less likely to sell labour and engage in *ganyu* work on other farms during the lean season. Hours worked on external land fell by an average of 23% across the programme. Consequently, farmers were able to spend seven additional work hours per week on their own farms, on average. At the same time, treated households were 25% more likely to hire *ganyu* labour for their own farms.

4. **Decreased dependency on informal or private loans**. The loan programme significantly reduced the need to borrow money on the informal market (at average monthly interest rates of 40%) or take loans from friends or family.

5. **Unclear persistence of effects**. The level of participants taking up a second loan in year two of the programme (98%) suggests a very high acceptance of the loan offers, even though they were at a substantial interest rate. However, the overall impact of the loan programme seems to be mostly down to first-year effects. Second-year effects were mostly substantially lower or insignificant, and the study does not find clear evidence of persistence. This result, though presumably due in part to drastically worse weather conditions in the second year, deserves further research attention.

Some core policy implications stem from the outcomes presented by Fink, Jack, and Masiye (2014, 2020):

1. **Timing of liquidity support is important**. Policies to relieve financial (and food) constraints during the lean agricultural season are effective in the presence of underdeveloped financial markets. They may lead to less consumption fluctuation and thus help households to escape from poverty traps.

2. **Targeted loan schemes address income inequality.** Resolving barriers to financial resources may contribute to reallocating labour towards more constrained farming households, and away from external activities. In the absence of functioning labour markets, more efficient investment of families' resources on their own farms will lead to improvements in the productivity, food-security, and total well-being of disadvantaged rural households, thus alleviating income inequality.

3. **Small-scale loans at moderate interest rates are efficient.** If well targeted, even low levels of loans may serve to substantially improve living conditions and increase agricultural output, while the willingness and ability of farmers to pay interest rates should not be underestimated.

4. **Lean season shortages may be further eased through tailored savings mechanisms.** In rural areas of developing countries, credit constraints are frequently accompanied by limited access to savings facilities and electronic banking technologies. Establishing trust in reliable banking infrastructure and shaping savings products to the needs of small-scale farmers may complement the loan approach well.

4.3 Are PWPs Effective in Rural Settings?

In the absence of functioning market solutions, many low-income countries operate large-scale public works—or workfare—programmes (PWPs) as a tool for increasing social protection and labour market attachment among the most vulnerable population groups in urban and rural areas. These programmes, frequently supported by international development aid, are based on a strict cash-for-work principle and are designed with a number of goals in mind, including employment creation, poverty reduction, and infrastructure development. They are not field of policy intervention unique to developing countries, though. Many developed countries run similar programmes to provide incentives to take up jobs and thus escape dependency on social transfers in the long run.

Whether such programmes are cost efficient and sufficiently well targeted to achieve the desired outcomes depends on their design and the (strong or weak) incentives to take part in the labour force provided by a country's socio-economic conditions. Subsidizing public work separately from the private markets may generate completely different overall effects than a strategy to support take-up of regular jobs by raising market wages to a level that workers will consider acceptable. However, defective labour market structures in most LICs leave only limited opportunity to pursue the latter strategy. Furthermore, developing countries' PWPs need to maintain a set of objectives that reach beyond the labour market attachment of workers, to tackle issues such as basic food security and fundamental social stability.

Against this general background, economic research has evaluated existing public work programmes in developing countries. The two largest PWPs worldwide—India's 'Mahatma Gandhi National Rural Employment Guarantee Scheme' (NREGS) and Ethiopia's Productive Safety Net Programme (PSNP)—have captured researchers' attention.

According to Berg et al. (2018), average agricultural wages among the poor increased significantly after the Indian NREGS programme was introduced at the district level, implying that its impact reaches beyond just active participants. Ravi and Engler (2015) found that participation in NREGS raised the probability of savings existing in poor households, while increasing both consumption and food security. Imbert and Papp (2015) showed indirect effects of the programme; higher private welfare gains appeared to result from a crowding-out effect of public sector hiring that in turn increased wages in the low-skill private sector. Indirect effects were also studied by Zimmermann (2020), providing evidence that the NREGS serves as a safety net without distorting the labour market, for example making self-employment less risky for the poor. Azam (2012) conducted a natural experiment, documenting the substantially positive impact of India's PWP on overall labour market participation. According to the study, which has been confirmed and enriched by GLM|LIC research (see Field et al. 2017, 2019, and Chapter 8 in this volume), this positive outcome is mostly driven by gender effects showing a larger increase in female participation rates and wages. Afridi, Mukhopadhyay, and Sahoo (2016) revealed that greater participation of mothers in the programme led to increased educational success for their children, whereas fathers' participation negatively affected children's education.

Turning to the second largest public works programme in Ethiopia, Hoddinott et al. (2012) investigated short-term food security effects as well as the longer-term impact on agricultural productivity, and the combined effect of participating in the PSNP and accompanying public programmes addressing food security and household asset building. Isolated PSNP participation showed no effect on productivity, while combined transfers were more effective in this respect. Berhane et al. (2014) revealed that longer PSNP participation yielded clearly positive outcomes, with respect to the length of households' lean season and livestock holdings. The study found that combined transfers through additional participation in the food- and asset-oriented programmes increase these effects even further.

4.3.1 The Malawian PWP Missed Its Goals

Research supported by GLM|LIC (Beegle, Galasso, and Goldberg 2017) enriched this picture by studying Malawi's PWP, which has operated under the Malawi Social Action Fund (MASAF) since the mid-1990s. The programme ranks just after

India's and Ethiopia's in terms of the size of the eligible population and aims to enhance food security as well as the use of agricultural inputs (for example fertilizers) by offering short-term employment to poor households. As of 2004, the programme has been directly linked to a fertilizer coupon intervention (Farm Input Subsidy Programme) available during the planting season. Unlike others, the Malawian PWP's timing does not focus on the lean season. Since 2012 it has covered roughly 500,000 households per year. Labour, allocated to eligible village households through a multi-stage decision process, mainly consists of construction, road rehabilitation, irrigation, and afforestation.

Work projects are segmented into two twenty-four-day cycles, with the first cycle aligned with the planting season of October to December, while the second cycle of public work projects is scheduled for June and July, immediately after harvest. At the time of the study, the daily wage rate was 300 Malawian Kwacha (0.92 USD), to be paid in four twelve-day intervals. Participants could thus earn a maximum of 44.16 USD over forty-eight total PWP working days. Given low national income in Malawi, this sum is not negligible. It is rather low, however, when compared to existing social protection transfers.

For the randomised control trial conducted by Beegle, Galasso, and Goldberg (2017) during the 2012–2013 agricultural calendar, selected villages were assigned to a control and four treatment groups. These were treated identically in the first cycle but differently in the second cycle. The research team varied both the timing of the programme (lean season replacing the standard timing aligned with the end of harvest) to capture buffer and consumption smoothing effects, and the schedule of payments (split payment after each three days of public work, instead of the standard arrangement of lump sum after twelve days) to examine changes in consumption patterns. The combined effects were studied to identify possible effects with regards to higher investment, when receiving lump-sum payment in the planting season, or smoothed consumption due to split payment in the lean season. Four survey waves investigated how households responded to the intervention.

The findings presented by Beegle, Galasso, and Goldberg (2017) are mostly rather disappointing with respect to the programme's main objective of improving food security.

1. Treated households worked more for the programme than the control group did, and this did not crowd out labour supply to the private sector. However, **the study does not find evidence for any positive effect on food security in the lean season** when compared to households in villages without access to PWP jobs. There is also no indication that PWP households were enabled to use more agricultural input via the programme, or that they transferred PWP income to savings. This cannot be traced back to households using programme earnings to purchase durable goods instead of food, according

to the study. Ownership of durable goods did not increase, and market prices did not change.

2. **The Malawian public works programme did not lead to tightening of labour markets**. The study did not find evidence of increased reservation wages (the lowest wage a worker will accept) and reduced labour supply.

3. **Rescheduling the second cycle of public work to the lean season did not generate any considerable improvements in food security**. This lack of any positive effects from shifting half of the forty-eight-day PWP to the lean season undermines the argument that raising the level of income provided by the PWP would result in a different impact. **Varying timing and payment frequency does not seem to induce changes in behaviour.**

4. Furthermore, **even the desired interlinkage effect with the specific fertilizer subsidy scheme was not present**, thus suggesting no complementary relationship. The programme neither increased short-term food security through additional household income, nor did it generate any such effect in the longer term through intensified use of fertilizers.

5. Instead, the study finds some indication of a **negative indirect effect of PWP participation on the food security of neighbouring, untreated households** in villages with PWP presence. This undesired outcome may at least partly be explained by untreated households' immediate reaction to changes in the consumption of PWP participants after receiving payment. Assuming that untreated households increase their consumption along the lines of their PWP neighbours, they would need to reduce consumption later on and thus may suffer greater food insecurity. Which variables explain this effect remains unclear, though studies on other PWPs do find rather positive spillover effects, for example on the casual wage rate (for India, see for example Deiniger and Liu 2013; Imbert and Papp 2015).

6. The study does not exclude the possibility that small-scale effects, not detected in the data, may have occurred and increased participants' welfare to a certain extent, even if the PWP failed to achieve its main goals. This would explain why the take-up rate of the programme is rather high. **Financial diaries could provide a way for future studies to investigate this.**

Overall, the results provided by Beegle, Galasso, and Goldberg (2017) seem to strongly contradict most of these studies on the public works programmes in India and Ethiopia. However, it should be noted that the Malawian PWP significantly differs from these more positively evaluated programme settings. Both the Indian and Ethiopian PWPs are designed as insurance schemes guaranteeing work and income over an extended period and at a higher intensity of transfer. It is possible that the magnitude of earnings in the Malawi programme, given the low wage and limited number of days of work provided, was simply too small to have measurable effects on food consumption, especially if households spread the income over many weeks. A programme with longer duration and higher wages might be more successful. Designers of PWPs should carefully evaluate the magnitude of earnings and the duration and flexibility of work in order to be sure that programmes have a significant impact on participating households.

Given that thirty-nine out of forty-eight sub-Saharan countries run PWPs, and that research has not yet been able to deliver an in-depth cross-country analysis of their socio-economic reach (due to constraints in comparable data), the reminder by Beegle, Galasso, and Goldberg (2017, p. 22) that 'PWPs will not always have significant and measurable welfare effects' should not go unheard.

Key Takeaways from this Chapter

- Due to underdeveloped manufacturing and secondary sectors in many African countries, better skilled workers may actually face higher unemployment risks.
- Labour market policies should not focus solely on manufacturing as key to economic growth in sub-Saharan Africa.
- More mechanization would reduce farm labour demand, which is often highly seasonal, but must be paired with policies to improve non-farm opportunities in rural areas.
- To enhance poor households' income prospects, productivity needs to be stimulated across sectors as switching from farm to non-farm work is not always an option.
- Timing access to credit along seasonal lines could allow farmers to buy and sell near optimal price, thus relieving their financial constraints during the lean season.
- Loan schemes targeted to small-scale farmers could be complemented with better access to savings facilities and electronic banking technologies.
- Public works programmes, though often positively assessed, may fail to achieve better food security if the duration is too short and the timing not flexible enough.

References

Afridi, F., Mukhopadhyay, A., and Sahoo, S., 2016. Female Labor Force Participation and Child Education in India: Evidence from the National Rural Employment Guarantee Scheme. *IZA Journal of Labor and Development*, 5(7).

Arthi, V., Beegle, K., De Weerdt, J., and Palacios-López, A., 2017. Not Your Average Job: Measuring Farm Labor in Tanzania. GLM|LIC Policy Brief No. 6.

Arthi, V., Beegle, K., De Weerdt, J., and Palacios-López, A., 2018. Not Your Average Job: Measuring Farm Labor in Tanzania. *Journal of Development Economics*, 130: 160–72.

Azam, M., 2012. The Impact of Indian Job Guarantee Scheme on Labor Market Outcomes: Evidence from a Natural Experiment. IZA Discussion Paper No. 6548.

Bazzi, S., Sumarto, S., and Suryahadi, A., 2015. It's All in the Timing: Cash Transfers and Consumption Smoothing in a Developing Country. *Journal of Economic Behavior & Organization*, 119: 267–88.

Beaman, L., Karlan, D., Thuysbaert, B., and Udry, C., 2014. Self-Selection into Credit Markets: Evidence from Agriculture in Mali (No. w20387). Cambridge, MA: National Bureau of Economic Research.

Beegle, K., Galasso, E., and Goldberg, J., 2017. Direct and Indirect Effects of Malawi's Public Works Program on Food Security. *Journal of Development Economics*, 128: 1–23.

Benjamin, D., 1992. Household Composition, Labor Markets, and Labor Demand: Testing for Separation in Agricultural Household Models. *Econometrica*, 60, 287–322.

Berg, E., 2013. Are Poor People Credit-Constrained or Myopic? Evidence from a South African Panel. *Journal of Development Economics*, 101: 195–205.

Berg, E., Bhattacharyya, S., Rajasekhar, D., and Manjula, R., 2018. Can Public Works Increase Equilibrium Wages? Evidence from India's National Rural Employment Guarantee. *World Development*, 103: 239–54.

Berhane, G., Gilligan, D. O., Hoddinott, J., Kumar, N., and Taffesse, A. S., 2014. Can Social Protection Work in Africa? The Impact of Ethiopia's Productive Safety Net Programme. *Economic Development and Cultural Change*, 63: 1–26.

Bhorat, H., Lilenstein, K., Oosthuizen, M., Sharp, M., and Yu, D., 2017. Modelling Labour Markets in Low Income Countries with Imperfect Data. GLM|LIC Working Paper No. 39.

Brummund, P., and Merfeld, J. D., 2016. Allocative Efficiency of Non-Farm Enterprises in Agricultural Households: Evidence from Malawi. GLM|LIC Working Paper No. 33.

Bryan, G., Chowdhury, S., and Mobarak, A. M., 2014. Underinvestment in a Profitable Technology: The Case of Seasonal Migration in Bangladesh. *Econometrica*, 82, 1671–1748.

Burke, M., Bergquist, L. F., and Miguel, E., 2019. Sell Low and Buy High: Arbitrage and Local Price Effects in Kenyan Markets. *Quarterly Journal of Economics*, 134: 785–842.

Chaudhuri, S., and Paxson, C., 2002. Smoothing Consumption under Income Seasonality: Buffer Stocks vs. Credit Markets. Columbia University Department of Economics Discussion Paper No. 0102-54.

Deininger, K., and Liu, Y., 2013. Welfare and Poverty Impacts of India's National Rural Employment Guarantee Scheme: Evidence from Andhra Pradesh. World Bank Policy Research Working Paper 6543.

Dercon, S., and Krishnan, P., 2000. Vulnerability, Seasonality and Poverty in Ethiopia. *Journal of Development Studies*, 36: 25–53.

Dillon, B., Brummund, P., and Mwabu, G., 2017. How Complete are Labor Markets in East Africa? Evidence from Panel Data in Four Countries. GLM|LIC Working Paper No. 31.

Dillon, B., Brummund, P., and Mwabu, G., 2019. Asymmetric Non-Separation and Rural Labor Markets. *Journal of Development Economics*, 139: 78–96.

Field, E., Pande, R., Rigol, N., Schaner, S., and Moore, C. T., 2017. On Her Account: Can Strengthening Women's Financial Control Boost Female Labor Supply? GLIM|LIC Working Paper No. 32.

Field, E., Pande, R., Rigol, N., Schaner, S., and Moore, C. T., 2019. On Her Account: Can Strengthening Women's Financial Control Boost Female Labor Supply? Cowles Foundation Discussion Paper No. 2201, Yale University.

Fields, G. S., 2006. Employment in Low-Income Countries: Beyond Labour Market Segmentation? Cornell University, Digital Commons. Available from: https://digitalcommons.ilr.cornell.edu/cgi/viewcontent.cgi?article=1462&context=articles.

Fink, G., Jack, K., and Masiye, F., 2014. Seasonal Credit Constraints and Agricultural Labour Supply. GLM|LIC Working Paper No. 1.

Fink, G., Jack, K., and Masiye, F., 2017. The Impact of Seasonal Food and Cash Loans on Small-Scale Farmers in Zambia. GLM|LIC Policy Brief No. 3.

Fink, G., Jack, B. K., and Masiye, F., 2020. Seasonal Liquidity, Rural Labor Markets and Agricultural Production. *American Economic Review*, 110(11): 3351–92.

Galdo, J., Dammert, A. C., and Abebaw, D., 2018. Child Labor Measurement in Agricultural Households. GLM|LIC Working Paper No. 43.

Hoddinott, J., Berhane, G., Gilligan, D., Kumar, N., and Taffesse, A., 2012. The Impact of Ethiopia's Productive Safety Net Programme and Related Transfers on Agricultural Productivity. *Journal of African Economies*, 21(5): 761–86.

Imbert, C., and Papp, J., 2015. Labor Market Effects of Social Programs: Evidence from India's Employment Guarantee. *American Economic Journal: Applied Economics*, 7: 233–63.

Karlan, D., Osei, R., Osei-Akoto, I., and Udry, C., 2014. Agricultural Decisions after Relaxing Credit and Risk Constraints. Qauarterly Journal of Economics, 129(2): 597–652.

Khandker, S. R., 2012. Seasonality of Income and Poverty in Bangladesh. *Journal of Development Economics*, 97: 244–56.

Lewis, W. A., 1954. Economic Development with Unlimited Supplies of Labour. *The Manchester School*, 22: 139–91.

Nagler, P., and Naudé, W., 2014. Non-Farm Entrepreneurship in Rural Africa: Patterns and Determinants. IZA Discussion Paper No. 8008.

Ravi, S., and Engler, M., 2015. Workfare as an Effective Way to Fight Poverty: The Case of India's NREGS. *World Development*, 67: 57–71.

Zimmermann, L., 2020. Why Guarantee Employment? Evidence from a Large Indian Public-Works Program. Global Labor Organization Discussion Paper No. 504.

5

The Impact of Migration on Employment Outcomes

Migration flows caused by precarious living conditions, civil wars, or environmental shocks in low-income countries are widely discussed in policy debates in the countries receiving migrants. Many development aid programmes focus on overcoming so-called push factors that drive emigration, especially among young people. While the reasons behind emigration are manifold, a key aim for policymakers is the creation and stabilization of employment conditions and labour market structures, in order to offer better local prospects to potential emigrants.

However, securing better prospects for higher-qualified and employed people does not guarantee a reduction in migration incentives. On the contrary, many studies reveal that it is mostly the better qualified that aim to emigrate when faced with a lack of prospects, or with uncertainty about their societies' future prospects. Most of these migrants, though, remain in the region or move to a neighbouring country—only a smaller share migrate internationally. For this group, better qualifications, information, and networking lead to the rising power of economic 'pull factors' in destination countries. 'Brain drain' effects, with respect to a country's stock of human capital and supply of qualified labour, may exacerbate the deficits.

At the same time, positive effects of emigration from low-income regions to developed-destination countries should not be underestimated. It is not only migrants who may benefit from employment and education abroad; their families and entire society may gain from the returning migration of better-qualified workers as well as from money sent home while working in a developed country. Also, emigration of qualified workers faced with ineffective labour markets, high unemployment or social upheaval may relieve tension from a society, at least for a limited period of time, while increasing the chances of 'brain gains' later on. Under certain conditions, migration may also be seen as a stepping stone for emerging and developing countries to better integrate into the world economy, as they benefit from migrants' networking. 'Brain drain versus brain gain' is a lcontroversial topic in migration economics and the debate is ongoing.

Policymakers should not overlook another aspect. From most developing and low-income countries' perspectives, migration presents a dual challenge: international migration is often accompanied by rural–urban migration. This migration

Labour Markets in Low-Income Countries. David Lam and Ahmed Elsayed, Oxford University Press.
© David Lam and Ahmed Elsayed (2022). DOI: 10.1093/oso/9780192897107.003.0005

on the national level may bring economic and social benefits to disadvantaged population groups, as well as overall economic gains, and thus should be advanced and well organized. But it may also aggravate unemployment and generate precarious employment scenarios in metropolitan areas in the absence of functioning regular labour markets. Policies aimed at controlling or stimulating internal migration flows need to take this into account.

Furthermore, many less-developed countries have experienced long-lasting or repeated violent conflicts that have caused massive forced migration and refugee flows into neighbouring LICs. Both the host and the origin societies are faced with severe challenges: how to host refugees without generating social tensions and labour market frictions, and how to later reintegrate returning migrants without the creation of economic disadvantages and a new vicious circle of conflicts. Supported by GLM|LIC, a number of studies and ongoing research projects are shining new light on this important research area.

5.1 Migration and Globalization: What Do We Know?

A rich economic literature has studied the interaction of migration and globalization, and evaluated whether the networking of migrants abroad helps to facilitate the access of their less-developed home countries to the global economy. On behalf of GLM|LIC, a thorough literature survey (Rapoport, 2016) summed up recent research findings and offered an idea of how migration may explicitly support LICs' efforts to catch up with globalization trends.

Heated public debates in Western developed societies on 'mass inflows' of immigrants may lead to the impression that the twenty-first century is experiencing migration of an unprecedented intensity. In reality, however, we are a long way from the level of global migration of the late nineteenth and early twentieth century, which saw a mass migration of poor Europeans emigrating in search of better living conditions elsewhere. During this episode, the share of migrants in the world population had been up to three times higher than it is today, with a remarkably stable share of around 3% sustained over several decades.

As Rapoport (2016) pointed out, the role of migration as part of ongoing globalization has changed since the 1960s. More than half of the current total world migration takes place as South–North migration, from developing countries to the highly developed world. It does not—as during the European emigration episode—substantially reduce population growth in the origin countries, but it is a crucial factor in building links between LICs and the world's most advanced economies. An increasing number of migrants are highly qualified—as of today, more than 40% have passed tertiary education. While earlier literature argued that a resulting brain drain could severely delay a developing country's economic progress, more recent research contradicts this with the argument that

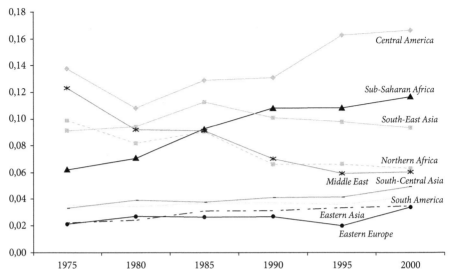

Fig. 5.1 Intensity of the Brain Drain (as Share of Human Capital Stock) by Region, 1975–2000

Source: Rapoport (2016)

the prospect of migration could act as an incentive for countries to provide additional education that could balance the brain drain effects. In fact, brain drain intensity has been decreasing in some global regions during the last decades, with only a few—mainly sub-Saharan Africa and Central America—experiencing a slight increase (see Figure 5.1).

Qualified emigrants help their origin countries connect to advanced societies by establishing their own networks, sharing their economic success with their families at home, returning home with newly accumulated human capital and finances, and by overcoming cultural and informational barriers to further economic integration. As a result, the prospects of less-developed countries better participating in international trade, and of attracting the inflow of capital and technologies into their markets, may rise. According to Rapoport (2016, p. 1211), 'These are the growth ingredients brought about by globalisation that developing countries need the most, and skilled emigrants have a strong comparative advantage in "shipping" them to the home country.'

The literature review clearly underlines the trade-creating effect of migration—that is, of migration networks. Emigrants establish new information channels, know about the market and institutional environments in both the home and host countries, create trust among negotiating parties, and accumulate foreign language skills that enable them to develop business activities in both directions. Another relevant trade-stimulating effect results from their own interest in consuming goods from their home countries, and their ability to affect natives' preferences. Most recent studies (for example Parsons and Vézina 2018, studying the trade-effect of Vietnamese immigrants in the USA) have enriched earlier findings with natural experiment insights showing that migration networks—and their contribution to removing information barriers—are indeed stimulating bilateral trade.

As seen by Parsons and Vézina (2018), similar effects have been observed by various studies with respect to foreign direct investments (FDI) and other financial flows into the home countries of migrants. Skilled migrants at their destination countries may help reduce uncertainties about the profitability of FDI in their home countries, as they share information about the labour force at home, local logistics, procurement, and regulations. Migration fosters new networks that diffuse business information, making a strong impact on FDI intensity. At the same time, better information on a developing country's specific financial and institutional framework may lead to lower transaction costs and risk premiums, thus enhancing financial transactions between migrants' host and home countries. For LICs these migration effects are highly relevant, as FDI plays a much larger role in developing economies than advanced economies.

The diffusion of knowledge and technology adoption is another highly relevant aspect of migration. Recent studies have explored to what extent migration networks drive innovation in their origin countries, by studying aspects including: networks of inventors; co-authorship of patents; the evolution of export baskets; and international knowledge flows. In sum, similar factors come into play here: to overcome information asymmetries, create trust, and stimulate collaborations is an obvious prerequisite for knowledge diffusion. New studies (for example Miguelez 2018) also found that, in the field of scientific knowledge and technology migration, networks help establish important contacts that enable host country partners to take the initiative in knowledge transfer.

In light of this recent empirical evidence, the role of migration and migrant networking as a stimulus of further integration of low-income countries into the world economy—and thus a generator of brain gain—should not be underestimated. **Migrant networks improve access to foreign markets, foreign investments and global knowledge networks—essential ingredients for growth and development**.

Nevertheless, it should not be forgotten just how multifaceted migration is, from the perspective of a low-income society: while labour migration of the better qualified may help to spur economic progress, brain drain effects cannot be ruled out completely, and other migration forms pose huge challenges. The remainder of this chapter addresses these challenges, and ways of coping with them, in the field of international development policies.

5.2 Rural–Urban Migration: Learning from Mobile Phone Tracking Data

According to a recent study (De Brauw, Mueller, and Lee 2014), migration rates in sub-Saharan Africa have been remarkably low in several countries with high population shares in rural areas—despite the clear rural–urban wage gap and other benefits of migration, such as enabling urban–rural financial transfers or better risk sharing among household members. Possible explanations for relatively low rural–urban migration rates include policy restrictions for land owners renting their properties, an absence of members of the same ethnic group in the destination area, and a lack of household networks to replace migrants' labour. This may create a challenge for economic development, since studies suggest that significant income growth at the national level is difficult for developing countries without a shift of jobs from agriculture to manufacturing and services sectors (see McMillan, Rodrik, and Verduzco-Gallo 2014).

An innovative GLM|LIC research project (see Blumenstock and Donaldson 2017 for a summary of the initial results) builds on these findings by looking deeper into internal migration flows in a number of LICs. Given the lack of reliable survey data, the authors innovate by using tracking data from mobile phones, which are widespread on the African continent (see Blumenstock 2018 to learn more about the method of using phone data). This 'big data' method allows the authors to identify migration patterns and observe how migration affects labour markets in LICs. Based on a terabytes-large data set covering four years, the research project tracks the daily location of several million individuals—among them tens of thousands of internal migrants. For the LIC of Rwanda, the results have already been quantified 'at a spatial and temporal resolution that has not been achieved in prior research or policy' (Blumenstock and Donaldson 2017, p. 1f)). To enrich their 'big data' and allow for further assessment, the authors combine data on changes in local weather, commodity prices, and agricultural yields, that help identify spatially differentiated shocks to local labour demand—and the migration response.

According to the analysis, the majority of migrations take place between rural areas and are not targeted towards larger urban regions. Furthermore, most of this internal migration lasts less than three months, suggesting a rather cyclical mobility—driven by demand, season, and weather—of rural workers who return to their origin at the end of a season. However, the research project reveals that a substantial share of migrants move on in a circular manner, staying at one or more other locations before returning home.

These findings indicate that internal migration, on the one hand, responds directly to seasonal changes in labour demand: workers are 'pushed' and 'pulled', in that they decide to temporarily leave their home region due to local negative demand changes, or they choose a destination based on expected positive demand in that destination. On the other hand, the findings underline the limited spatial range of labour mobility in many LICs, and give policymakers reasons to focus on rural–urban migration incentives once again.

Further research within the project aims to better understand the root causes of internal migration by investigating the value of social networks in migration decisions (Blumenstock, Chi, and Tan 2019). The social network acts not only in the form of a conduit of information, but also as a source of social and economic support. According to Blumenstock, Chi, and Tan (2019), the average migrant benefits more from 'interconnected' networks that provide social support than from 'expansive' networks that could act more efficiently in terms of transmitting information. The paper finds evidence of rivalry in information transmission, especially in settings where a migrant's direct contacts have a large number of 'strong ties' in the destination (where tie strength is defined by the frequency of communication). This suggests that there may be rivalry in information sharing in networks, which suggests that the probability that two people share information is roughly inversely proportional to the (square root of the) size of their social networks.

This innovative research approach can be further used to better understand how internal migration responds to wage differences in labour markets and generates an optimal allocation of a low-income country's resources. Innovative research of this kind is highly relevant in learning more about the causes and dynamics of national migration flows in LICs, and the types of migration that respond to different labour market interventions, in order to inform effective policy.

Until now, there has been little empirical knowledge on the short- and long-term effects of internal migration, and the characteristics of migrants in LICs. Future studies using the same innovative approach and tools to explore anonymized mobile phone records will help answer open questions and add to our picture of LICs' internal migration patterns, as well as other issues relevant when tailoring development and labour market policies.

5.3 Circular Migration: Remittances, Human Capital Accumulation, and Labour Market Outcomes

The dynamic spread of mobile phones and phone-based payment services facilitates international remittances and contributes to a substantial reduction in transaction costs, thus overcoming barriers and speeding up processes. Empirical evidence indicates that emigrants respond to these trends by sending more remittances to family members and other recipients back home, while further financial service innovations enable them to diversify the nature of remittances and direct them to savings or investments in human capital and businesses (see for

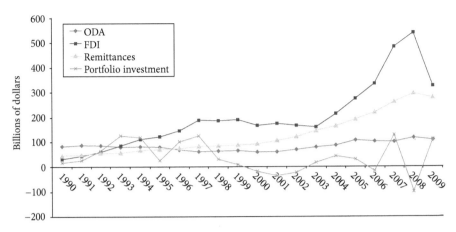

Fig. 5.2 Remittances vs. Other International Financial Flows to Developing Countries, 1990–2009

Note: Billions of constant 2005 USD in total across developing countries (low- and middle-income as classified by World Bank). Variables displayed are: 'Net official development assistance and official aid received (current USD)', 'Foreign direct investment (FDI), net inflows (Balance of Payments/BoP, current USD)', 'Workers' remittances and compensation of employees, received (current USD)', and 'Portfolio investment, excluding LCFAR (Liabilities Constituting Foreign Authorities Reserve/LCFAR; BoP, current USD)'. Data for all flows except Official Development Assistance (ODA) from the World Bank's World Development Indicators (WDI) 2010. Data on ODA up to 2008 from WDI 2010, for 2009 from OECD.
Source: Yang (2011)

example Yang 2011). These technological advances will presumably even increase the importance of emigrants' remittances as a means of stimulating economic and social development in their countries of origin.

Remarkably, international remittances have surpassed total official development aid transactions and total portfolio investments in developing countries since the late 1990s, and almost reached the level of total foreign direct investment flows in 2009. More importantly, while portfolio and direct investments are the results of strategic decisions, and respond immediately to the business cycle, remittances have been rising continuously. Even in 2008–9, in the wake of the global financial crisis, remittances have been almost stable—in contrast to sharply falling amounts of foreign direct investments (see Yang 2011, p. 129f and Figure 5.2) and mirroring similar stability seen during other economic slowdowns in the recent past (see for example World Bank 2016).

Remittances represent a substantial share of many migrant workers' earnings, revealing a high motivation to insure their families against economic risks and natural disasters, support their education, or enable savings, entrepreneurship, and small business survival (see Yang 2011 for details on the motivations behind remittances). Some studies (for example Ashraf et al. 2011) have emphasized that new financial services boosted by technological progress may serve the need of emigrants to better control the use of their remittances.

However, mobile money technologies are still very unequally distributed worldwide—with sub-Saharan Africa still facing a large backlog, despite the dynamic spread of mobile phones in the region. This backlog results in high costs and risks when sending or receiving remittances. Sub-Saharan Africa represents the most expensive corridors for remittances, while also struggling with substantial deficits in terms of uptake of bank accounts.

5.3.1 Does Access to Mobile Banking Impact Remittances?

In a recent research project supported by the Growth and Labour Markets in Low-Income Countries Programme, Batista and Vicente (2017, 2018, 2020) conducted a behavioural experiment to understand: (1) mobile money adoption patterns; (2) fundamental outcomes related to welfare, such as consumption and investment; and (3) the patterns of remittances and savings as mediators for the impact on the more fundamental economic outcomes. The experiment took place in 102 rural Enumeration Areas (EAs) of southern Mozambique. In half of these locations, randomly chosen, a set of mobile money dissemination activities took place. These activities included the recruitment and training of agents, community theatres, and community meetings where mobile money services were explained to the local population, as well as a set of individual dissemination activities including registration and experimentation of several mobile money transactions with trial e-money provided by the campaign team.

Using a combination of administrative and household data, the project shows that the adoption of mobile money tends to be positively self-selected. Early adopters are better educated and often already have a bank account. This positive self-selection raises the question of whether mobile money is an effective tool for financial inclusion. Indeed, if those who first adopt mobile money and keep using this technology over time are disproportionately those who already had bank accounts, this could be an effective tool for financial deepening but may be less effective for financial widening. New approaches may be needed to promote financial inclusion together with strategies for organic technology adoption following its initial dissemination (Batista and Vicente 2020).

The overall results over the three years following the initial introduction of the programme indicate significant levels of adoption of mobile money, which substitutes for traditional alternative methods to send remittances and save (Batista and Vicente 2018). The treatment also improved consumption smoothing given that treated households became less vulnerable to both adverse geo-located weather and idiosyncratic shocks. However, mobile money led to reduced investment, especially in agriculture. These findings suggest that mobile money facilitated rural outmigration by reducing the transaction costs associated with migrant remittances and thereby improving insurance possibilities.

The availability of mobile money in treated rural areas also increased the willingness of targeted individuals to send transfers. The overall increase relative to the control was 11 percentage points over three years according to experimental games. The magnitude of these effects increased over time, presumably as trust in the mobile money system improved. The authors also found a positive effect on the willingness to use mobile money to conduct transfers instead of alternative transfer methods. Given the very poor remittance channels available before the introduction of mobile money, namely making in-person visits to the rural receivers or using bus drivers as expensive and risky transfer carriers, it is not surprising that the marginal willingness to transfer increases—in particular using mobile money as a substitute for traditional remittance channels.

The findings of this research project provide central banks in low-income countries with substantial evidence on the effects of mobile banking technologies on economic development and social welfare. The findings illustrate potential approaches for implementing mobile banking structures by using tailored dissemination strategies and shaping supportive regulation that also takes into account how to facilitate remittances from one country to the other.

5.3.2 Do Remittances Induce Structural Change?

From this perspective, understanding whether emigration and remittances have persistent impacts on origin communities, or if these effects collapse at the end of labour migration, becomes even more important. New research supported by GLM|LIC (Dinkelman and Mariotti 2016; Dinkelman, Kumchulesi, and Mariotti 2017) looked in depth into the economics of capital accumulation via labour migration, in the specific case of the low-income country of Malawi.

Two studies have focused on the temporary and thus later return-migration (circular migration) of Malawians to South Africa in the 1960s and 1970s, and explored long-term effects in terms of capital accumulation, restructuring of rural labour markets, and human capital formation of the next generation. Both studies presented an analysis covering several decades following a significant migration shock triggered by the opening and closing of the labour market of a nearby 'pulling' country for the first time. This long-term evaluation built on existing studies documenting the positive short-term impacts of circular migration and remittances on the income and well-being of migrant families (see for example Yang 2008; Gibson, McKenzie, and Stillman 2013); Kosac, 2015), and delivered important insights for development policies.

Dinkelman, Kumchulesi, and Mariotti (2017) studied whether receiving migrant capital may stimulate structural change in regional labour markets. While the influence of new, labour-saving agricultural technologies, trade liberalizations, and environmental change on labour reallocation towards higher productivity non-farm jobs is rather well studied by recent analyses (see Hornbeck and Naidu 2014; Bustos, Caprettini, and Ponticelli 2016; McCaig and Pavcnik 2018), thorough empirical evidence on the role of capital is rare.

In the absence of present data covering an extended period, Dinkelman, Kumchulesi, and Mariotti (2017) explored unique historical data from a 'natural experiment', allowing insights into the lasting effects of circular migration and remittances. Sub-Saharan Africa has a long tradition of circular migration, with Malawi serving as a traditional supplier of unskilled male workers to the gold mining companies in South Africa since the 1930s. The Witwatersrand Native Labour Association (Wenela)—South Africa's Chamber of Mines' centralized labour recruitment organization—coordinated local recruitment stations in Malawi. The jobs they offered provided annual earnings around 2.5 times higher than the average for agricultural jobs in Malawi (see Dinkelman and Mariotti 2016 for a detailed account of this migration episode).

The Malawian government, however, brought in strict emigration quotas that by the end of the 1950s accounted for 20,000 workers per year (around 2% of the working-age male population), mainly in response to lobbying from European plantation owners in Malawi and Zimbabwe wanting to recruit cheap labour. Contracts with the Wenela company were tailored towards the economic interests of Malawi. Contracts were typically limited to two years (with each contract renewal including a standard earnings raise) and forced Malawians working in South Africa to accept so-called deferred pay, whereby two-thirds of miners' earnings were withheld until their return to Malawi. This institutional circular migration setup ensured a large share of the additional income earned would be saved and returned to the country as compulsory remittances along with the workers themselves.

This arrangement changed drastically in 1967, when all quotas were officially abandoned due to shrinking employment prospects in other neighbouring regions. The number of emigrants exploded from 40,000 in 1967 to 120,000 in 1973, while the labour contract standards remained in place. In some Malawian communities during this period, up to 20% of the male working age population was working in South Africa.

The next drastic change took place in 1974, when the crash of a plane carrying Malawian miners led the Malawian government to stop all recruiting and order all miners to return home from South Africa. Although this policy was in place for just three years, a change in the recruitment policies of mining companies (see Figure 5.3) meant that Malawian southbound labour migration never again reached pre-1974 levels.

Against this historical background, Dinkelman, Kumchulesi, and Mariotti (2017) analysed the capital flows back to Malawian districts, and their structural impact on rural labour markets, over three decades. The authors highlight the relevance of migration-driven capital accumulation for sub-Saharan Africa,

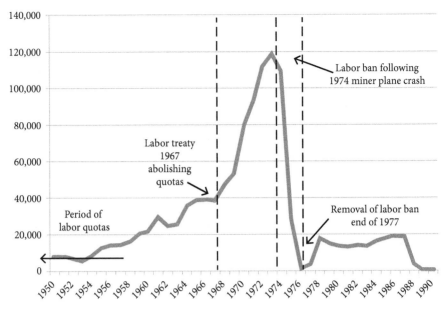

Fig. 5.3 Annual Employment of Malawian Miners on South African Mines, 1950–94

Note: Number of workers contracted by Wenela to work on South African mines in each year; dotted lines represent (from left to right) the abolition of labour quotas in August 1967, the moratorium on migration after the April 1974 Malawian plane crash, and the legal resumption of mine migration in 1978.

Source: Dinkelman, Kumchulesi, and Mariotti (2017)

given its potential for structural change. Controlled circular migration that is combined with the channelling of labour earnings back to home regions 'may present a practical tool for boosting structural change in communities where industrial, agricultural, and trade revolutions have been slow to arrive' (Dinkelman, Kumchulesi, and Mariotti 2017, p. 7).

Flows of money to home regions mirrored the significant rise in migration from and to Malawi between 1967 and 1975, and underline the crucial importance of capital accumulation strategies for LICs. During this period total deferred pay inflows represented almost 90% of all money flowing from Malawian migrants working in South Africa, totalling 53 million USD (1975 exchange rate).

When migration peaked in 1973, the average monthly money transfer to each Malawian district was 115,000 USD, totalling 2.75 million USD nationally (Dinkelman, Kumchulesi, and Mariotti 2017; see Figure 5.4). The distribution of capital flows across the districts was uneven: some districts benefited more due to having: more migrants; different migration timing (mine wages were increased by over 200% between 1966 and 1974); more migrants closer to the end of their contract in 1974; or a higher share of repeat contracts with higher earnings. The study combines these data with district-level differences in the composition of migrants.

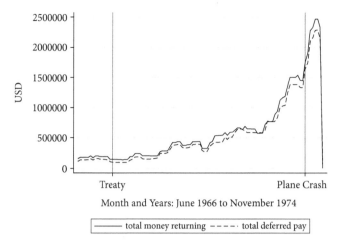

Fig. 5.4 Migrant Capital Flows over Time, 1966–75
Source: Dinkelman, Kumchulesi, and Mariotti (2017), archival material collected by the authors

From a theoretical perspective, what outcomes should we expect these substantial remittances to have in terms of driving structural change in relatively closed economies such as many Malawian districts? Additional capital in the form of remittances and deferred pay transfers should offer households significant help to break out of poverty traps and invest in more than mere daily living (see for example Rosenstein-Rodan 1943; Lewis 1954; Kuznets 1955). The supply of financial capital may stimulate investments in better housing, better quality farming equipment, and more land, seeds, and fertilizers (if available), allowing farmers and their families to either work more efficiently or reduce their labour input.

Excess labour can then be orientated towards non-farm sectors with additional—and better—earnings prospects. As a consequence, another channel of structural change may be encouraged: the higher local incomes generated by returning migrants may increase the demand for small non-farm businesses and service providers. Along with the easing of credit constraints brought by additional capital, this may enable workers to enter the non-farm sectors as entrepreneurs, and increase the viability of new businesses (see Banerjee and Newman 1993; Buera, Kaboski, and Shin, 2013). Last, but not least, a positive income shock may be an incentive to invest in human capital accumulation for the next generation. Educational progress may then strengthen productivity and employability in non-farm sectors, and hence promote structural change in the labour market.

Dinkelman, Kumchulesi, and Mariotti (2017) thoroughly explored these channels for long-term changes in their empirical work. A first look at census data revealed that, for male workers, different trends in districts with low and high migrant capital inflows occurred rather soon after all migrants returned to Malawi in 1975. For female workers, these trends started some years later. For both men and women, **those districts that received more migrant capital transitioned more quickly out of agriculture and into the manufacturing and services sectors, with the effects clearly persisting**, increasing over time, and not being the result of internal migration between districts (see Figures 5.5 and 5.6).

Further investigation revealed that **this impact of migrant capital on the reallocation of labour lasted for at least thirty years**. A higher number of returning migrants within a district reinforced the effects of the capital inflow, although to a lesser extent over time. 'In an average district, with 58,000 women and 57,000 men in the economically active population, each additional one million USD received created 1,402 more jobs in the non-farm sector over three decades. This translates into a cost of 713 USD per non-farm job created' (Dinkelman, Kumchulesi, and Mariotti 2017, p. 21).

The authors concluded that overall migrant capital accounted for around 5% of male labour reallocation into non-farm work, while at the same time being responsible for 17% of structural changes of female labour. Non-farm jobs were mostly concentrated in construction, retail sales, transport, and communications, with men more likely to be self-employed and women more likely to take over unpaid family enterprise jobs.

These persistent effects also caused a moderate growth in population and an urbanization trend of rural districts in response to migrant capital. Roughly three decades after the end of returning migration from South Africa, districts that had received more capital were around 15% more urbanized than districts that had not experienced any shock to migration capital. At the same time, urbanization may have accelerated structural changes in rural labour markets.

Economic theory suggests that remittances and migrant capital should increase farm-specific investments. Interestingly, this does not hold in the Malawian case study: there is no evidence that districts with more capital invested in more farm-specific capital over time. Instead, there was an increase in households with durable walls and roofs, indicating investments in better housing quality and property security—which is also a prerequisite for retail trade and service-orientated jobs.

5.3.3 Remittances Affect the Upgrading of Human Capital

The long-term impact of migrant capital on education and human capital accumulation is of crucial importance in terms of any upward shift of low-income countries' labour markets. Do remittances and other capital transfers raise the average number of years spent in school? Does having more money affect the education investment behaviour of parents, and does this result in higher long-term levels of education in communities with high(er) migration? Dinkelman and Mariotti (2016) provided empirical evidence that persistent migration does

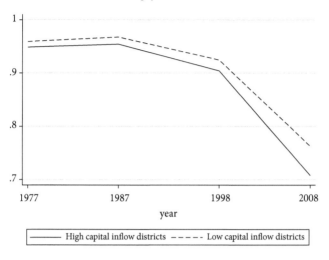

Share of workers in agricultural sector by decade and size of deferred pay shock to district: women

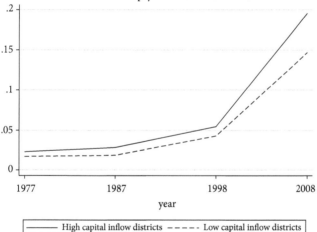

Share of workers in service sector by decade and size of deferred pay shock to district: women

Fig. 5.5 Sectoral Shifts in the Labour Market: Women

Notes: Share of employed women working in agricultural (top) or services (bottom) sectors over time and by type of district.High capital inflow districts are the districts receiving above median levels of migrant deferred pay before 1977. Low capital inflow districts are those receiving below median levels of deferred pay. Means are weighted using census weights.
Source: Dinkelman, Kumchulesi, and Mariotti (2017)

indeed lead to substantial gains in human capital, although the effects shrink over time Their study confirmed and broadened the findings of Edwards and Ureta

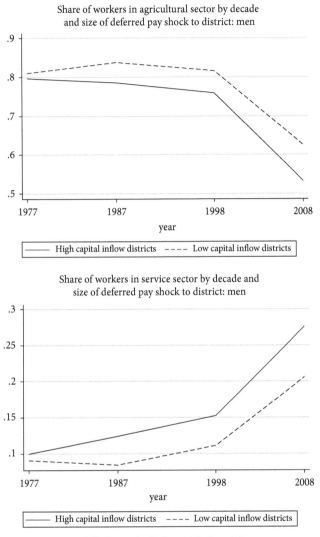

Fig. 5.6 Sectoral Shifts in the Labour Market: Men

Notes: Share of male workers in agricultural (top) or services (bottom) sectors over time and by type of district. High capital inflow districts are the districts receiving above median levels of migrant deferred pay before 1977. Low capital inflow districts are those receiving below median levels of deferred pay. Means are weighted using census weights.

Source: Dinkelman, Kumchulesi, and Mariotti (2017)

(2003), who also found—in the context of the low-income country of El Salvador—that remittances have a large impact on the schooling decisions of poor rural households, even if parents themselves have low levels of schooling.

Dinkelman and Mariotti (2016) used a difference-in-differences strategy to estimate gaps in the education level of individuals who were age-eligible for primary school immediately after the expansion of mining migration in Malawian districts, with and without migrant recruitment. Control cohorts of children above primary school age were also studied, to factor in any differences in educational attainment across districts.

The main finding was that, two decades after the migration expansion, **primary school cohorts in migrant-recruiting districts were 4.8% to 6.9% more educated**. This was a result of more children attending school, and of a longer average stay in school between 1967 and 1977—it was a remarkable effect given the very low average level of just two and a half years of completed education in this adult population.

As might be expected, the effect on human capital formation was greater during the period when labour migration was prohibited (as more migrants returned with their earnings) compared to when migration was ongoing and more workers were leaving their households. Districts without agricultural estates, and hence with a lower value of child labour, saw the largest positive impacts on education. Furthermore, the study finds no difference in the education impact on men and women. This shows that, although only men were recruited to work in the gold mines, increases in education were not driven by the expectation of higher returns as future gold mine workers.

Dinkelman, Kumchulesi, and Mariotti (2017) quantified the structural shift of work towards services, based on additional human capital, for the period 1998–2008. According to these estimates, roughly 17% of the shift of women away from agriculture (men show lower rates) in the third decade after labour migration had stopped can be traced back to an upgrading of human capital via circular migration and remittances. These rates are lower in earlier periods, which can be explained by the long time-frame that is needed to create human capital.

These results enrich our picture of the long-term effects of migration-driven human capital accumulation beyond the end of a migration episode. Earlier research, mostly studying a shorter period and not covering African countries (see Dinkelman and Mariotti 2016 for a brief discussion of the literature), has found mixed evidence on the effects of labour migration on the formation of next-generation human capital. These showed positive effects from relaxing credit constraints and expected higher wages, as well as negative effects from children dropping out of school to replace a migrant and as a potential consequence of changes to the bargaining power of households in the absence of a migrant. **Overall, migration and remittance flows may generate positive or negative education effects on non-migrant households by affecting levels of wages, prices, and infrastructure.**

Dinkelman and Mariotti (2016) underlined that—in their studied scenario—the positive long-term effects of migration and remittances on the demand for education clearly surpassed any negative impacts, making it possible to 'generalise the patterns of positive short run results to the long run in an African setting, despite the different context for schooling and child labour decisions' (Dinkelman and Mariotti 2016, p. 4). Better access to jobs and labour incomes abroad through circular migration could help poor, rural regions to escape poverty, reduce child labour, and invest in the education of their children as a first step towards future economic growth. **As a prerequisite, remittances should be further facilitated through modern technologies that allow migrants to better control their investments and savings.** From a development policy perspective, the historical case of Malawi provides some important lessons for shaping future—time-limited—guest-worker programmes in LICs to stimulate positive, long-term effects on human capital acquisition in migrants' home regions.

5.4 The Impact of Forced Migration on Education, Skills, and Employment

Besides rural–urban and circular migration, many low-income countries face large-scale forced migration of both refugees from neighbour countries and internally displaced persons due to natural disasters, civil wars, violence, or other external shocks. Most of the world's refugee flows are not directed towards developed regions—indeed the poorest countries often bear the greatest burden. According to the United Nations High Commissioner for Refugees (UNHCR 2018), there were 20.4 million refugees in 2018, with 31% of them in Africa, compared to only 14% in Europe (excluding Turkey), and a mere 3% in the Americas. There were also more than 41.4 million internally displaced people, with 17.7 million (42.6%) of them in Africa. Astonishingly, there is still little empirical evidence on the circumstances of forced migration in low-income countries and the effects of refugee inflows on host regions and their labour markets.

A comprehensive study by Alix-Garcia and Saah (2010) studied the impact of refugee flows into Tanzania in the 1990s following ethnic conflicts in neighbouring Burundi and Rwanda, focusing on price and general wealth effects. While food aid only partially compensated for a substantial price increase resulting from the rise of refugee numbers, the wealth effects were split in two opposite directions: rural regions apparently benefited from nearby refugee camps due to increases in the prices of goods needed to nourish refugees. The increased income enabled rural households to invest in more durable goods. Meanwhile, the opposite occurred in urban areas, with people suffering from higher price levels that reduced their spending power. The authors conclude that host governments and international development aid programmes should make every effort to mitigate the negative effects of hosting refugees in poor countries, to avoid a domino effect of humanitarian crises.

5.4.1 How Does Hosting Refugees from Neighbour Countries Affect Low-Income Labour Markets?

New research supported by GLM|LIC (Ruiz and Vargas-Silva 2015, 2016) has contributed important insights to this picture by studying the immediate labour market consequences in Tanzania of hosting refugees from Burundi and Rwanda in the 1990s. The research project pursued a natural experiment based on the fact that the distribution of refugees was extremely uneven. This disparity was due to the geographical barriers between western and eastern regions, and logistical aspects that caused most UNHCR refugee camps to be placed in the western region of Kagera, close to the Rwanda and Burundi borders. Overall, more than 1 million people were received as forced migrants in Tanzania between 1993 and 1998, with some parts of Kagera far more affected than others. In some regions, refugees outnumbered natives by a factor of five.

Longitudinal data from the Kagera Health and Development Survey allowed the authors to study households affected by forced migration, from prior to this external shock (1991) up until 2010. From a theoretical perspective, an inflow of refugees may increase competition for jobs, generating wage pressure as labour supply rises, depending on whether refugee labour is able to substitute for native workers (see Braun and Mahmoud 2014). At the same time, new jobs may emerge in the context of government and non-government institutions engaging in refugee aid programmes. As the broad literature on unforced labour migration shows, additional migrant labour may also push natives towards jobs that need higher qualification or specific skills (see for example Peri and Sparber 2011). The increase in population may stimulate native production of goods related to refugee aid and boost productivity in rural regions. This could also give some momentum to human capital acquisition among young people.

Ruiz and Vargas-Silva (2015, 2016) focused on the direct labour market outcomes and found that, for those aged 16–46 in 1991 (first survey), **the probability of working as an employee outside their own household (instead of being self-employed or engaging in rural subsistence work) shrank significantly as the intensity of the forced-migration shock increased**. In particular, these cohorts were less likely to be formally employed in the agricultural sector, indicating a degree of refugees substituting for natives. There is also hardly any evidence that the external shock resulted in a tendency to change the types of crops cultivated and increase rural productivity.

The studies controlled for changes in population due to movement of people to other regions, finding no indication that the refugee inflow resulted in a diversification of economic activities; subsistence activities still dominated at a very high 80%. Temporary workers exposed to the refugee inflow and job competition showed a reduced probability of being employed in the non-rural sector, but were more likely to move to self-employment after the shock. For the younger cohorts (those younger than 16 in 1991), exposure to a forced-migration shock tended to increase the likelihood of being employed. However, only those from wealthy households were more likely to be employed in non-agricultural jobs—others appeared to be stuck in the rural sector. A possible explanation may be that exposure to the forced-migration shock prevents households from acquiring human capital.

These negative labour market impacts are accompanied by limited positive outcomes for those recruited for jobs in the field of refugee aid. Natives already employed regularly in regions with a high inflow of refugees partly benefited from taking over better jobs that included substantially better social security standards. Nevertheless, the overall results underline the crucial importance of policy strategies that account for the impact of forced migration on the host societies, and for potential substitution effects in the labour markets. **Policies need to be informed by the risks to the well-being of the natives who are most likely to compete with refugees in agricultural labour markets or casual wage jobs.** Given that by far the most refugees stay in the region of origin, migrating from one poor country to another, a better understanding of how labour markets and native workers react to forced-migration shocks is a prerequisite for any targeted development programme. The research supported by GLM|LIC provides important new insights that should help policy makers tailor future programmes.

5.4.2 Returning Refugees Are Highly Disadvantaged

While many LICs experience significant inflows of refugees, others face problems resulting from massive return migration of refugees into post-conflict home regions. Overcoming civil war and other conflicts does not necessarily raise the economic chances of returning refugees, and it is important to understand that the well-studied positive effects of voluntary migrants returning home do not apply here: refugees heading towards poor neighbour countries' crowded camps are hardly accumulating human capital, sending remittances, or enriching their home regions with new capacities when they return years later. The acute conflicts and violence driving refugee migration reduce subsequent options to a minimum and most often leave no choice other than to move to a region deemed more secure, even in the absence of any favourable economic prospects.

Depending on the destination country's laws around labour market activities, some refugees may join the host labour market while others take the chance to establish some trade (for example, of food aid products) between refugee camps and neighbouring host communities (see Enghoff et al. 2010). But since massive refugee inflows tend to overstrain many host countries, the economic prospects for refugees remain rather limited and host countries may even prohibit refugees from accessing the labour market or conducting economic activities within camps (see Harild, Christensen, and Zetter 2015). The resulting forced inactivity may then lead to behavioural effects in terms of work ethics (Lehrer 2010). Also, an acute conflict forces many refugee households to leave behind their only assets, livestock and land, which are then difficult to reclaim after returning home (see Ruiz and Vargas-Silva 2013). The situation of many refugees is further complicated by them being typically unable to choose when they return—voluntary return when violence decreases may result in different outcomes to involuntary repatriation.

Against this high-risk background, a recent case study of Burundi supported by GLM|LIC (Fransen, Ruiz, and Vargas-Silva 2017) revealed substantial negative economic effects for returning forced migrants compared to non-migrant households: overall, returnee households showed lower subjective socio-economic well-being (slightly reducing over time) and were in most cases set back to lower levels of economic activities as a result of an extended period of inactivity during their displacement.

Burundi experienced a large-scale emigration to Tanzania due to violent civil war conflicts between 1993 and 2000, followed by a massive post-war refugee return triggered by the Tanzanian government stopping refugee aid and closing all camps step by step. Between 2001 and 2009, roughly 500,000 refugees returned to Burundi, mostly to their region of birth, with the most recent peak in 2012 due to the closing of the last large refugee camp (see Figure 5.7). Initially, many refugees had found casual agricultural employment in villages near their camps. Over the years however, the government of Tanzania imposed strict limits on movement and economic activity, making many refugees fully dependent on international aid programmes for their entire stay.

The study explores rich panel data collected in 2011 (total 1,500 households) and 2015 offering detailed information on the economic activities of non-migrants and refugees before, during, and after their displacement. A thorough analysis controlling for exposure to conflict, time abroad, time since return, geographical proximity to Tanzania, and costs of migration shows that returnee households suffer from a large livestock gap compared to remaining households (fewer and/or lower-level livestock per adult) and are more likely to engage in mere agricultural subsistence work or similar employment activities.

The results further suggest that returnees have lower chances to be self-employed—in contrast to returning 'traditional' economic migrants from abroad—while boosting the likelihood of being stuck with agricultural-worker status. Both findings—dependency on agricultural subsistence and low chances of self-employment—emphasize that **returning refugees face a higher risk of precarious income than their non-migrant neighbours**. According to the study, legal and practical restrictions on economic activities in Tanzania were the main reasons

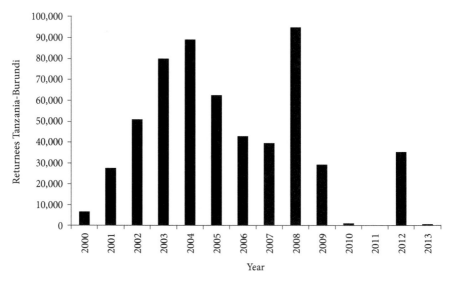

Fig. 5.7 Returnees from Tanzania to Burundi
Source: Fransen, Ruiz, and Vargas-Silva, 2017, based on UNHCR data

behind this obvious gap between former refugees and non-migrants. While returnees showed no higher vulnerability to crime and health complications, and loss or theft of property left behind does not seem to have played a relevant role, it appears that a clear disadvantage was posed by forced inactivity and the potential deterioration of skills and motivation to work. This is consistent with the finding that those refugees who stayed abroad longer and were then forced to return have worse economic outcomes after coming home.

Given these effects only began to diminish over a long period, the study offers clear lessons for development policies: **to avoid long-term setbacks and a loss of socio-economic perspectives for sending and receiving low-income societies, it is critically important to allow refugees to engage in employment and other economic activities while displaced, and to support them continuously after their return**. Initiatives that aim to stimulate an early return of refugees need to take into account that such measures, while possibly easing the host country's burden, may also invoke a new cycle of tension and violence in the origin/home country which is likely already struggling for stability. International policy efforts will be needed to support host countries to establish labour market opportunities for refugees, and to reintegrate returning refugees more successfully. Right now, remedying these issues is still an underdeveloped topic in both research and policy.

Key Takeways from this Chapter

- South–North migration makes up more than half of current global migration.
- While migration may cause a 'brain drain', it can also stimulate growth and development by improving access to global markets, investments, and knowledge networks.
- Remittances help accelerate the transition from the agricultural to the manufacturing and service sectors.
- Voluntary migration along with remittances can have a positive effect on human capital accumulation in the origin countries.
- The positive effect of remittances can be increased with modern technologies that allow migrants to better control their savings and investments.
- Forced migration to low-income countries makes natives less likely to find a job outside their own household.
- Allowing refugees to work while displaced, and supporting them upon return, is important to prevent long-term income losses due to forced inactivity and deterioration of skills.

References

Alix-Garcia, J., and Saah, D., 2010. The Effect of Refugee Inflows on Host Communities. *World Bank Economic Review*, 24: 148–70.

Ashraf, N., Aycinena, D., Martínez A. C., and Yang, D., 2011. Remittances and the Problem of Control: A Field Experiment among Migrants from El Salvador (Working Paper). University of Chile, Department of Economics.

Banerjee, A., and Newman, A., 1993. Occupational Choice and the Process of Development. *Journal of Political Economy*, 101(2): 274–98.

Batista, C., and Vicente, P. C., 2017. Introducing Mobile Money in Rural Mozambique. GLM|LIC Working Paper No. 30.

Batista, C., and Vicente, P. C., 2018. Is Mobile Money Changing rural Africa? Evidence from a Field Experiment (No. wp1805). Universidade Nova de Lisboa, Faculdade de Economia, NOVAFRICA.

Batista, C., and Vicente, P. C., 2020. Adopting Mobile Money: Evidence from an Experiment in Rural Africa. *AEA Papers and Proceedings*, 110: 594–8.

Blumenstock, J. E., 2018. Estimating Economic Characteristics with Phone Data. *AEA Papers and Proceedings*, 108: 72–6.

Blumenstock, J. E., Chi, G., and Tan, X., 2019. Migration and the Value of Social Networks. CEPR Discussion Paper No. 13611.

Blumenstock, J., and Donaldson, D., 2017. Using Mobile Phone Records to Estimate the Effect of Local Labor Demand Shocks on Internal Migration and Local Wages. GLIM|LIC Policy Brief No. 11.

Braun, S., and Mahmoud, T. O., 2014. The Employment Effects of Immigration: Evidence from the Mass Arrival of German Expellees in Postwar Germany. *Journal of Economic History*, 74: 69–108.

Buera, F. J., Kaboski, J. P., and Shin, Y., 2013. Macro-Perspective on Asset Grants Programs: Occupational and Wealth Mobility. *American Economic Review Papers and Proceedings*, 104(5): 159–64.

Bustos, P., Caprettini, B., and Ponticelli, J., 2016. Agricultural Productivity and Structural Transformation: Evidence from Brazil. *American Economic Review*, 106: 1320–65.

De Brauw, A., Mueller, V., and Lee, H. L., 2014. The Role of Rural–Urban Migration in the Structural Transformation of Sub-Saharan Africa. *World Development*, 63: 33–42.

Dinkelman, T., Kumchulesi, G., and Mariotti, M., 2017. Labor Migration, Capital Accumulation, and the Structure of Rural Labor Markets. GLIM|LIC Working Paper No. 22.

Dinkelman, T., Mariotti, M., 2016. The Long-Run Effects of Labor Migration on Human Capital Formation in Communities of Origin. *American Economic Journal: Applied Economics*, 8: 1–35.

Edwards, A. C., and Ureta, M., 2003. International Migration, Remittances, and Schooling: Evidence from El Salvador. *Journal of Development Economics*, 14th Inter-American Seminar on Economics, 72: 429–61.

Enghoff, M., Hansen, B., Umar, A., Gildestad, B., Owen, M., and Obara, A., 2010. In Search of Protection and Livelihoods: Socio-Economic and Environmental Impacts of Dadaab Refugee Camps on Host Communities. Danish Refugee Council.

Fransen, S., Ruiz, I., and Vargas-Silva, C., 2017. Return Migration and Economic Outcomes in the Conflict Context. *World Development*, 95: 196–210.

Gibson, J., McKenzie, D., and Stillman, S., 2013. Accounting for Selectivity and Duration-Dependent Heterogeneity When Estimating the Impact of Emigration on Incomes and Poverty in Sending Areas. *Economic Development and Cultural Change*, 61: 247–80.

Harild, N., Christensen, A., and Zetter, R., 2015. Sustainable Refugee Return: Triggers, Constraints, and Lessons on Addressing the Development Challenges of Forced Displacement. GPFD Issue Note Series.

Hornbeck, R., and Naidu, S., 2014. When the Levee Breaks: Black Migration and Economic Development in the American South. *American Economic Review*, 104: 963–90.

Kosack, E., 2015. The Bracero Program and Entrepreneurial Investment in Mexico (SSRN Scholarly Paper No. ID 2603535). Social Science Research Network, Rochester, NY.

Kuznets, S., 1955. Economic Growth and Income Inequality. *American Economic Review*, 45(1): 1–28.

Lehrer, K. J., 2010. Economic Behaviour during Conflict: Education and Labour Market Participation in Internally Displaced People's Camps in Northern Uganda. PhD thesis, University of British Columbia. Available from: https://doi.org/10.14288/1.0071050.

Lewis, W. A., 1954. Economic Development with Unlimited Supplies of Labor. *The Manchester School*, 22(2): 139–91.

McCaig, B., and Pavcnik, N., 2018. Export Markets and Labor Allocation in a Low-Income Country. *American Economic Review*, 108, 1899–1941.

McMillan, M., Rodrik, D., and Verduzco-Gallo, Í., 2014. Globalization, Structural Change, and Productivity Growth, with an Update on Africa. *World Development*, 63: 11–32.

Miguelez, E., 2018. Inventor Diasporas and the Internationalization of Technology. *World Bank Economic Review*, 32: 41–63.

Parsons, C., and Vézina, P.-L., 2018. Migrant Networks and Trade: The Vietnamese Boat People as a Natural Experiment. *Economic Journal*, 128: F210–F234.

Peri, G., and Sparber, C., 2011. Highly Educated Immigrants and Native Occupational Choice. *Industrial Relations: A Journal of Economy and Society*, 50: 385–411.

Rapoport, H., 2016. Migration and Globalization: What's in It for Developing Countries? *International Journal of Manpower*, 37: 1209–26.

Rosenstein-Rodan, P. N., 1943. Problems of Industrialisation of Eastern and South-Eastern Europe. *Economic Journal*, 53: 202–11.

Ruiz, I., and Vargas-Silva, C., 2013. The Economics of Forced Migration. *The Journal of Development Studies*, 49: 772–84.

Ruiz, I., and Vargas-Silva, C., 2015. The Labor Market Impacts of Forced Migration. *American Economic Review*, 105: 581–6.

Ruiz, I., and Vargas-Silva, C., 2016. The Labor Market Consequences of Hosting Refugees. *Journal of Economic Geography*, 16: 667–94.

UNHCR, 2018. Global Report 2018. Geneva: UNHCR—The UN Refugee Agency. Available from: https://www.unhcr.org/en-us/5e4ff98f7.pdf

World Bank, 2016. *Migration and Remittances Factbook 2016*. Washington, DC: World Bank.

Yang, D., 2008. International Migration, Remittances and Household Investment: Evidence from Philippine Migrants' Exchange Rate Shocks. *Economic Journal*, 118: 591–630.

Yang, D., 2011. Migrant Remittances. *Journal of Economic Perspectives*, 25: 129–52.

6

The Interrelationship of Growth, Formality, Informality, and Regulation

Low-income countries often face huge challenges in building up formal labour market structures that allow labour supply and demand to balance more efficiently. While it is widely accepted that the formal sector is a driver of economic growth and additional social security, in a number of developing regions there is no alternative to the informal sector, since this accounts for the majority of available jobs.

Recent economic growth in many developing countries, far from contributing to a decline in the informal sector, has actually done the opposite. This is a concern not only for rural areas but also—and possibly even more so—for congested urban centres with dysfunctional labour markets. The absence of stable formal structures may put people at risk and increase uncertainty, while premature policy strategies to reduce informality may result in undesired outcomes and aggravate the living conditions and socio-economic prospects of disadvantaged households.

Governments in LICs, as well as international development aid agencies, need to accept that informality will remain a central feature of the economic landscape for the foreseeable future. There is substantial evidence that informality does not prevent countries from developing. Furthermore, since there does not seem to be an impermeable barrier between the two sectors, transition patterns need the full attention of research and policy advice. However, the role of informality in the process of economic growth and sectoral transformation, and its link to the formal sector is not yet well established by economic research.

Economic development has nevertheless contributed to a slow increase of formal employment in some developing regions in the recent past. This calls for careful, measured regulation of emerging formal labour markets—even more so if the trend is negatively impacted by the COVID-19 pandemic. Policy interventions such as minimum wages and other wage regulation, or mandatory social insurance, may help to organize vulnerable labour markets and aid individuals' economic success, but could also have the opposite effect.

GLM|LIC research has addressed these topics in a number of insightful projects that show the relevance of the informal sector in the process of development. These projects have shed new light on sectoral transformation between formal and

Labour Markets in Low-Income Countries. David Lam and Ahmed Elsayed, Oxford University Press.
© David Lam and Ahmed Elsayed (2022). DOI: 10.1093/oso/9780192897107.003.0006

informal employment, and investigated the relationship between trade, employment, regulation, and productivity. This chapter presents some core findings and connects them to other studies in the field.

6.1 Is There a Close Link between Sectoral Transformation, Economic Growth, and Employment?

Given the high prevalence of informal employment in the developing world, a thorough understanding of its mechanisms is central to any evidence-based labour market and economic policy. While definitions can vary, informal employment is generally characterized by the absence of legal contracts and limited protection schemes for workers such as minimum wage, sick leave, paid holiday, or unemployment insurance. The classic one-dimensional view of informality is still present in ongoing debate: less-educated workers, unable to find jobs in the regular market, are forced to look for informal employment or engage in self-employment. Without written contracts, paid leave, and any other social security, they are at high risk of being locked into informality and poverty, as the sector seems stagnant and unproductive. It offers only precarious employment at the lowest wages with poor working conditions, or small-scale self-employment, and fails to contribute significantly to economic growth. From this perspective, the informal sector merely provides a subsistence fall-back option for the disadvantaged, but has no long-term benefit to offer other than to pool surplus labour. At best, economic development will crowd out informality and dispense with it over the long run.

A study by La Porta and Shleifer (2014) mostly confirmed this pessimistic view of informality, arguing that the formal and informal sectors are too disconnected to expect any transition in between, or any contribution from informality to economic growth. From this point of view, neither policy strategies to support the sector nor interventions to regulate it seem feasible. Instead, policies would need to focus strictly on empowering the formal sector and enhancing educated entrepreneurship.

However, this perspective is not without controversy among economists, and statistics reveal that reality is more complex: quite a number of developing countries experienced substantial growth rates in recent years, with hardly any change in the share of informal (self-)employment. Although this is in part due to demographic change driving many young workers into informality in the absence of formal jobs, it is doubtful that informality necessarily inhibits economic growth, or that development can be induced by formalization only.

This raises the provocative question of whether the informal sector should even be supported by acknowledging voluntary informal self-employment, and providing better opportunities for disadvantaged groups outside the regular labour market. A GLM|LIC study emphasized this argument using the example of the youth employment challenge in sub-Saharan Africa (Fox 2016; see also Chapter 7 in this volume). This challenge is not likely to be solved without the 'help' of informal employment since the rate of growth of formal jobs is unlikely to keep up with the growth of the working-age population. Hence organizing informal employment better, and raising its productivity, could serve as a byway to empowering population groups at risk and strengthening their labour market attachment and welfare. Specifically, **supporting informal agricultural self-employment and entrepreneurship among the young may provide a way to overcome extreme poverty and drive inclusive growth, by reducing the welfare gap versus private sector employment.**

This recommendation deserves full attention, even if research has so far found only small potential gains from interventions that aim to improve productivity among informal businesses. Strategies towards more formal registration among informal entrepreneurs do not inevitably lead to significant productivity gains (see Bruhn and McKenzie 2014), while providing business training and better access to microcredit does not necessarily promote growth (see Karlan and Zinman 2011; McKenzie and Woodruff 2014).

6.1.1 Informal Employment Is not Always the 'Last Resort'

To further assess the economic rationale of the approach suggested by Fox (2016), it is essential to know the permeability between the formal and informal labour market segments, and what this contributes to aggregate productivity. Only if individuals can choose which sector to engage in, and not have their hand forced entirely by necessity, should sustainable positive outcomes be expected. Gelb et al. (2009) addressed this topic by investigating the internal barriers—in terms of management quality and productivity—that prevent firms from taking advantage of the wider opportunities provided by the formal sector. The study revealed the high opportunity costs of switching to formal employment as one main reason why the informal sector has a high share of 'survivalist firms'.

These findings raise the question of whether transition will promote or discourage upward mobility that brings higher returns to labour, and of which factors are most important in attracting workers to the formal labour market. These issues have been investigated by two GLM|LIC studies that surveyed workers in Bangladesh on their de facto transition activities. The studies used a choice experiment to identify the aspects of formality most valued among workers (Gutierrez et al. 2019; Mahmud et al. 2021, see also the summary of the main results in Kumar, Nataraj, and Gutierrez 2017). The survey-based study found evidence for a dual role of the informal sector: on the one hand, it fosters segmentation with limited upward mobility or even a risk of downward mobility; on the other hand, it

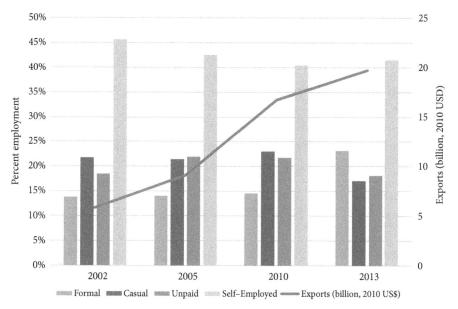

Fig. 6.1 Growth in Exports and Shares of Formal, Casual, Unpaid, and Self-Employment, Bangladesh
Source: Kumar et al. (2017)

provides an entrepreneurial alternative to paid jobs in the formal sector. According to the choice experiment, the average worker ranked the promise of job stability—gained through a longer-term formal job contract—as the most attractive feature of formal labour compared to other work.

Bangladesh is a good example of a low-income country experiencing significant economic growth at a stubbornly low (though increasing) rate of regular paid work in the formal sector. A clear rise in per capita GDP and an even stronger increase in export growth have not yet overcome the predominance of informal self-employment in the country's economy (see Figure 6.1).

Against this background, Gutierrez et al. (2019) conducted a large survey of 2,000 adult workers in the metropolitan areas of Dhaka and Chittagong, collecting rich data on their current jobs and their job history over the past fifteen years. This unusually long survey period allowed for extensive analysis. To measure trends of formality and informality, the survey included questions focusing on working conditions, training, reasons for job change, and total job satisfaction, as well as the take-up of job benefits (sick or casual leave, holidays, maternity leave, bonus payments, retirement benefits) and the design of job contracts (written work contract, timely termination notice).

Roughly 18% of participants were female, while more than 20% of the sample workers were aged 25 or below. More than 40% were self-employed or family workers in household businesses; 40% had paid jobs in the private sector; 12% were casual workers (including seasonal workers, day labourers, domestic workers, apprentices, trainees, and interns). Government workers made up some 6% of the sample. Around 40% of the workers reported low education (primary or less), while 20% had some secondary education, and about 25% reported having completed high school or higher education. The garments industry was the most frequent sector of employment (20%), followed by manufacturing (15%) (see Table 6.1).

Table 6.1 Characteristics of Workers in the Formal and Informal Sector in Bangladesh

Variable	%
Female	17.8%
Age	
18–25	21.9%
26–35	35.6%
36–45	22.8%
46–55	12.7%
56+	7.1%
Education	
Pre-school or less	16.6%
Some primary (Class 1–5)	22.7%
Some secondary (Class 6–9)	19.6%
Class 10 or SSC	15.9%
HSC or Diploma	9.6%
Bachelor's degree or higher	15.4%
Missing	0.3%
Vocational Training	
No vocational training	89.0%
Vocational training without certification	3.2%
Vocational training with certification	7.9%
Employment Type	
Government employees	6.4%
Private employees	40.3%
Casual workers	11.7%
Self-employed alone/with family	25.8%
Self-employed (with non family)	12.7%
Family worker	3.1%
Industry	
Garments	20.5%
Other Manufacturing	15.5%
Trade/Transportation	27.8%
Other services	36.3%
Total	1,966

Note: Summary statistics from sample of 1,966 working adults who completed the survey. Employment type and industry are based on current employment type at the time of the survey. Sampling weights are applied.
Source: Gutierrez et al. (2019)

Table 6.2 Reasons for Informal Self-Employment

Reason	%
Because I was unable find other work	18.2%
Because I wanted independence/be my own boss	45.3%
Because I wanted to have flexible working hours	4.5%
Because I wanted higher income	12.2%
Because I wanted to be close to home	3.3%
Because parents, relatives, or friends have their own business	6.4%
Because I wanted do grow professionally	1.8%
Because I wanted to have job security	0.3%
Because family members wanted me to work in the business	3.6%
Other	4.4%
Total	100.0%

Note: Reported reasons for self-employment among self-employed individuals. Sampling weights are applied.
Source: Gutierrez et al. (2019)

With regards to overall self-employment, owners of businesses both with and without additional employees were surveyed (see Table 6.2). The data reveal that self-employment is mostly chosen voluntarily—only 18% said they were unable to find other work, whereas independence (45%) and better income prospects (12%) were reported as the decisive factors in choosing it.

The clear distinction between wage workers in the private and public sectors, and casual workers, with respect to benefits received, seems self-descriptive. However, it should be emphasized that only a minority of private market wage employees, according to the survey, had written work contracts—48% of them relied on verbal contracts, reaching almost the same level as casual workers, where 51% relied on such contracts. Maternity leave and paid overtime were particularly rare among casual workers, whereas a majority reported being offered sick leave (see Table 6.3).

Monthly and daily labour incomes showed government workers earning the most. The self-employed reported the next highest income, resulting from their business profits, with a higher income among those who employ non-family workers. This finding aligns with workers' expectations when deciding to be self-employed. Private sector wages rank only third, according to the survey, while casual and family workers reported the lowest incomes (see Table 6.4).

Furthermore, and stunningly, a majority of survey participants across all groups reported being fully satisfied in their jobs, with government workers most likely to be fully satisfied (95%) and the self-employed (92%) following closely behind. The survey also revealed, though, that poor working conditions are widespread across all forms of employment with regard to exposure to hazards or physical violence, being highest among casual workers (78% and 40%, respectively). Conversely,

Table 6.3 Work Benefits by Type of Employment

	Government Employees	Private Employees	Casual Workers
Written contract	91.9%	25.0%	1.6%
Verbal contract	5.0%	48.1%	51.3%
Sick leave	98.5%	87.8%	63.7%
Casual leave	96.6%	61.2%	26.0%
Holiday leave	87.9%	83.0%	17.0%
Maternity leave	93.8%	85.1%	27.0%
Paid overtime	19.3%	33.5%	7.3%
Bonus	95.8%	86.1%	26.1%
Provident fund	93.5%	12.6%	0.6%
Gratuity	72.6%	6.4%	0.6%
Pension	82.8%	0.7%	0.8%
Termination notice	73.6%	45.2%	14.4%

Note: Reported benefits by employment type, based on current employment type at the time of the survey. Casual worker category includes day labourers, seasonal workers, domestic workers, and apprentices, interns, or trainees. Sampling weights are applied.
Source: Gutierrez et al. (2019)

Table 6.4 Earnings by Type of Employment

Employment Type	(a) Monthly Earnings (2016 Taka)		
	25% percentile	50% percentile	75% percentile
Government employee	15,200	25,000	35,000
Private employee	7,000	9,500	15,000
Casual worker	6,000	7,500	12,000
Self-employed (alone/with family)	7,500	15,000	20,000
Self-employed (with non- family)	15,000	20,000	35000
Family worker	2,500	7,500	15,000
	(b) Hourly Earnings (2016 Taka)		
	25% percentile	50% percentile	75% percentile
Government employee	303	480	837
Private employee	114	166	267
Casual worker	111	143	222
Self-employed (alone/with family)	111	222	370
Self-employed (with non- family)	222	370	519
Family worker	91	178	286

Note: Monthly earnings (panel (a)) and hourly earnings (panel (b)), by employment type. Hourly earnings are calculated based on reported monthly earnings and working hours. Earnings information is based on current job at time of survey. Casual worker category includes day labourers, seasonal workers, domestic workers, and apprentices, interns, or trainees. Sampling weights are applied.
Source: Gutierrez et al. (2019)

Table 6.5 Working Conditions by Type of Employment

Statement	% who Agree or Strongly Agree				
	Government employee	Private employee	Casual worker	Self-employed	Family worker
I am exposed to hazards at work	35.5	53.2	77.9	47.1	47.4
I have been exposed to threats of physical violence	11.3	21.6	39.8	20.4	14.2
The hygiene in my workplace is good	91.4	76.6	57.4	72.2	76.0
My employer gives the benefits I am supposed to get for my work	97.7	86.7	86.2	88.1	95.0
My employer always pays me on time	97.5	92.9	90.9	89.7	100.0
I have the training opportunities to perform my job well	87.7	60.0	31.6	42.2	31.0
I have the opportunity to progress/get promoted	92.0	80.9	58.4	91.8	91.8
I am fully satisfied with my job	95.3	87.3	76.4	92.1	89.1

Note: Reported working conditions by employment type, for current job at time of survey. Casual worker category includes day labourers, seasonal workers, domestic workers, and apprentices, interns, or trainees. Sampling weights are applied.
Source: Gutierrez et al. (2019)

above 80% or even 90% of all workers stated that—besides being paid in a timely way—they received their benefits as agreed, which may explain the high level of job satisfaction. However, few casual workers reported training opportunities (32%) (see Table 6.5).

The study also reported calculations of the median time workers had spent in their current job, at the time of the survey (see Table 6.6). These numbers showed that the self-employed had a rather high median duration of eight to ten years in their current business, which was surpassed only by government employees (fifteen years), possibly contradicting the more classical perception of self-employment as a temporary necessity for those unable to obtain a formal employment (see, for example, Harris and Todaro 1970; Fields 1975). However, as the calculated figures obviously cannot reveal future job duration, they need to be complemented by information on the number of jobs actually held over the survey period.

Table 6.6 Median Employment Duration in Current Jobs (Years)

	Median Duration
Government employee	14.8
Private employee	4.3
Casual worker	6.3
Self-employed (with no employees or with family employees)	8.3
Self-employed (with non-family employees)	10.1
Family worker	6.3

Note: Calculations of median employment duration by employment type, based on current job. Casual worker category includes day labourers, seasonal workers, domestic workers, and apprentices, interns, or trainees. Duration for casual workers measures type of work, although not necessarily for the same employer. Sampling weights are applied.
Source: Gutierrez et al. (2019)

According to Gutierrez et al. (2019), around 57% of all workers across all types of employment had only one job (their current one) in the last fifteen years. When combined with workers reporting two jobs (32%), they make up roughly 90% of the spectrum (see Figure 6.2, first panel). Rather high job stability appears to have been driven by government employment and the self-employed.

This finding is confirmed by the authors' further investigation, which—by estimating the 'survival curves' of jobs for all types of employment—revealed the longest duration for these two groups (see Figure 6.2, second panel). Self-employed individuals were the second most likely to 'survive' in their job in the short and long term, with only a marginal difference from government employees over the first five years. Just 5% of government workers had left their job within five years, while the rates for the self-employed were 6% (for those with external employees) and 9% (for those with only family employees or no employees at all). Despite an increasing gap between both groups over time (15% of government employees and 24–29% of the self-employed left their job after fifteen years), the self-employed stayed second in terms of job survival, and even increased the gap with respect to private, family, and casual workers. **This appears to be a clear signal that voluntary informal self-employment lasts for an extended period**.

In a next step, Gutierrez et al. (2019) explored whether worker or job characteristics affect employment duration and the probability of switching jobs (see Table 6.7), finding that:

1. **private sector employees were the group most likely to change their job**, with the main reasons being finding a preferred one or choosing self-employment, and thus switching voluntarily;

(a)   Cumulative Number of Jobs since 2000

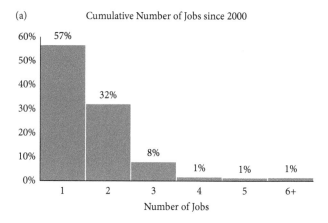

(b)   Survival Curves by Employment Type

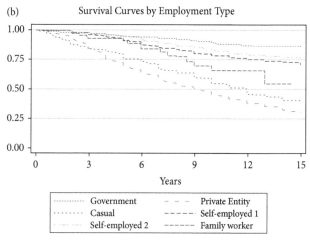

Self-employed 1: no employees or employ only family worker
Self-employed 2: employ non-family worker

Fig. 6.2 Frequency of Job Turnover and Survival Curves

Note: Panel (b) shows Kaplan-Meier survival curves by employment
type. Calculations are based on all observed jobs. Casual worker
category includes day laborers, seasonal workers, domestic workers, and
apprentices, interns, or trainees. Sampling weights are applied.
Source: Gutierrez et al. (2019)

2. **self-employed individuals had a low likelihood of turning to wage employment** if their business failed; they mostly decided to stay self-employed and start a new business;

3. among the self-employed, a voluntary move from a wage job to another type of employment was much more likely than a voluntary move to wage employment;

Table 6.7 Main Reason for Leaving Previous Job

(a) Among Government Employees, Private Employees, and Casual Workers

Main Reason for Separation	Government Employees	Private Employees	Casual Workers
Terminated	0%	5%	12%
Firm closed	5%	8%	2%
Job completed	21%	2%	3%
Found preferred job	32%	38%	26%
Dedicated to start my own business	5%	18%	16%
Dedicated to work for family business	0%	2%	2%
Retired	11%	2%	0%
Still work at this job but it is no longer the main activity	0%	1%	8%
Other	26%	23%	31%
Don't know	0%	0%	0%
Refused	0%	0%	0%
Total	100%	100%	100%

(b) Among Self-Employed and Family Workers

Main Reason for Separation	Self-employed (w/o employees or w/family employees)	Self-employed (w/non-family employees)	Family worker
Firm did not make enough profit	39%	55%	10%
Found preferred job	13%	2%	10%
Decided to start another business	19%	11%	25%
Decided to work for another family business	2%	0%	5%
Retired	2%	0%	0%
Still work in this business but it is no longer the main activity	9%	11%	15%
Other	13%	21%	20%
Refused	3%	0%	15%
Total	100%	100%	100%

Note: Reported reason for leaving previous jobs, for wage workers (panel (a)) and workers in household businesses (panel (b)). Casual worker category includes day labourers, seasonal workers, domestic workers, and apprentices, interns, or trainees. Sampling weights are applied.
Source: Gutierrez et al. (2019)

4. **shorter job duration was associated with higher levels of education for wage workers** (government, private, casual), reflecting increased demand for skilled labour;

5. **women showed lower job mobility than men in both wage and household business employment**, due to constraints in taking over a new job (time-conflicting family and household responsibilities, travel restrictions);

6. **higher earnings and access to social transfers such as retirement benefits were associated with an extended job duration for wage employees** (mainly driven, of course, by the high prevalence of retirement benefits among government workers);

7. **upward mobility was revealed by the changes in earnings and job benefits among private wage employees who transition to another job**, but the risk of downward mobility was rather high among those workers moving into casual employment.

Turning to the most prevalent transition patterns, the study presented some instructive results. Most importantly, **the majority of workers stayed in the same type of job**. This pattern was most pronounced among the self-employed (60%), followed by private employees (58%), government workers (47%), and casual workers (42%). Only family workers were more likely to move on to self-employment. Nevertheless, it should be noted that there was a substantial amount of (voluntary) transition between private sector employment and self-employment. More than one-quarter of self-employed workers who left their business decided to take up jobs in the wage sector. Conversely, almost one-third of wage workers who left private employment chose entrepreneurship or joined a family business. Of those leaving casual work, almost one-quarter entered the private market (see Table 6.8). There are many interpretations to this: self-employment or a family business may give more contentment than working in an enterprise (see Fajnzylber, Maloney, and Rojas 2006), while for others a higher cash income may be more attractive than job benefits (see Maloney 1999).

Some additional findings further underline the conclusion that job and worker characteristics matter. Higher private wage income and longer tenure seemed to raise the probability of moving on to another sector, with a high preference for self-employment among wage employees with longer tenure. At the same time, educated workers leaving the private sector were less likely to start their own business. Access to retirement benefits—of a sufficient level—reduced the likelihood of moving into types of work that lack these benefits. Casual workers were more likely to transition towards formality—by moving on to private wage jobs or self-employment—if they were better educated or had been working casually for a longer period of time, thus gaining work experience. Interestingly, there seemed to be no correlation between gender and transition to certain types of jobs, while controlling for age effects reveals that older self-employed workers were more likely to start a new business after ending previous self-employment.

Table 6.8 Transition between Employment Categories

		Current Employment				
		Government employee	Private employee	Casual workers	Self-employed	Family worker	Total
Previous Employment	Government employee	47.37%	47.37%	5.26%	10.53%	0.00%	100%
	Private employee	3.59%	57.57%	8.96%	28.09%	1.79%	100%
	Casual workers	0.00%	22.54%	42.25%	30.99%	4.23%	100%
	Self-employed	0.60%	26.51%	12.05%	60.24%	0.60%	100%
	Family worker	0.00%	30.00%	20.00%	45.00%	5.00%	100%

Note: Rows show previous type of employment, while columns show current type of employment. Each cell shows the probability that a worker who leaves a previous job of a certain type (given by row headings) transitions to a new job of a certain type (given by column headings). Casual worker category includes day labourers, seasonal workers, domestic workers, and apprentices, interns, or trainees. Sampling weights are applied.
Source: Gutierrez et al. (2019)

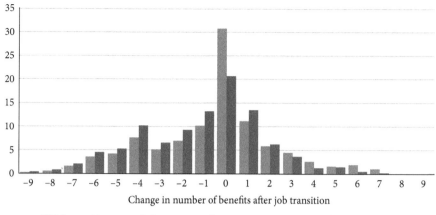

Fig. 6.3 Change in Number of Benefits after Job Transitions

Note: Change in the number of benefits between the previous job and current job. Sampling weights are applied.

Source: Gutierrez et al. (2019)

Studying earnings outcomes reveals large variation in wage changes after transition. In most cases—corresponding to voluntary transition from this sector—private employees gained additional income when they moved on to other types of employment. This effect is especially pronounced for private wage workers who started a business and employed non-family workers (42% increase in median monthly earnings). At a far lower level (2–10%), those casual workers who turned to self-employment also saw a rise in earnings. The observation that replacing self-employment with other types of work does not lead to income gains, but instead induces significant losses, is consistent with the general finding that the majority of self-employed workers stayed business orientated, even in the event that they needed to terminate a business.

Does moving between types of employment lead to workers acquiring more job-based benefits? The study shows this was largely not the case. Most often, benefits were retained at the same level, while the probability of increasing them was outweighed by a higher risk of losing benefit entitlements when moving (see Figure 6.3). This finding is not surprising, given the abovementioned results that transition from private wage employment to self-employment was rather frequent (higher risk of losing benefits), while transition from self-employment and family work to private sector employment drove benefit effects in the opposite direction (higher likelihood of gaining benefits).

In an accompanying study, Mahmud et al. (2021) introduced a choice experiment that aimed to identify the values of wage employment seen as the most beneficiary among those surveyed. Participants were given two hypothetical job offers with different levels of job benefits ranging from zero to a maximum level (short-/longer-term written contract, timing of advance termination notice, amount of paid holidays, number of working hours, and access to retirement funds). The monthly income offered was varied, up to a 50% increase above current labour earnings. This allowed the authors to examine the notional 'price' that workers would pay for receiving single benefits, and put a monetary value on their willingness to substitute between the benefits offered. Furthermore, it allowed them to capture the preferences of the self-employed about benefits not available in their current type of employment.

According to the experiment, job stability was the most valued attribute across all types of worker. Compared with receiving no job contract, average workers would waive 44% of their earnings for a permanent contract. While this could be explained by the scarcity of permanent work contracts in many low-income countries, the figures for shorter contracts are the more revealing: workers would sacrifice 27% of their earnings for a one-year contract and 19% for a half-year contract. Early contract termination was another attribute highly welcomed by average workers (12% of monthly income).

When distinguishing between types of workers it becomes obvious, according to Mahmoud et al. (2021), that private sector employees place lower value on long-term contracts. Meanwhile casual workers have the strongest preference for higher-paid jobs, and the self-employed are more likely to value a broad range of benefits, but do not greatly prefer long-term contracts. Loss aversion and sorting effects may explain these preferences. For policymakers, these results imply that increasing job stability could yield positive labour market outcomes.

Summing up these intriguing GLM|LIC studies, the authors investigated a topic that is underdeveloped in economic research and provided some important insights for future development policies. **The formal and informal sector do not face off irreconcilably, but allow transition to happen voluntarily to a significant extent.** Also, transition is a two-way street: almost one-third of the surveyed Bangladeshi workers moved from private wage employment to self-employment and household businesses, accepting a loss of employment benefits but gaining earnings. Most of the self-employed stayed in the sector even after termination of a business, but a significant minority moved to wage employment.

By and large, the informal sector—at least in an urban and peri-urban setting such as that being studied here—appears to consist of two elements. Firstly, employment segments that provide only limited upward mobility while putting some groups at risk of downward mobility, and secondly, a significant share of voluntary entrepreneurship serving as a true and stable alternative to wage employment.

According to Gutierrez et al. (2019), 'Self-employment is not always an activity of last resort'. Hence the informal sector should no longer be viewed (and stigmatized) as a dead end for workers whose distance from 'regular' employment is too far. **Informal self-employment seems far more driven by entrepreneurship and**

choice than often thought. Gutierrez et al. (2019) provided convincing evidence on the permeability of, and transition patterns between, the formal and informal sector under the conditions of low-income urban settings. The resilience of the findings deserves to be tested for other regions and (rural) settings also.

6.1.2 Formality and Informality across and within Birth Cohorts: the Case of Vietnam

Another study supported by GLM|LIC (McCaig and Pavcnik 2015) widens the perspective and adds some important findings on the permeability of the informal and formal sector in Vietnam, and the characteristics of those informal workers who are most likely to move on to formal employment. The study showed that rapid economic growth and shifting demographics in Vietnam have led to a faster transition to the formal sector than in other low-income countries, and some decline in informality that nevertheless left the share of the sector at an extremely high level. The results of the study suggest that focusing on productivity gains in the formal sector are the best strategy for improving working conditions among the poor.

Vietnam is an ideal setting for investigating these complex relationships, as it has experienced high growth rates from 1999 to 2009, with GDP per capita exploding by 78%, and 35% growth of the labour force. At first sight, this remarkable development has not allowed the country to reduce its share of informal employment substantially. Informality fell by 7 percentage points, but aggregate informal employment still made up 79% of total employment in 2009.

Further examination reveals, however, that this moderate trend masks a clear shift of employment. Agricultural employment saw a significant decline, while manufacturing and services expanded; even more importantly, as McCaig and Pavcnik (2015) noted, the share of informal jobs within the manufacturing sector dropped by 15 percentage points.

This confirms a generally decreasing trend in informality as economies grow (see La Porta and Shleifer 2014). However, it should be noted that cyclical fluctuations or severe global crises may dramatically alter these trends, given the high vulnerability of labour markets in LICs to fundamental external shocks. In such circumstances, informality will prevail and may even—in light of the economic consequences of the COVID-19 pandemic—increase in many developing countries. Policymakers are thus confronted with the dual challenge of increasing productivity of the informal sector while also facilitating transition to higher-productivity formal employment. The potential contribution to aggregate productivity from the transition of individual workers between the informal and formal sectors remains an understudied research area.

Starting from this baseline, McCaig and Pavcnik (2015) enriched the literature by investigating these interrelations based on representative data from the Vietnam Household Living Standards Surveys (VHLSS: 2002, 2004, 2006, 2008), which allowed the tracking of working-age individuals over four years, and the Vietnam Population Census (1999, 2009). These data sets cover all industries, including formal and informal employment. They were used to identify the characteristics of informal workers most likely to formalize when low-income economies grow rapidly, and to analyse whether the job tasks of workers change as they transition to formal employment.

The study found that demographics are a crucial determinant of transition by examining the aggregate decline in informality across different birth cohorts. Young workers who entered Vietnam's labour force during the growth period of 1999 to 2009 (aged 10–19 in 1999) were substantially less likely to work in the informal sector than workers in older birth cohorts (55–59, 60–64 in 1999) that entered the labour force in earlier years with lower economic growth rates. In fact, the young cohorts contributed the most to the aggregate decrease in informality in Vietnam between 1999 and 2009. With an average informality level of roughly 70% in 2009, they ranked more than 20 percentage points below older workers. The share of informal workers rather consistently increased with the age of the cohorts (see Table 6.9). According to the calculations given by McCaig and Pavcnik (2015), this demographic effect accounted for 69% of the decline in total nationwide informality during the study period.

Informality within cohorts confirmed this trend, accounting for another 31% of aggregate informality decline: workers of older cohorts (over 40 years of age in 1999) experienced an increase of informality over the ten-year period of up to 8 percentage points, whereas the younger birth cohorts aged 20–24 and 25–29 in 1999 saw a clear drop by 11 and 5 percentage points respectively.

The rise of the manufacturing sector in Vietnam was accompanied by a 14.5% decrease in informality over the decade. Thus, it should not surprise that the young birth cohorts' contribution to informality decline was even larger in manufacturing than it was economy wide. The share of this group employed informally was about 30% in manufacturing in 2009, while cohorts above the age of 40 showed rates of 67% and higher. Analysing by gender did not reveal strongly deviating results—only that the gap in the share of the informally employed across female birth cohorts appears to be larger than for males.

Manufacturing in developing countries is usually clustered in urban areas and their peripheries. Vietnam is no exception to this 'rule', with five provinces accounting for 63% of formal employment in this sector in 1999. Moving from informal employment to formal jobs in manufacturing may thus involve (temporary) labour migration within the country. The study found that internal migration in fact has a key function in increasing formalization in Vietnam, and that young internal migrants were far less likely to be employed informally. The growth decade

Table 6.9 Informality across and within Age Cohorts

Panel A: Share of information workers in cohort

Year of birth	Age in 1999	Economy-wide			Manufacturing		
		1999	2009	Change	1999	2009	Change
1985–9	10–14		0.716			0.287	
1980–4	15–19		0.687			0.325	
1975–9	20–24	0.873	0.761	−0.112	0.569	0.440	−0.129
1970–4	25–29	0.864	0.816	−0.047	0.585	0.527	−0.059
1965–9	30–34	0.868	0.843	−0.025	0.590	0.586	−0.004
1960–4	35–39	0.850	0.835	−0.014	0.561	0.61	0.049
1955–9	40–44	0.838	0.849	0.011	0.545	0.669	0.123
1950–4	45–49	0.844	0.906	0.061	0.587	0.762	0.175
1945–9	50–54	0.872	0.956	0.083	0.605	0.858	0.253
1940–4	55–59	0.924			0.723		
1935–9	60–64	0.967			0.866		
Total		0.864	0.790	−0.074	0.580	0.435	−0.145

Panel B: Decomposition of aggregate informality change 2009–1999

	Within cohorts	Between cohorts	Total change	Within cohorts	Between cohorts	Total change
Decomposition	−0.023	−0.051	−0.074	−0.014	−0.131	−0.145

Note: Authors' calculations based on Vietnam Population Census data for 1999 and 2009 on workers aged 20–64.
Source: McCaig and Pavcnik (2015)

clearly stimulated migration to the manufacturing areas, particularly among the young cohorts, while the effect declined with age. Between 2005 and 2009 around 12% of workers aged 20–24 migrated, according to the survey data, while the share of manufacturing workers in the same age and migration cohort rose to 29%.

The informality gap between migrants and non-migrants in the same cohort is striking: the share of informality among male and female migrants in the youngest cohort (33% and 31% respectively) was over 40 and 35 percentage points below the average rate for all male female workers in this cohort respectively. Just 42% of all workers who recently migrated were employed informally, with an even lower share of 14% among recent migrants in manufacturing—a stark contrast with the figure for workers overall (79%). These results suggest that younger workers may transition from informality to formality more quickly if they have a greater willingness and readiness to migrate. In other words, the decision to migrate substantially increases the probability of being formally employed.

6.1.3 Who Is More Likely to Transition between the Formal and Informal Sectors?

The study further examined the actual transition of workers to the formal sector within birth cohorts and the duration of these switches. Learning more about the underlying patterns is important in order to better target potential policy approaches. A close look at the shares of workers who were always employed formally or informally, or who moved between the sectors between 2002 and 2005, gives a rather clear picture: although most workers stayed in one sector, younger cohorts were more likely to move sectors or to stay longer in the formal sector (see Table 6.10).

Using cross-sectional analyses to account for individual attributes that may influence transition behaviour, McCaig and Pavcnik (2015) concluded that workers who switch into formality, and workers already working formally, share similar observable characteristics: they were more likely to be younger, better educated,

Table 6.10 Aggregate Transition between the Informal and Formal Sectors

Age of workers at start of panel	Share of workers			Share of switchers		
	Always informal	Always formal	Switchers	Informal at start	Informal at end	Permanently move to formal
20–29	0.698	0.151	0.151	0.652	0.443	0.217
30–39	0.795	0.111	0.094	0.572	0.533	0.174
40–49	0.785	0.13	0.085	0.528	0.597	0.136
50–64	0.868	0.057	0.075	0.444	0.64	0.14
All	0.784	0.116	0.099	0.569	0.536	0.173
Manufacturing	0.606	0.182	0.211	0.57	0.467	0.187

Notes: The sample of manufacturing workers is defined based on working on manufacturing at either the start or the end of the period. A worker is defined as permanently moving to the formal sector if they were initially working in the informal sector and subsequently working in the formal sector in the surveys two and four years later
Source: McCaig and Pavcnik (2015)

male, non-minorities, and urban. In contrast, older, low-educated, female, and rural workers were relatively less likely to move to the formal sector. The opposite
seems true as well: those workers moving to informality had a similar education,
age, and area of residence to workers already in the sector. Women were less likely
to switch to the informal sector but more likely to be employed there. The authors
suggested that this puzzling finding may be explained by occupational sorting and
the higher share of women working in urban, trade-intensive manufacturing that
makes other formal jobs (or informality) undesirable.

It remained unclear, however, to what extent these individual characteristics
actually determine decisions to move sector; they *influenced* the likelihood of
switching to another sector but did not *predict* this behaviour. That is, many
surveyed workers, although being likely to move sector according to their characteristics, actually did not move at all. Additional research may be able to explore
these findings further.

6.1.4 Is There Occupational Upgrading along with Transition?

In a final step McCaig and Pavcnik (2015) asked whether transition between
the informal and formal sector helps workers to upgrade their occupation. The
data revealed that elementary occupations were the most prevalent among informal workers (85%) and 'switchers' (67%), but were low among formal workers
(11%). According to the study, those switching from the informal to the formal
sector actually increased their employment—and thus their earnings—in skilled
occupations (for example manual workers, skilled handicraftsmen, skilled service
workers) and in assembly, mechanical, or professional occupations over time.

Even those workers moving to low-skill manufacturing jobs experienced a skills
and earnings upgrade compared to their former jobs in agriculture or informal
manufacturing and services. However, workers already in formal employment
at the start of the period kept their leading position in terms of higher-skilled
occupations (for example machinists, assemblers, professionals).

In summary, McCaig and Pavcnik (2015) presented a number of findings that
should give cause for reflection, since they paint a more optimistic picture of
the informal sector than does mainstream economic thinking. While the study
confirmed the importance of policies that promote growth in the formal sector, as a prerequisite to enabling informal workers to upgrade occupation and
earnings by moving sector, it also highlighted another aspect: **the combination
of demographic trends, educational progress and economic growth may increase permeability and accelerate transition dynamics, as the young cohorts
appear to be more likely to step into formality**. Over two-thirds of the decrease
in informality in Vietnam appeared to be due to changing labour force cohorts.

Upward job mobility by moving sectors may be viewed as an important contribution to further economic growth, as it raises sectoral and aggregate productivity. This leads us back to the interrelationship between economic growth, trends in informality and formality, and the observation that Vietnam appears to have transitioned towards the formal sector more quickly than other developing countries. McCaig and Pavcnik (2018) provided evidence on the impact of additional export opportunities in Vietnam on transition between formality and informality, showing that reallocation was more frequent in more trade-orientated regions of the country and among younger workers. This finding adds neatly to the results presented and discussed above. Exposure to globalization and international trade—as well as repeated setbacks that may occur in the longer term—will certainly affect transition trends, since it expands formal employment opportunities and occupational quality.

6.1.5   Poor Prospects for Non-Farm Microenterprises in Vietnam

In a further study supported by GLM|LIC, McCaig and Pavcnik (2017) drew attention from the individual to the firm level of transition. Given that non-farm microenterprises—mostly operated on an informal, small, single-person level—employ roughly 60% share of the Vietnamese labour force, better knowledge on the entry, exit, hiring, and transition behaviour of these household businesses is highly valuable. A lack of large-scale, representative data on non-registered microenterprises restricts this field of study. The Vietnam Household Living Standard Survey, also used in the studies presented above, allows the dynamics of non-farm microenterprises to be investigated and linked to characteristics of the business owner over almost a decade. The core findings can be summarized:

1. **The decreasing share of informal employment during Vietnam's period of growth between 1999 and 2009 is not linked to formalization of informal microenterprises** but can instead be explained by the new entry and expansion of private sector firms offering wage employment.
2. **Since the large majority of non-farm household businesses do not transition from informality to formality, their expansion prospects are rather limited.**
3. Successful non-rural microenterprises are the exception to the rule. They adapted different characteristics of formality, and were more likely to hire external workers and increase their workforce, or even to register formally. But while only 10% in this group hired workers overall, less than 5% of those who did not hire at baseline changed their hiring behaviour over time.

4. **There is no positive correlation between the age of a household business and firm growth**. Small businesses with a longer market presence did not perform better than younger firms on average.
5. When poorly performing enterprises leave the market, they are largely replaced by new firms with similarly poor market prospects.
6. **Business entry and exit, productivity, hiring, and transition probability are strongly correlated to the owner's education**. While many individuals with lower levels of education operated non-farm household businesses, only the better-educated hired employees. Even this group had lower levels of education than formal sector employees.
7. **The business skills needed to operate a successful microenterprise are rare among owners.**
8. **Most owners of microenterprises enter the market from self-employment in agriculture**. Private wage workers starting a business were rare.

Overall, the analysis presented by McCaig and Pavcnik (2017) suggests that, in the case of Vietnam, there is only very limited potential for sustained growth and employment expansion among non-rural household businesses. This was true even during the period of remarkable growth experienced in the first decade of the twenty-first century. This hints once more at the **urgent need to enhance (business) education among workers in the informal sector, to either improve their business and entrepreneurial skills or to facilitate a move to formal employment**. A lack of business education appears to be the most relevant constraint (see La Porta and Shleifer 2014).

6.2 How Do Low-Income Labour Markets Respond to Economic Crises?

While Vietnam and many other low-income countries saw significant economic growth in the years before the global financial crisis, this was not the common pattern across all developing regions. For instance, Zimbabwe suffered a collapse of its economy in the same period, due to hyperinflation, macroeconomic shocks, and the negative consequences of a land-reform intervention. Although the Zimbabwean economy slowly recovered, the manufacturing sector in particular lagged behind and experienced a further fall in employment.

Against this background, GLM|LIC research projects address the specific challenges posed to the Zimbabwean labour market, as an example of how low-income societies are affected by severe economic crisis. A set of three instructive policy briefs (Edwards et al. 2018; Oostendorp et al. 2018; Rankin et al. 2018) offered meaningful policy instructions based on ongoing research activities.

By studying the performance of more than 200 manufacturing formal sector firms (with at least five employees), Edwards et al. (2018) examined the effect of the crisis on firm behaviour and survival. A so-called 'tracer survey' exploited rich 2015 data on the further business history of firms initially surveyed under the Zimbabwean Regional Programme on Enterprise Development (RPED) between 1993 and 1995. Combining data from trade directories, business associations, firm registers, tax clearance certificates, and other sources with the RPED data, allowed the research group to detect initial firm-based attributes that determined firm performance over time.

The composition of the sample hints at a rather low survival rate of the surveyed firms: out of a sample of 203 firms initially surveyed in the 1990s, seventy-eight still existed in the same market segment, forty were closed, and eight merged, while a high share of thirty-two firms could no longer be traced. Further investigation identified three main firm-specific characteristics associated with firm survival (see Figure 6.4):

1. **Firm survival depends on firm size.** While the survival rate of businesses with twenty or fewer employees was just 9%, it was a relatively high 57% among firms with one hundred workers or more.
2. **Firm age is a determinant of survival.** Less than five years of market experience reduced the likelihood of survival to 9%, whereas firms at least fifteen years old survived at a rate of 55%.
3. **Survival rates reveal a striking gap in firm productivity.** Survival probabilities were six times higher in the top third (most productive) than the bottom third (least productive) of firms.

According to the analysis, other important firm characteristics (for example market share, export-orientation, business sector, ownership (foreign or national), education of manager) were surprisingly not systematically related to firm survival likelihood.

It should be noted as well that Zimbabwe's firm survival rates are not the lowest in the sub-Saharan region but rank at a rather average level—despite the country's huge economic challenges. For instance, Kenya and Tanzania show lower survival rates. Following Edwards et al. (2018), this may be explained by the fact that—given relatively low entry rates—Zimbabwean manufacturing firms were larger, older and more experienced already in the 1990s when compared to other countries in the region, and thus were more likely to survive the 2000–9 crisis period. Also, hyperinflation may have partly offset firms' cost disadvantages, and the absence of other economic options led many firms to operate below capacity rather than close. Further research within this project will reveal whether the surviving firms will be able to expand in better times, and to weather upcoming crises also.

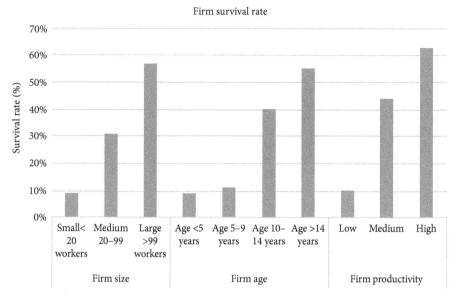

Fig. 6.4 Determinants of Firm Survival Rates among Manufacturing Firms in
Zimbabwe
Source: Edwards et al. (2018)

6.2.1 Economic Uncertainty Affects the Reliability of Workers' Wage Payments

One important aspect of firm performance is economic volatility and policy uncertainty. Firms are directly affected by a lack of planning and revenue security,
and pass on risks to their employees. In a LIC, this will result in far more severe
outcomes than in a developed country.

Additional research within the GLM|LIC project (Rankin et al. 2018) investi-
gated the impact of prevalent uncertainties in Zimbabwe on the welfare of workers
employed by firms in formal and informal manufacturing. The research focused on
the steadiness of wage payments, showing a high share of outstanding pay among
surveyed workers. This finding is highly relevant when examining the transition
between formality and informality, as workers at high risk of going unpaid may
leave formal employment.

Survey data were collected in 2015, from 170 informal workers (131 informal
firms) and over 1,300 formal workers (the same roughly 200 formal firms, with at
least five employees, that were examined in Edwards et al. 2018) across six sectors.
A year later, more than 1,000 formal workers were surveyed again. The findings
Rankin et al. (2018) are revealing (see Figure 6.5) and deserve attention:

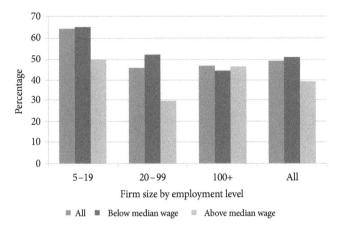

Fig. 6.5 Share of Zimbabwean Workers with Outstanding Pay by Firm Size and Wage Level
Note: 2016 numbers for outstanding pay; 2015 data on firm size and wage level.
Source: Rankin et al. (2018)

1. **Almost half of workers reported outstanding wages** in the second wave of the survey.
2. Roughly **two-thirds of small-firm employees were owed wages**, whereas larger firms paid earnings more reliably.
3. **Workers earning below the median wage were more likely to be owed part of their pay.** Better-paid employees showed an almost 25 percentage points lower risk of being owed earnings in firms with twenty to ninety-nine workers, and an average advantage of 10 percentage points across all firms.
4. **Workers who had been at their firm longer were more likely to be paid reliably.**
5. There is no evidence of significant gender effects.
6. These results were widespread across geographical regions and industries within the manufacturing sector, with only a few exceptions (for example wood and furniture industries).

The amount of earnings owed to manufacturing workers in 2016 is even more stunning: according to Rankin et al. (2018), median outstanding pay was worth almost five months of 2015 wages. More than half of workers were owed at least a full year's earnings, regardless of their individual wage level. Compensation for outstanding earnings was only received by a very small minority of workers (for example housing and transportation, in-kind payments).

In better-functioning labour markets, this high wage uncertainty would either: not occur; induce firms to reduce their workforce; or simply cause workers to leave their jobs for other options. However, given the severe constraints of many low-income countries' labour markets, worker reactions may be quite different.

Rankin et al. (2018) highlighted some reasons why manufacturing workers surveyed in Zimbabwe did not leave firms, despite outstanding wages. Besides just optimistically waiting for better times to come, regulation appears to be one main reason. Zimbabwean labour legislation forces firms to pay out to workers in case of dismissal, depending on their length of service. This regulation gives workers a significant incentive to not leave voluntarily and thus stay entitled to this claim.

Survey data may confirm this: the average tenure of workers owed wages was two years longer than the average twelve years of fully paid workers. Furthermore, by exploring additional data collected to measure risk behaviour and time preferences, the authors indicated that workers with outstanding pay may have a slightly greater readiness to take risks. Additional labour activities do not seem to be an explanatory factor, as the data show no differing proportions for fully and incompletely paid workers; both groups had a roughly 25% share engaged in such activities.

In the course of this chapter, one other reason for accepting owed earnings seems particularly important: the informal sector in Zimbabwe is not likely to offer a serious alternative to those facing wage uncertainty in the formal sector. By estimating alternative earnings through informal employment, based on the survey data on informal manufacturing, Rankin et al. (2018) showed that moving into informality was hardly an attractive option for formal workers. On average, workers that were owed formal sector wages still earned around 50% more in 2015 than their labour earnings would have been in the informal (manufacturing) sector. Within one single year, however, the formality premium fell to 35%.

If it declines further in the face of persistent economic uncertainty affecting the manufacturing sector, it will not just increase the share of workers waiting for earnings payments and the level of owed wages. The gap in earnings between the formal and informal sectors would then shrink, raising the likelihood of workers moving into informality. In turn, this would put informal earnings under significant pressure and enlarge the welfare gap between formal and informal workers.

At least as important are the findings presented by Rankin et al. (2018) showing that **demographics may accelerate a process of distancing between manufacturing in the formal and informal sectors**. If the trend persists, and if older workers tend to benefit from their tenure and face a lower risk of being owed wages, while younger cohorts are far more affected, this could pose a risk of sectoral separation between age groups that must not be ignored. In the case of Zimbabwe, such undesirable outcomes could be tackled best by strengthening the formal manufacturing sector, which is particularly exposed to economic instability.

6.2.2 Productivity Gains versus Allocation Inefficiency among Manufacturing Firms

Exploring the same combination of 2015 survey data on around 200 formal manufacturing firms in Zimbabwe and the 1993–1995 RPED survey, Oostendorp et al. (2018) analysed how the unusual frequency of economic shocks and structural change affected firm characteristics, productivity and allocative efficiency over a twenty-year period (1994–2014). Sectors covered in the study include food processing, textile/garment/leather industries, woodworking/furniture, and metalworking, in selected Zimbabwean regions.

According to the analysis, firm productivity levels increased substantially on aggregate between 1994 and 2014 (see Figure 6.6), while productivity differences across types of business widely diminished. However, export-orientated firms even expanded their clear advantage in terms of productivity over non-exporting firms, despite a substantial loss in external competitiveness due to the 'dollarization' of the Zimbabwean economy in 2009. Remarkably, half of the productivity gap between domestic-owned and foreign-owned manufacturing enterprises has been closed over time.

Notwithstanding these trends, formal manufacturing was exposed to high economic pressure leading to structural adjustments and inefficiencies. The decrease in small-firm market entries indicates that the sector has lost attractiveness and that entrepreneurs may have turned to informal manufacturing instead. This would explain why the share of foreign-owned firms has not decreased, although

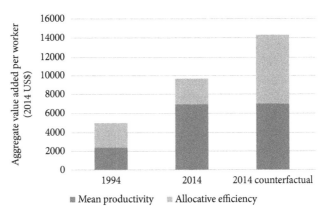

Fig. 6.6 Changes in Aggregate Manufacturing Productivity in Zimbabwe

Note: The counterfactual aggregate productivity level reported for 2014 keeps allocative efficiency at its 1994 level.
Source: Oostendorp et al. (2018)

Zimbabwean indigenization policies resulted in the market exit of many businesses. Low entry rates resulted in a strong rise in the average market age of formal manufacturing firms, which almost doubled from 1994 (16 years) to 2014 (30 years).

Further analysis by Oostendorp et al. (2018) revealed that aggregate productivity within the formal manufacturing sector would have substantially increased (up to 4,600 USD per worker in 2014 prices) if allocative efficiency had been at least stable. Instead, the allocation of resources towards higher productivity businesses worsened over the 1994–2014 period across most manufacturing subsectors and firm characteristics, leading to a dramatic decline in total allocative efficiency. Notably, allocative efficiency among exporting firms fell even more sharply than among non-exporting firms, thus preventing them from gaining an even wider productivity advantage.

These are rather worrying outcomes; despite raising their average productivity, more productive firms were unable to grow as fast as their advantage over less productive businesses should have indicated. **Inefficient allocation of resources has, to a significant extent, dampened aggregate productivity growth within the manufacturing sector**, allowing firms to survive, yet hardly to expand and contribute more to overall economic growth.

The policy implications of these findings are rather straightforward but all the more difficult to implement. Given the apparent market entry barriers and the decline in allocative efficiency, facilitating investment will not be enough. The functioning of factor markets should be improved in order to increase efficiency in the allocation of resources. Furthermore, export-orientated subsectors have shown a remarkable resilience to repeated shocks suggesting that policies stimulating them and reallocating resources can significantly impact total manufacturing productivity in Zimbabwe. Last but not least, given the trend towards increasing informality of the Zimbabwean economy, it becomes obvious that, rather than condemn this sector, policy should seek to improve wellbeing conditions within it.

Further research should investigate whether the patterns of structural change identified by Oostendorp et al. (2018) for the formal manufacturing sector also exist in agriculture and mining—and in the informal economy.

6.3 Does Manufacturing Offer a Chance to Take the Next Step in Development for sub-Saharan Africa?

The findings presented above lead to the question of whether low-income countries, in particular in sub-Saharan Africa, may have a realistic opportunity to expand their role in global manufacturing and enhance export-orientation of their domestic formal manufacturing sectors—and whether low labour costs may give them an advantage in this respect. If so, corresponding policy interventions could raise productivity in the (formal) manufacturing sector and benefit from competitiveness growth due to rising labour costs in emerging markets in other global regions. As a prerequisite, however, labour costs would need to be relatively low, to compensate for less favourable factors that may affect competitiveness. This is often assumed to be the case for sub-Saharan Africa, but does this assumption withstand scrutiny?

Economic research has studied this topic from a variety of perspectives. For example, Fox, Thomas, and Haines (2017) benchmarked the overall output, productivity, and employment performance of sub-Saharan Africa against their counterparts in Asia, concluding that this region mainly falls short in terms of manufacturing productivity and employment dynamics, while overall prospects are better for other (services) sectors. Page (2012) argued in favour of speeding up industrialization through export-orientated policies and investments to enhance education and firm capabilities, rather than focusing on regulation. Gelb, Meyer, and Ramachandran (2013) showed 'enclave effects' to be a potential cause of higher labour costs in sub-Saharan Africa and observed that firm expansion led to a stronger increase in labour costs than among low-income competitors in other regions.

Supported by GLM|LIC, Gelb et al. (2020) enriched the latter study by thoroughly examining panel data. The authors explored firm-level data from the World Bank's Enterprise Surveys to assess the level of actual labour costs of manufacturing businesses in a number of low- and middle-income countries in Africa, while also measuring their hypothetical labour costs if they had been located outside of Africa. In summary, the study finds that **labour is indeed more costly for manufacturing firms than expected—and more expensive in most sub-Saharan African countries when compared to international low-income countries**. Strategies to foster export-orientated manufacturing in the region may thus not achieve their objectives.

The survey sample covers multi-year periods for each country, comprising a total of almost 5,500 manufacturing firms with five and more workers in twelve African and seventeen non-African countries. Around 1,200 firms were located in Africa (see Figure 6.7).

To account for the imbalance of the sample in terms of total economic performance (only two non-African countries had GDP per capita below 1,000 USD, compared with six African), the authors assigned higher respective weights to firms in poor non-African countries and controlled for capital cost per worker. Total labour costs were defined as the total of annual wages and all benefits (including transport, food, and social insurance).

The study found only modest differences in basic firm characteristics: median African firms were smaller than their competitors (thirty-eight to forty-seven employees), younger (14 to 19 years), and more likely to be foreign-owned

Argentina (2006–2010)
Bangladesh (2007–2013)
Bhutan (2009–2015)
Bolivia (2006–2010)
Brazil (2003–2009)
Chile (2006–2010)
Colombia (2006–2010)
Indonesia (2009–2015)
Lao PDR (2012–2016)
Mexico (2006–2010)
Nepal (2009–2013)
Pakistan (2007–2013)
Philippines (2009–2015)
Turkey (2005–2008)
Turkey (2008–2013)
Ukraine (2008–2013)
Uruguay (2006–2010)
Vietnam (2005–2009)
Vietnam (2009–2015)

Botswana (2006–2010)
Cameroon (2006–2009)
Congo, Dem. Rep. (2006–2010)
Congo, Dem. Rep. (2010–2013)
Ethiopia (2011–2015)
Kenya (2007–2013)
Malawi (2009–2014)
Mali (2003–2007)
Mali (2007–2010)
Senegal (2003–2007)
Senegal (2007–2014)
South Africa (2003–2007)
Tanzania (2006–2013)
Uganda (2006–2013)
Zambia (2002–2007)
Zambia (2007–2013)

Fig. 6.7 Analytical Sample: Are Labour Costs Lower in (sub-Saharan) Africa?
Source: Gelb et al. (2020)

(17% to 9%), while the share of skilled and unskilled workers was almost the same. The differences in productivity were huge, however: for non-African firms, the calculated level of median value added per worker was roughly 11,400 USD, whereas the median African firm reach just 5,200 USD. Although poorer, African manufacturing firms faced higher capital costs per worker. In summary, **lower values added, higher capital costs, and similar levels of human capital, hint at lower productivity levels for African firms**.

Furthermore, the data provided by Gelb et al. (2020) refute the simplified picture of generally lower labour costs in African economies. This is true in absolute terms only—the differences versus other countries were rather small when labour costs were adjusted by GDP per capita (see Figure 6.8). The general observation that poorer countries face higher labour costs than those suggested by their income levels is all the more valid for the African countries, where the ratio of labour cost per worker to GDP per capita was also substantially higher. Most African economies had a ratio level clearly above 1.0, while most non-African economies stayed below (see Figure 6.9).

The study dug deeper into these striking differences by comparing a set of countries (Tanzania, Ethiopia, Kenya, Senegal, Bangladesh) that ranked rather similar in terms of their competitiveness and GDP per capita, according to the 2016–2017 Global Competitiveness Report of the World Economic Forum (see Schwab and Sala-i-Martín 2016). The data (see Table 6.11) highlight that **even African countries viewed as more competitive had far higher labour costs (with one exception) and capital costs compared to a country like Bangladesh**.

As a major manufacturing country, Bangladesh could, in principle, serve as a role model for sub-Saharan countries with regards to expanding their

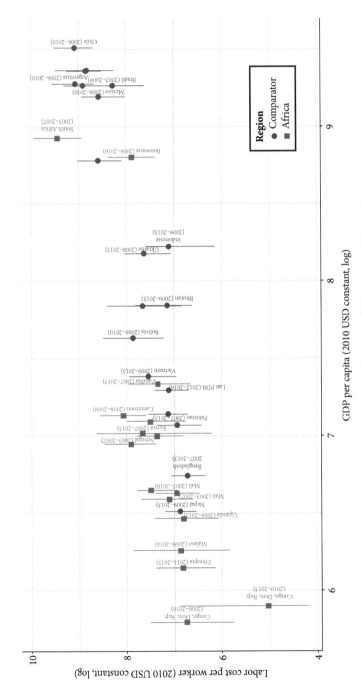

Fig. 6.8 Median Labour Cost Relative to GDP per Capita in African and Comparator Countries

Note: Data for each country shows values for the median, 25th and 75th percentile.

Source: Gelb et al. (2020)

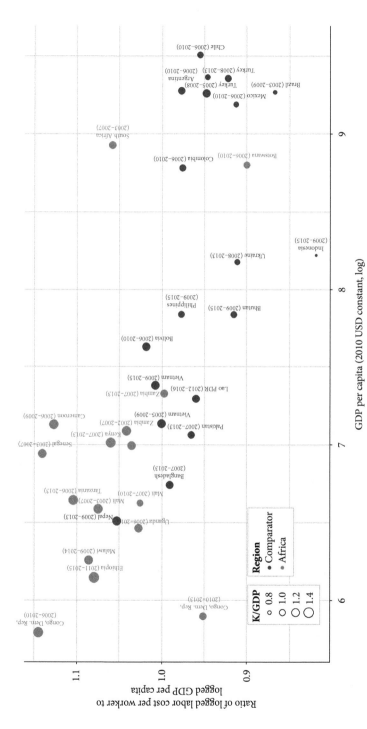

Fig. 6.9 Average Ratio of Labour Cost and GDP per Capita Relative to GDP per Capita in African and Comparator Countries

Note: K/GDP refers to the ratio of logged capital cost per worker to logged GDP per capita.

Source: Gelb et al. (2020)

Table 6.11 Higher Labour Costs in sub-Saharan Africa

	Labour cost per worker	Capital cost per worker	GDP per capita	WEF competitiveness rankings
		(in USD)		
Bangladesh	835.31	1,069.84	853.02	106
Kenya	2,118.01	9,775.45	1,116.69	96
Tanzania	1,776.65	5,740.99	1,094.95	116
Senegal	1,561.64	2,421.98	775.45	112
Ethiopia	909.28	6,137.98	471.19	109

Source: Gelb et al. (2020)

manufacturing sector—but the country appears to have much more favourable firm costs. Labour costs in Kenya, Tanzania, and Senegal were roughly twice as high as both their own GDP per capita and labour costs in Bangladesh. Only Ethiopia faced a labour cost per capita comparable to Bangladesh, though its GDP per capita was only half as high as Bangladesh's.

Capital cost per capita showed Bangladesh far ahead of the African countries as well; here the figures are even more stunning and reveal the gap African countries will have to make up to gain productivity and global competitiveness within their manufacturing sectors.

Estimates presented by Gelb et al. (2020) further emphasized the disadvantages of most manufacturing sectors in sub-Saharan Africa. If they were to operate outside Africa, their total labour costs would have been just one-third of the actual costs, whereas non-African firms would face double the labour costs if they were in Africa. This effect increased with firm size thus clearly signalling the existence of an 'Africa premium': small African firms were roughly 39% more expensive in terms of labour cost per worker than a small non-African firm. Medium-size firms in Africa were 52% more expensive, while very large firms were almost 55% more expensive than their non-African counterparts.

The findings also reveal a pay gradient: **across all countries, labour in smaller firms is cheaper than in larger enterprises.** However, comparison between African and non-African countries paints a mixed picture. The pay gradient between medium-size and small firms is steeper in Africa; conversely, it is steeper outside Africa between large and medium-size firms.

Gelb et al. (2020) distinguished three main groups of African countries with respect to their manufacturing prospects:

1. **Middle-income countries** like South Africa and Botswana operate highly capital-intensive industrial sectors and are rather unlikely to compete in labour-intensive manufacturing.

2. **Low- and lower-middle income countries (for example Kenya, Tanzania, Senegal) offer relatively stable conditions** for foreign investment and an expansion of the manufacturing sector. Yet their labour costs are presumably too high and their firms too small to compete with international rivals such as Bangladesh.

3. **Lowest-income countries like the Democratic Republic of the Congo may be suffering from governance failings that prevent any increase of manufacturing.** If these failures do not occur and instead, as in the case of Ethiopia, low labour costs are accompanied by significant progress with regards to stable administration and easing of transport and logistics constraints, then there is a good chance of successfully entering the international manufacturing market.

Ethiopia is a good example of a sub-Saharan country that could even take the opportunity to compete with Bangladesh in manufacturing in the long term, the authors argue. The country's low labour costs and level of prices were equal to Bangladesh's, for the most part. Also, the Bangladeshi economy is enjoying significant growth, leading to rising labour costs that will in turn encourage more foreign-owned manufacturing firms to scour the globe for alternative low-wage locations. Ethiopia has already appeared on the radar in some early cases.

In summary, this GLM|LIC study revealed the obstacles in the way of most sub-Saharan countries' admission to the export-orientated manufacturing sector. **High labour costs relative to GDP per capita hint at market constraints and compromise the region's competitiveness to a significant extent.** Ethiopia aside, the chances that sub-Saharan Africa may follow Asia in using the manufacturing sector as a launch ramp to further development appear to be limited.

6.4 Social Insurance Mandates, Compliance, and Employment in Sub-Saharan Africa

Ethiopia has also been at the centre of attention of GLM|LIC research in a different context that is no less important when evaluating development potential in a low-income setting: social protection has gained significant importance in developing countries. Compared with middle-income regions like Latin America, where social insurance and assistance has a rather long tradition, and covers a majority of the labour force, similar programmes are only partially implemented in low-income sub-Saharan Africa. Hence most economic research has so far focused on the impact of social insurance in middle-income economies.

From a theoretical perspective, implementing mandatory social insurance will not negatively affect employment if workers' valuation of the benefits matches the additional labour costs to firms. This match will result in lower wages, reflecting the 'price' employees are willing to pay to receive the benefits, and in additional labour supply inducing further wage pressure. A negative impact on employment, in the form of lower employment growth or rising unemployment, may occur if firms are not able to pass on the resulting cost of the programmes or to increase their efficiency to compensate for the cost burden, or if they substitute capital for labour. Existing wage regulation (for example minimum wages) may further hinder employment. At the same time, productivity may increase if firms react to the additional cost of benefits by adjusting their production.

While these mechanisms also apply to developed economies, the absence of frictionless labour markets in many low-income countries poses an additional risk of labour market distortions and other unintended outcomes following social insurance reforms. In particular, if workers value benefits lower than expected, they may instead choose informal employment to avoid mandatory social insurance contributions, which may in turn reduce formal employment, tax revenues, and overall productivity.

This effect may result either from switching to the informal sector or from working informally in the formal sector (for the same or another employer). It may also affect low-skilled workers more, given that pension benefits, for example, are mostly related to work experience and shorter unemployment spells. A lack of enforcement may lead to uncertainties in terms of benefit receipt among workers, changing both employers' and employees' behaviour, and thus further limiting the effect of social insurance interventions.

Recent research, though not focused on the poorest countries and sub-Saharan Africa in particular, has drawn attention to mixed outcomes of social insurance implementation and the challenge of enforcement. Joubert (2015) noted that a sizeable informal sector such as Chile's complicates enforcement of mandatory pension contributions and may encourage informality. Almeida and Carneiro (2012) studied the economic effects of mandatory severance benefits in Brazil, showing the positive effects of more intensive enforcement in terms of raising the attractiveness of the formal sector among informal workers, while localities with lower enforcement observed an increase in informality. Jung and Tran (2012) revealed the positive welfare effects of a pension scheme for older informal sector workers in Brazil, despite an increase in informal employment. Aterido, Hallward-Driemeier, and Pagés (2011), and Bosch and Campos-Vazuguex (2014), provided evidence that the provision of public health insurance to informal sector workers in Mexico increased informal employment, while decreasing the number of small and medium-size firms, and workers, in the formal sector.

6.4.1 The Mixed Outcomes of a Social Insurance Scheme in Ethiopia

Similar studies for sub-Saharan Africa have so far been lacking. Given the conditions of LICs facing high risk and uncertainty, and high exposure to shocks, it is even more important to learn more about the impact of social insurance programmes. To examine the impact of social insurance implementation in sub-Saharan Africa, GLM|LIC has supported a study by Shiferaw et al. (2017) on the labour market outcomes of a mandatory social insurance scheme in Ethiopia, which appear to be rather mixed in terms of employment shifts and resulting informality.

Ethiopia has undertaken a swift, major pension reform in 2011 ('Private Organizations Pension Fund', POPF), for the first time granting retirement and disability benefits to not only civil servants and those working in the armed forces, but to all permanent employees in the formal private sector. Self-employed and informal workers are excluded from the programme, while participation is mandatory for formal sector workers. If an employer operates a voluntary 'provident fund', workers may choose to either continue this fund or transfer their benefit savings to the government fund. Employers' contribution rates to the POPF were raised in stages, from 7% of the gross monthly wage in 2011 to 11% in 2015. Employee contributions meanwhile increased gradually from 5% to 7% over the same period. The pension benefit was set at 30% of the average three-year wage preceding retirement. To receive pension benefits at the age of 62, workers need to make contributions for at least ten years. Since the programme is focused on permanent workers, firms are required by law to give permanent employment status to all employees after forty-five days.

Importantly, the new pension programme was introduced in the midst of a period of substantial economic growth in Ethiopia between 2005 and 2015, when annual growth rates reached 10%, roughly twice as high as in the decade before. Hence the timing of the reform seems very appropriate to avoid a decline in labour demand, by allowing firms to better balance the cost of contributions. Overall, labour demand in the manufacturing sector has been growing before and after the 2011 pension reform. It should be further noted that Ethiopia has no minimum wage legislation for the private sector (only for public sector employees), but guarantees a minimum pension, thus potentially encouraging additional labour supply from low-wage workers looking to secure pension benefits that go beyond their contributions. It may thus be in firms' interest to pass on the cost of pension contributions by paying lower wages.

The Private Organizations' Employees' Pension Agency (POEPA) operates the pension programme, registers all employers and workers, and is authorized to collect untimely firm contributions from their bank accounts. Incomplete pension contributions prevent firms from filing their taxes, thus risking high penalties.

However, whether these enforcement mechanisms are effective in practice, remains unclear. Shiferaw et al. (2017) argued that enforcement is relatively strong in Ethiopia with respect to workers already registered, while subsequent monitoring of employment changes and verifying employers' contributions may be weaker. Census data provided by the Central Statistical Agency (CSA) of Ethiopia suggest a compliance rate of under 50%.

The census data further show a clear rise in the number of firms making pension contributions in the years after the pension reform was introduced, while employment and sales of the firms also increased (see Figures 6.10 and 6.11). While the first observation is rather self-descriptive, the latter cannot exclude the possibility that rates may have been even higher without the pension reform.

Against this background, the study differentiated between firms with pre-existing voluntary provident funds, and those firms facing mandatory pension contributions for the first time. While the first group should have exhibited neither low compliance nor a significant increase in non-wage labour costs, the second group was likely to react to additional costs by adjusting wages and labour demand. To examine this hypothesis the authors used firm-level panel data collected by the Ethiopian Electric Power Authority for billing reasons, and CSA census data for the pre-reform (2008–11) and post-reform (2012–13) periods, to measure the impact of the pension reform on wage levels, employment trends, the composition of the workforce, and labour productivity.

A closer examination of the data reveals some interesting findings:

1. **Manufacturing firms with pre-existing provident funds were larger and older**, and had higher wage rates, productivity and investment per worker than those without any earlier pension scheme.
2. **The gap between large and small firms in terms of employment, sales and real wage rates** decreased in the years prior to the reform, but **increased after the mandatory pension system was introduced**.
3. The panel data support the expected patterns of compliance: **about 75% of firms with provident funds complied with the new scheme** and made pension contributions. In contrast, only 43% of firms without such funds complied.
4. **Pension contributions increased significantly for firms with pre-existing provident funds**, indicating the mandatory pension scheme was more generous.

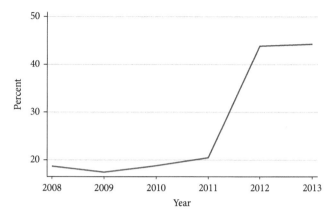

Fig. 6.10 Proportion of Manufacturing Firms Making Pension
Contributions in Ethiopia

Note: Compliance with the 2011 pension scheme was below 50%. Graph is
based on firm-level panel data.
Source: Shiferaw et al. (2017)

5. Firm size plays a role in this respect: 72% of large firms reported pension contributions compared with only 45% of small businesses. **Smaller
   firms were more likely to respond to the reform by reducing pre-existing
   bonuses**.

6. Notably, **small enterprises showed the same compliance behaviour** related to the (non-) existence of provident funds. Compliance of small firms
   was 64% for those with pre-existing funds, but only around 41% for firms
   without.

7. **Changes in firm size were an important outcome of the pension reform**.
   While the average size of businesses with pre-existing pension funds
   increased by 5%, firms without funds reduced in size by an average 8%
   after the reform.

8. Both **the increase and decrease of firm size can be linked to a shift
   of the human capital composition of firms** in reaction to the pension
   reform. In average firms with provident funds, the share of low-wage
   workers declined from 58% before the pension reform (2008–11) to
   47% after (2012–13), while in firms without funds the shares fell from
   72 to 57%. However, this can only be partly attributed to the pension
   reform.

9. **Real wages increased substantially after the reform,** on average—and at
   an even higher rate for firms without any pre-existing provident funds.
   This is consistent with a decline in low-skilled labour in the average
   manufacturing firm.

10. **The increase in non-wage labour costs due to the pension reform has
    been partly offset by productivity gains** in larger firms, whereas small
    firms have mostly not experienced such gains.

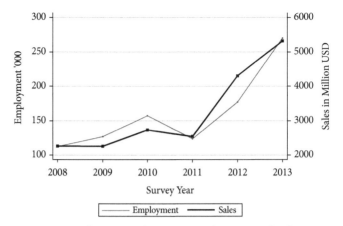

Fig. 6.11 Trends in Manufacturing Employment and Sales in
Ethiopia

Note: Graph is based on annual census data (CSA Large and Medium Scale
Manufacturing Survey) including all manufacturing firms with at least ten
employees.
Source: Shiferaw et al. (2017)

11. Adjusting production costs only marginally contributed to offsetting the
    pension reform burden across firms.
12. **Employment effects were negative for small manufacturing firms or
    those without pre-existing pension funds**, although overall employment
    in Ethiopian manufacturing continued to increase after 2011. Job reduc-
    tion reached levels of 23% and 27% in 2012 and 2013 respectively among
    firms without funds, while small firms saw almost the same decline in em-
    ployment (20% and 24%, in 2012 and 2013, respectively). Combining both
    attributes led to only a modest decline, as small firms without funds had
    even fewer employees and were the most likely not to complain about the
    pension scheme.
13. **Firm size is a driver of employment effects**. Small firms initially expe-
    rienced a significant reduction in skilled labour (and thus an increasing
    share of low-skilled workers) after the reform. The overall rise in skilled
    manufacturing employment was due to the expansion of larger firms.
14. **The pension reform appears to have induced a rise in total labour pro-
    ductivity in the manufacturing sector**. Capital intensity increased among
    larger firms along with increasing non-wage labour cost. Small firms, how-
    ever, experienced a decline in their productivity, which may be explained
    by the greater difficulties they face in attracting higher-skilled workers due
    to lower levels of wages and bonuses.
15. **Evasion was a non-negligible factor**. The study suggests an increased
    number of former formal workers were hired informally by registered
    enterprises after the reform.

In summary, the GLM|LIC study by Shiferaw et al. (2017) provided multifaceted evidence on the impact of a major social insurance reform (starting from scratch) on the manufacturing labour market of a sub-Saharan African low-income country. In a difference from study settings that examine small-level changes to existing social protection schemes, the findings presented here addressed the quasi-natural experiment of an entirely new policy intervention, thus showing accentuated effects and policy implications.

Overall, this Ethiopian case study yielded mixed results. Firm-level employment declined substantially after the reform, particularly among smaller firms. Low-skilled formal labour was induced away from larger firms into informality, while larger firms' labour forces shifted in favour of higher-skilled workers. Real wages and labour productivity levels increased, though these effects may in part be attributed to the period of economic growth.

Positive outcomes should thus not be overlooked—the impact of the pension reform on workers' welfare may have been significant and deserves additional research. Unintended employment effects on the side of low-wage workers and small firms could be tackled by Ethiopian pension policies, through more flexible contribution rates.

Last but not least, the example of Ethiopia proves that implementing major social insurance reforms requires good timing. Introducing them in times of economic growth allows firms to cope better with the additional costs, and thus show more trust and compliance.

6.5 The Impact of Minimum Wages in Sub-Saharan Africa

The share of formal workers is still small in low-income countries, given the low rates of formality and urbanization. Recent economic growth has led to a significant increase in formal sector employment, but economic shocks may pose severe setbacks for vulnerable economies in particular. Yet economic growth and the (slow) rise of the formal sector have enlarged governments' desire for labour market regulation. In most sub-Saharan African countries, regulation is on the advance, following up on standards implemented earlier in other developing regions. Its main focus is usually the issue of widespread poverty, protecting low-wage workers, and introducing minimum standards for working conditions in a rapidly changing economic environment.

Wage governance is among the most used regulation tools—almost all sub-Saharan African countries have now implemented some form of minimum wage legislation, either aimed at the entire formal economy or at specific industries or occupations. However, limited enforcement capabilities and low compliance are serious barriers on the road to more successful and sustainable regulation of minimum wages and beyond.

Economic research has extensively analysed regulation efforts in middle-income regions revealing, among other insights, that enforcement may strengthen the formal sector, particularly in the presence of minimum wages (see, for example, Almeida and Carneiro 2012). Rani et al. (2013) provided evidence for low levels of compliance with minimum wage laws across a number of countries.

A recent summary of existing literature on the effects of raising minimum wages and the impact on poverty reduction (Gindling 2018) captured the limited effect on overall poverty whereby, on average, only a minority of workers in developing countries are covered by such legislation. Yet the potential spill-over effects on the informal sector, in terms of raising wages, should be taken into account. Undesired outcomes mainly occur when excessively high minimum wages result in job losses in the formal labour market.

In principle, the prospects of minimum wages in LICs are mixed. The simple assumption—that introducing minimum wages necessarily induces wage-employment trade-offs and a decrease in employment—does not hold as a general rule. However, negative effects beyond potential unemployment may include reduced work hours and a shift in human capital among firms—both disadvantaging low-skilled workers. Forced moves from formal to informal work may cause additional negative outcomes.

In contrast, minimum wage legislation may raise the welfare of low-skilled workers and lead to rising average wages, thus stimulating demand and consumption. The resulting higher prices may have a dampening effect, though. Behavioural aspects with regards to a rise in reservation wages and education investments (see Falk, Fehr, and Zehnder 2006) may not only apply in developed economies but also in low-income settings.

These factors notwithstanding, vulnerable economic and political conditions are certainly key determinants of policy interventions in the labour markets of LICs. Exposure to shocks and other issues related to timing, are of the highest importance when introducing programmes aimed at tackling poverty. The most decisive factor of minimum wage efficiency in a low-income country setting may be found in law enforcement and compliance.

The impact of minimum wages and related compliance in sub-Saharan Africa is still understudied, with limited findings available, for only a few countries. To thoroughly examine the impact of minimum wages, researchers would need pre- and post-legislation data, which is scarce on the national level, while data on wages and levels of compliance do not exist for many countries in the region. The South African minimum wage has attracted most attention. Studies by Dinkelman and Ranchhod (2012), Bhorat, Kanbur, and Mayet (2013), and Bhorat, Kanbur, and Stanwix (2012), largely documented job losses in agriculture as a result of the minimum wage introduction yet found no employment decreases in other sectors.

6.5.1 Comparative Analysis of Minimum Wage Schemes Reveals Higher Levels in sub-Saharan Africa

Supported by GLM|LIC a comprehensive study by Bhorat, Kanbur, and Stanwix (2017) aimed to narrow this gap by providing an assessment of minimum wage legislation, compliance, and economic effects in sub-Saharan Africa and other countries. The analysis revealed that lowest-income countries in sub-Saharan Africa operated the most generous minimum wage scheme relative to their regular levels, while rather low compliance was a common feature across countries.

First, it should be noted again that minimum wage coverage is inevitably rather narrow in sub-Saharan Africa, since only around 20% of the labour force are wage employees (see Figure 6.12), while legislation is mostly applied to formal wage workers only. The variety of minimum wage schemes is the highest of all global regions, with a share of countries (around 60%) operating sectoral or occupational minimum wages instead of an economy-wide minimum wage. Within this variety of schemes, the actual determination of minimum wages may be rather complex. **Differentiated minimum wage schedules can be useful to address gaps between sectors, geographical regions, or skill levels, yet complexity may complicate enforcement and compliance.**

Furthermore, the levels of minimum wages vary significantly between countries in different regions of sub-Saharan Africa, depending on the country's income levels. Central African countries (Cameroon, Chad, Congo, Gabon) show higher levels on average compared to East African countries (Burundi, Ethiopia, Kenya, Tanzania) (see Figure 6.13). Across sub-Saharan Africa and other countries, minimum wage levels are positively correlated with gross national income per capita, with sub-Saharan Africa at the bottom of the scale (see Figure 6.14).

The relationship between economic growth and minimum wage levels appears to be rather clear—higher levels of GDP per capita are accompanied by higher minimum wages. Compared to developing countries outside sub-Saharan Africa, minimum wages in the region appear to be both lower relative to, and less responsive to increases in, GDP (see Figures 6.15, 6.16).

When looking at country income groups, the positive correlation between minimum wage levels and national income becomes obvious again, albeit with variation across countries within single-income groups. There is no obvious tendency, on average, towards a more progressive minimum wage policy in sub-Saharan Africa than in other regions.

However, the ratio of minimum wage to mean wage signals that low-income countries in sub-Saharan Africa are setting higher minimum wages—relative to their domestic average wages—than countries in higher-income groups in the same region (a higher ratio indicates a more pro-minimum wage policy, see Table 6.11), yet lower than most other global regions. While lower- and upper middle-income countries in sub-Saharan Africa are setting minimum wages at roughly a

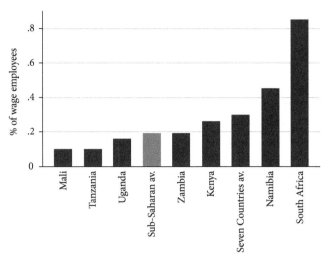

Fig. 6.12 Wage Employees as a Percentage of Total Employment in Africa

Note: South Africa: Labour Market Dynamics Study (2013); Kenya: Kenya Integrated Household Budget Survey (2005/06); Uganda: Uganda National Panel Survey (2012); Mali: Rani et al. (2013); Zambia: Living Conditions Monitoring Survey (2010); Tanzania: Integrated Labour Force Survey (2005/06); Namibia: Labour Force Survey (2012); Bhorat, Naidoo and Pillay (2016).

Source: Bhorat, Kanbur, and Stanwix (2015, 2017)

third of their average wages, LICs show a substantially higher ratio on average that appears to be driven by large variation among this group.

As already mentioned, minimum wage schemes in sub-Saharan Africa tend to be somewhat complex in nature. To assess whether different minimum wages within a country are properly set, relative to its wage distribution, Bhorat, Kanbur, and Stanwix (2017) defined a 'lower floor' sector (low-paid, unskilled sector such as agriculture) and 'upper floor' sector (higher paid, medium-skilled sector such as retail trade). Applying these 'floors' to the wage distribution in Zambia, Tanzania, South Africa, Namibia, Uganda, and Kenya confirms that minimum wages in these countries were set at a relatively high level, and further reveals that there was hardly any 'spike' in any of the minimum wage schedules (see Figure 6.17). Considerable tails to the left of the minimum wage schedules in each of the depicted economies, however, indicate a substantial share of workers that were not adhering to the minimum wage.

The study revealed large variations in both the level of minimum wages and in lower and upper floor earnings within the same country. Lower-floor wages were 54% below upper-floor wages, on average. This indicates substantial intrasectoral wage inequality, resulting from a large gap between average and median wages. Adding data for Mali, the authors calculate this mean–median gap at an

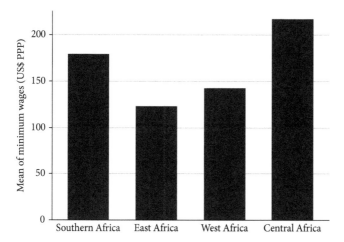

Fig. 6.13 Monthly Minimum Wage Levels in sub-Saharan Africa by Region

Note: Data from ILO Global Wage Database and World Bank World Development Indicators, with the latest available data for each country used for a sample of thirty-five countries.
Source: Bhorat, Kanbur, and Stanwix (2015)

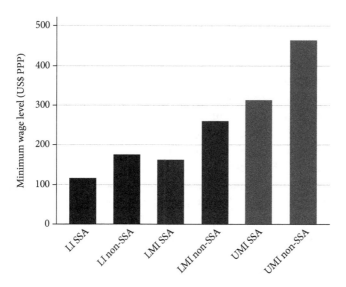

Fig. 6.14 Monthly Minimum Wage Levels by Country Income Group

Notes: LI = Low Income, LMI = Lower-Middle Income, UMI = Upper-Middle Income; SSA = sub-Saharan Africa; PPP = purchasing power parity.
Source: Bhorat, Kanbur, and Stanwix (2015, 2017)

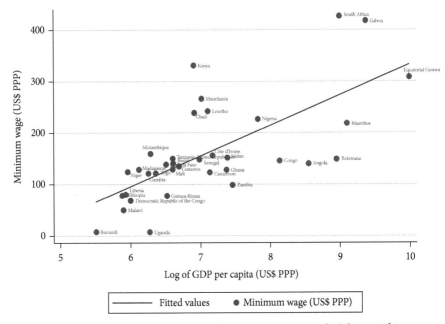

Fig. 6.15 Monthly Minimum Wages and GDP per Capita in sub-Saharan Africa
Note: Data from ILO Global Wage Database and World Bank World Development Indicators, with the latest available data for each country used for a sample of thirty-seven countries.
Source: Bhorat, Kanbur, and Stanwix (2015, 2017)

average 55% across the seven countries. Conversely, this finding hints at the fact that, despite frequent variety of minimum wage levels in all countries apart from Uganda and Mali (national minimum wage), a significant share of workers are not covered by legislated minimum wages. Overall coverage of sectoral minimum wages in sub-Saharan Africa appears to be rather low.

The sectoral ratios of minimum to mean and median wages for the lower- and upper-floor sectors show how high minimum wages were set relative to average sectoral wages. The average minimum-to-mean ratio was 0.93 for lower-floor and 0.63 for upper-floor workers. That is, within the lower floor, the minimum wage almost equalled the average wage. Accounting for the mean–median gap reveals substantially higher minimum-to-median ratios for both sectors, above 1.0 on average (see Figures 6.18 and 6.19).

These figures show sub-Saharan Africa significantly above non-sub-Saharan developing countries, where Rani et al. (2013) reported a minimum-to-mean ratio of 0.54 and a minimum-to-median wage ratio of 0.76 (average figures across Brazil, Costa Rica, India, Indonesia, Mexico, Philippines, Peru, Turkey, Vietnam). In other words: **sub-Saharan Africa appears to set minimum wages that are very high relative to regular wages, thus risking low compliance**.

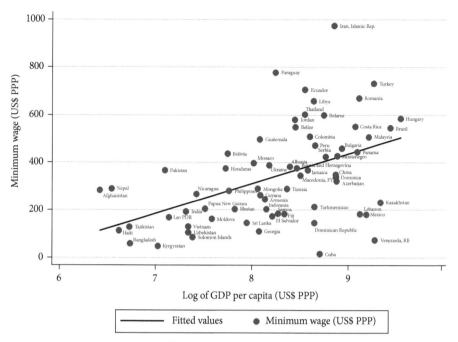

Fig. 6.16 Minimum Wages and GDP per Capita in non-sub-Saharan Countries

Note: Data from ILO Global Wage Database and World Bank World Development Indicators, with the latest available data for each country used for a sample of sixty-seven countries.

Source: Bhorat, Kanbur, and Stanwix (2015, 2017)

6.5.2 Do Relatively High Minimum Wages Lead to Low Compliance?

To measure compliance with the minimum wages operated in sub-Saharan Africa, the GLM|LIC study examined the share of workers who earned below the minimum wage they were entitled to, and the distance between their earnings and the minimum wages, as an 'index of violation'. The resulting estimates are highly instructive (see Figures 6.20 and 6.21).

On average, 58% of workers in the sectors under scrutiny earned below the minimum wage in sub-Saharan Africa, with a significant variation across countries—from 36% (Zambia) to 80% (Tanzania). Developing countries outside Africa showed an average of 30%. These figures clearly indicate relatively low rates of compliance with minimum wage legislation in sub-Saharan Africa.

Investigating the average shortfall in workers' earnings below the minimum wage alters the picture slightly: while sub-Saharan Africa lags behind in terms of the share of workers who earn less than the minimum wage, the average shortfall is higher among workers in developing countries outside Africa. Meanwhile levels of non-compliance appear to be lower in sub-Saharan Africa.

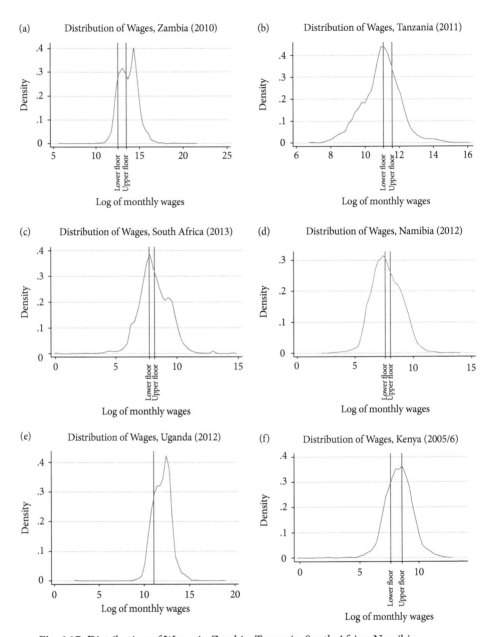

Fig. 6.17 Distribution of Wages in Zambia, Tanzania, South Africa, Namibia, Uganda, and Kenya

Notes: Kernel density estimates. Zambia: Living Conditions Monitoring Survey (2010); Tanzania: Integrated Labour Force Survey (2005–6); South Africa: Labour Market Dynamics Study (2013); Namibia: Labour Force Survey (2012); Uganda: Uganda National Panel Survey (2012); Kenya: Kenya Integrated Household Budget Survey (2005–6).
Source: Bhorat, Kanbur, and Stanwix (2017)

Table 6.12 Monthly Minimum Wage Estimates for sub-Saharan Africa

Country	Minimum Wage (USD PPP)	Mean wage (USD PPP)	Minimum-to-mean-wage ratio
Low-income economies			
Burkina Faso	138	210	0.66
Burundi	26	256	0.10
Chad	239	371	0.64
Congo, Dem Rep	68	53	1.27
Ethiopia	77	175	0.44
Madagascar	128	183	0.7
Malawi	49	368	0.13
Tanzania	149	624	0.24
Uganda	65	464	0.10
Group mean	104	300	0.46
Group median	77	256	0.44
Lower-middle-income economies			
Congo, Rep	145	526	0.28
Ghana	128	469	0.27
Kenya	331	979	0.34
Lesotho	242	377	0.64
Senegal	148	983	0.15
Swaziland	94	815	0.12
Zambia	98	252	0.39
Group mean	169	629	0.31
Group median	145	526	0.28
Upper-middle-income economies			
Algeria	531	1,003	0.53
Botswana	148	1,287	0.12
Gabon	418	2,356	0.18
Mauritius	218	1,424	0.15

Continued

Table 6.12 *Continued*

Country	Minimum Wage (USD PPP)	Mean wage (USD PPP)	Minimum-to-mean-wage ratio
South Africa	517	1,251	0.41
Group mean	366	1,464	0.28
Group median	418	1,287	0.18
Total SSA mean	188	687	**0.37**
Total SSA median	145	469	**0.28**
Other regional averages			
LAC mean	369	937	0.46
			(1.24)*
LAC median	289	859	0.37
			(1.32)*
EAP mean	317	884	0.38
			(1.03)*
EAP median	284	739	0.32
			(1.14)*
SA mean	233	386	0.63
			(1.70)*
SA median	255	368	0.59
			(2.11)*
ECA mean	325	1,136	0.3
			(0.81)*
ECA median	344	1,183	0.28
			(1.00)*

Note: Data from ILO Global Wage Database and World Bank World Development Indicators, latest available data for each country. Aggregate estimates for sub-Saharan Africa (SSA) based on twenty-one countries; East Asia and Pacific (EAP) sample based on eight countries; Latin America/Caribbean (LAC) sample based on sixteen countries; South Asia (SA) sample based on four countries; Europe and Central Asia (ECA) sample based on seventeen countries. Monthly wages and average minimum wage (if variation applies in a country). All estimates are in 2015 USD PPP. Asterisk (*) indicates ratio of measure to SSA mean or median. Monthly wages in 2015 USD purchasing power parities (PPP). Column 3 would usually give the minimum-to median wage ('Kaitz') ratio, but data on median wages is rare in Sub-Saharan Africa.
Source: Bhorat, Kanbur, and Stanwix (2017)

In summary, this comprehensive GLM|LIC study provides illustrative evidence on the specific conditions of minimum wages in sub-Saharan Africa, opening the field for further research. From a policy perspective, the following aspects deserve attention:

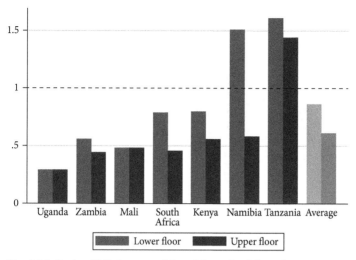

Fig. 6.18 Ratio of Minimum to Mean Wages for Selected sub-Saharan Countries

Note: Authors' calculations.
Source: Bhorat, Kanbur, and Stanwix (2015, 2017)

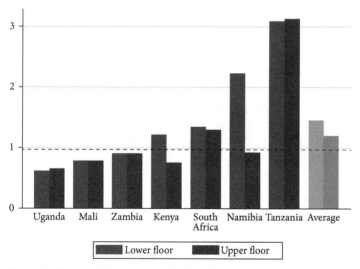

Fig. 6.19 Ratio of Minimum to Median Wages for Selected sub-Saharan Countries

Note: Authors' calculations.
Source: Bhorat, Kanbur, and Stanwix (2015, 2017)

1. **Almost all countries in sub-Saharan Africa run minimum wage schemes, while there is a positive correlation between minimum wage levels and economic growth** (GDP per capita) in the region. But the region does not stand out among other developing countries in this respect.

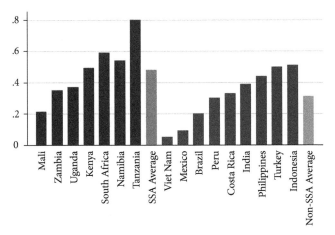

Fig. 6.20 Average Compliance Rates (Violation Index) in
sub-Saharan Africa and Other Countries

Note: Authors' calculations for sub-Saharan Africa, figures for other
countries based on Rani et al. (2013).
Source: Bhorat, Kanbur, and Stanwix (2015, 2017)

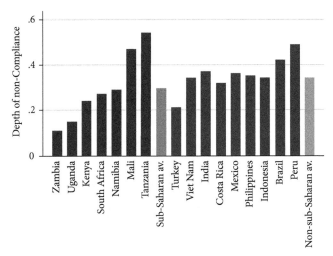

Fig. 6.21 Average Depth of non-Compliance in sub-Saharan
Africa and Other Countries

Note: Authors' calculations for sub-Saharan Africa, figures for other
countries based on Rani et al. (2013).
Source: Bhorat, Kanbur, and Stanwix (2015, 2017)

2. At first sight, minimum wage levels are lower in sub-Saharan Africa, according to broad income levels.
3. **What distinguishes sub-Saharan Africa from other developing regions is
the level of the minimum wage relative to countries' mean wages. This
ratio is substantially higher in sub-Saharan Africa.**

4. **Within sub-Saharan Africa, countries with the lowest income levels show the highest absolute levels of minimum wages.**

5. Findings presented for Ghana, Kenya, Malawi, and South Africa confirm that introducing and raising minimum wages has a **small negative or negligible effect on employment.**

6. **In the case of vulnerable sub-Saharan African countries, variation is a strong factor**—in terms of either labour market structures, variety of wages and productivity, or minimum wage schemes—which may lead to larger employment or compliance effects if the reform is not appropriate.

7. **Regulation efforts are met with rather low compliance in the absence of effective enforcement.** The variety of minimum wage legislation in favour of sectoral or occupational minimum wage requirements cannot disguise this common challenge. **Absolute levels of non-compliance are higher in sub-Saharan Africa than elsewhere** in terms of the percentage of workers earning below the minimum wage.

The topic of how to operate minimum wage schemes in sub-Saharan Africa will undoubtedly become more important as formality increases with economic growth. Yet insights on changes to productivity, workers' welfare, or sectoral transition as a consequence of minimum wage legislation, are difficult to reach because the available data is rudimentary. GLM|LIC research will continue to investigate this topic and the overall issue of labour market regulation in low-income countries.

Key Takeaways from this Chapter

- Despite the often negative perception of informal labour, it will remain a central feature of many LICs and does not necessarily inhibit growth and development.
- Supporting informal agricultural self-employment and entrepreneurship among the young my help overcome extreme poverty and drive inclusive growth.
- Policies to increase job stability could make formal labour more attractive, though not all workers value longer-term contracts.
- There is a lot of voluntary transition between formal and informal sectors, and informal self-employment is often driven by entrepreneurship and choice rather than by necessity.
- Policymakers are facing the dual challenge of increasing productivity of the informal sector while also facilitating transition to higher-productivity formal employment.

- Demographic trends, educational progress, and economic growth may accelerate transition dynamics, as the young generation appears more likely to step into formality.
- Exposure to globalization and international trade expands formal employment opportunities and occupational quality.
- Improving informal workers' business and entrepreneurial skills can help promote sustained growth in informal household businesses or facilitate a move to formal employment.
- Policies to boost development by promoting export-oriented manufacturing are less likely to succeed in sub-Saharan Africa due to relatively high labour costs.
- Differentiated minimum wage schedules can help address sectoral, regional, or skill-level gaps, yet complexity may complicate enforcement and compliance.

References

Almeida, R., and Carneiro, P., 2012. Enforcement of Labor Regulation and Informality. *American Economic Journal: Applied Economics*, 4(3): 64–89.

Aterido, R., Hallward-Driemeier, M., and Pagés, C., 2011. Does Expanding Health Insurance Beyond Formal-Sector Workers Encourage Informality? Measuring the Impact of Mexico's Seguro Popular. IZA Discussion Paper No. 5996.

Bhorat, H., Kanbur, R., and Mayet, N., 2013. The Impact of Sectoral Minimum Wage Laws on Employment Wages, and Hours of Work in South Africa. IZA Journal of Labor and Development, 2(1).

Bhorat, H., Kanbur, R., and Stanwix, B., 2012. Estimating the Impact of Minimum Wages on Employment, Wages and Non-wage Benefits: The Case of Agriculture in South Africa. DPRU Working Paper 12/149.

Bhorat, H., Kanbur, R., and Stanwix, B., 2015. Minimum Wages in Sub-Saharan Africa: A Primer. GLM|LIC Synthesis Paper No. 1.

Bhorat, H., Kanbur, R., and Stanwix, B., 2017. Minimum Wages in Sub-Saharan Africa: A Primer. *World Bank Research Observer*, 32(1): 21–74.

Bhorat, H., Naidoo, K., and Pillay, K., 2016. Growth, Poverty and Inequality Interactions in Africa: An Overview of Key Issues. UNDP Africa Economists Working Papers 267778.

Bosch, M., and Campos-Vazquez, R. M., 2014. The Trade-Offs of Welfare Policies in Labor Markets with Informal Jobs: The Case of the 'Seguro Popular' Program in Mexico. *American Economic Journal: Economic Policy*, 6(4): 71–99.

Bruhn, M., and McKenzie, D., 2014. Entry Regulation and the Formalization of Microenterprises in Developing Countries. *World Bank Research Observer*, 29(2): 186–201.

Dinkelman, T., and Ranchhod, V., 2012. Evidence on the Impact of Minimum Wage Laws in an Informal Sector: Domestic Workers in South Africa. *Journal of Development Economics*, 99(1): 27–45.

Edwards, L., Davies, R., Makochekanwa, A., Oostendorp, R., and Rankin, N., 2018. Manufacturing Firm Survival in the Face of Economic Crises. GLM|LIC Policy Brief No. 26.

Fajnzylber, P., Maloney, W., and Rojas, G. M., 2006. Microenterprise Dynamics in Developing Countries: How Similar Are They to Those in the Industrialized World? Evidence from Mexico. *World Bank Economic Review*, 20(3): 389–419.

Falk, A., Fehr, E., and Zehnder, C., 2006. Fairness Perceptions and Reservation Wages — the Behavioral Effects of Minimum Wage Laws. *Quarterly Journal of Economics*, 121(4): 1347–81.

Fields, G. S., 1975. Rural–Urban Migration, Urban Unemployment and Underemployment, and Job-Search Activity in LDCs. *Journal of Development Economics*, 2(2): 165–87.

Fox, L., 2016. What Will It Take to Meet the Youth Employment Challenge in Sub-Saharan Africa? GLM|LIC Working Paper No. 10.

Fox, L., Thomas, A., and Haines, C., 2017. Structural Transformation in Employment and Productivity: What Can Africa Hope for? Washington: International Monetary Fund.

Gelb, A., Mengistae, T., Ramachandran, V., and Kedia Shah, M., 2009. To Formalize or Not to Formalize? Comparisons of Microenterprise Data from Southern and East Africa. CGDEV Working Paper No. 175.

Gelb, A., Meyer, C., and Ramachandran, V., 2013. Does Poor Mean Cheap? A Comparative Look at Africa's Industrial Labor Costs. CGDEV Working Paper 325.

Gelb, A., Ramachandran, V., Gelb, A., Meyer, C., Wadhwa, D., and Navis, K., 2020. Can Africa Be a Manufacturing Destination? Labor Costs, Price Levels, and the Role of Industrial Policy. *Journal of Industry, Competition and Trade*, 20: 335–57.

Gindling, T. H., 2018. Does Increasing the Minimum Wage Reduce Poverty in Developing Countries? IZA World of Labor 2018: 30 doi: 10.15185/izawol.30.v2

Gutierrez, I. A., Kumar, K. B., Mahmud, M., Munshi, F., and Nataraj, S. (2019). Transitions between Informal and Formal Employment: Results from a Worker Survey in Bangladesh. *IZA Journal of Development and Migration*, 9(1).

Harris, J. R., and Todaro, M. P., 1970. Migration, Unemployment and Development: A Two-Sector Analysis. *American Economic Review*, 60(1): 126–42.

Joubert, C., 2015. Pension Design With a Large Informal Labor Market: Evidence From Chile. *International Economic Review*, 56(2): 673–94.

Jung, J., and Tran, C., 2012. The Extension of Social Security Coverage in Developing Countries. *Journal of Development Economics*, 99(2): 439–58.

Karlan, D., and Zinman, J., 2011. Microcredit in Theory and Pracice: Using Randomized Credit Scoring for Impact Evaluation. *Science*, 332(6035): 1278–84.

Kumar, K., Nataraj, S., and Gutierrez, I., 2017. Growth and Informality: The Case of Bangladesh. GLM|LIC Policy Brief No. 19.

La Porta, R., and Schleifer, A., 2014. Informality and Development. *Journal of Economic Perspectives*, 28(3): 109–26.

Mahmud, M., Gutierrez, I., Kumar, K., and Nataraj, S., 2021. What Aspects of Formality Do Workers Value? Evidence from a Choice Experiment in Bangladesh. *World Bank Economic Review*, 35(2): 303–27.

Maloney, W. F., 1999. Does Informality Imply Segmentation in Urban Labor Markets? Evidence from Sectoral Transitions in Mexico. *World Bank Economic Review*, 13(2): 275–302.

McCaig, B., and Pavcnik, N., 2015. Informal Employment in a Growing and Globalizing Low-Income Country. *American Economic Review*, 105(5): 545–50.

McCaig, B., and Pavcnik, N., 2017. Out with the Old and Unproductive, in with the New and Similarly Unproductive: Microenterprise Dynamics in a Growing Low-Income Economy. GLM|LIC Working Paper No. 23.

McCaig, B., and Pavcnik, N., 2018. Export Markets and Labor Allocation in a Low-Income Country. *American Economic Review*, 108(7): 1899–1941.

McKenzie, D., and Woodruff, C., 2014. What Are We Learning from Business Training and Entrepreneurship Evaluations around the Developing World? *World Bank Research Observer*, 29(1): 48–82.

Oostendorp, R., Edwards, L., Makochekanwa, A., Davies, R., and Rankin, N., 2018. Productivity under Twenty Years of Structural Change in Zimbabwe's Manufacturing Sector. GLM|LIC Policy Brief No. 28.

Page, J., 2012. Can Africa Industrialise? *Journal of African Economies*, 21(2): ii86–ii124.

Rani, U., Belser, P., Oelz, M., and Ranjbar, S., 2013. Minimum Wage Coverage and Compliance in Developing Countries. *International Labour Review*, 152(3–4): 381–410.

Rankin, N., Edwards, L., Davies, R., and Oostendorp, R., 2018. Wages in Zimbabwean Formal and Informal Manufacturing – Firm-Level Responses to Low Levels of Demand and Economic Uncertainty. GLM|LIC Policy Brief No. 27.

Schwab, K., and Sala-i-Martín, X., 2016. The Global Competitiveness Report 2016–2017. Geneva: World Economic Forum.

Shiferaw, A., Bedi, A. S., Söderbom, M., and Zewdu, G. A., 2017. Social Insurance Reform and Labor Market Outcomes in Sub-Saharan Africa: Evidence from Ethiopia. GLM|LIC Working Paper No. 35.

7

Child Labour and the Youth Employment Challenge

Child labour is a core topic in all low-income countries. Given unstable labour markets and a lack of sustainable economic growth, many families see no other way to ensure all family members' livelihood than to have their children take part in subsistence work or paid employment. According to recent statistics published by the International Labour Organization (ILO 2017) more than 150 million children aged 5–17 were engaged in child labour worldwide in 2016. While these figures represent a steep decline compared to the year 2000, when more than 245 million children were working around the globe, it is unclear whether this trend will continue. The negative impact of the COVID-19 pandemic is foreseeable: child labour statistics may rise again as a result of struggling economies, collapsing enterprises, and a decline in regular employment prospects.

Growth paths are vulnerable in the developing world. Rising productivity and labour incomes, leading to a fall in demand for child labour and a growing demand for better education, are not a matter of course. They may instead be exposed to severe setbacks. Child employment can dampen future economic growth through its negative impact on child development, schooling, and health, and may depress current growth by reducing unskilled wages and discouraging the adoption of skill-intensive technologies. Nevertheless, with a lack of alternatives, child labour is often poor families' insurance against external shocks. Hence policy strategies need to address these economic constraints if they are to succeed in further reducing child employment.

Low-income countries tend to have very young populations and high rates of population growth. The youth employment challenge will become even greater in the near future, and to earn the 'demographic dividend'—that is, the economic benefits of a younger society—would need far-reaching policy initiatives as well. The COVID-19 pandemic may severely affect the living prospects of the younger generation in developing countries, and further depress their economic opportunities. This generation, who are already facing a lack of opportunities to accumulate human capital or find stable employment in frictional labour markets, need the special attention of international development policies.

Labour Markets in Low-Income Countries. David Lam and Ahmed Elsayed, Oxford University Press.
© David Lam and Ahmed Elsayed (2022). DOI: 10.1093/oso/9780192897107.003.0007

Research supported by the Growth and Labour Markets in Low-Income Countries Programme offers new insights on the patterns of child labour and the barriers to better youth employment prospects. This chapter provides a brief overview on the main policy-relevant findings.

7.1 The Link between Child Labour and Economic Growth

In the context of developing countries, the existing body of recent literature on child labour has not yet delivered a clear understanding of how economic aspects and decisions interfere with children's labour market presence, their schooling, and the human capital capacities of the next generation of adults. One line of research argues that child labour may not just *signal* poverty but in fact *cause* it, by disrupting the next generation's human capital formation—whereas economic growth could reduce the need for child labour.

This relationship has been doubted, however, in recent studies (see the overview in Brown, Deardorff, and Stern 2003) based on cross-sectional data within a country that compare different households and their children's activities. Following these hypotheses, households would expand their economic activities if economic growth leads to higher income, and thus further rely on more profitable child labour or—more generally—consider child labour part of their cultural norms or parental preferences that continue, even if family welfare rises.

Edmonds (2005) addressed these contradictory positions by evaluating an identical set of Vietnamese agricultural households, their income changes, and their child labour activities over time (instead of comparing households at one point in time). The period studied was 1993 to 1997, when the country's GDP grew by almost 9% per year on average, while child labour declined by nearly 30%. This seminal study found strong evidence that 80% of this decline can be traced back to poor households escaping extreme poverty and improving their economic status, and that cultural norms or preferences were not barriers to reducing child labour. The results are the more remarkable and policy-relevant since, in the studied environment, growing agricultural productivity led to rising earnings opportunities for child workers as well.

Beegle, Dehejia, and Gatti (2006) presented a thorough examination of the relationship between (transitory) household income shocks and child labour. Based on a household panel survey in Tanzania, the study revealed that unpredictable crop shocks resulting in a substantial income loss increased a poor family's use of child labour and its willingness to disrupt their children's schooling if available assets were an insufficient buffer. These findings imply that policies to insure agricultural households against temporary income shocks—needed now more than any time in the past due to the COVID-19 pandemic—and easy access to credit will contribute to reducing child labour and increasing family welfare.

Edmonds (2006) complemented this study by analysing the impact of a foreseeable rise in a household's income on child labour and schooling decisions. When Black South Africans became eligible for an unconditional old-age pension, daily child labour of their co-resident grandchildren declined from three hours to less than two hours, while school attendance strongly increased. Until then, liquidity constraints prevented higher school attendance rates for children in low-income households that could not afford direct and indirect schooling costs. Hence reducing schooling costs and overcoming financial barriers may offer an effective means to fight child labour, whereas policies aimed at prohibiting child labour, for example via trade sanctions, may have the opposite effect by imposing costs on the poorest.

Most countries have a minimum-age regulation in place regarding child labour. A survey of recent empirical research provided in Edmonds (2014) has emphasized that such a policy should not be at the core of a strategy against child labour in developing countries, even if accompanied by compulsory schooling laws. An effective minimum-age regulation would need enforcement, which is not in place in most countries with widespread child labour. Findings from fifty-nine developing countries reveal that children's time allocation is, in fact, not significantly affected by such regulation. Combining enforced minimum-age and schooling legislation would have a stronger effect, but other policies seem more appropriate.

The main lesson, as Edmonds (2016) argued in a literature review commissioned by GLM|LIC, is to eliminate potential motives for child labour by promoting alternatives and providing stable social safety conditions for poor families. **Given that child labour is a cause as well as a consequence of a lack of economic growth, more attention should be paid to reducing it through sustainable development**, in line with the UN Sustainable Development Goals.

Child labour and economic growth (measured as GDP per capita) are closely connected (see Figure 7.1). The rate of economic activities of children aged 7–14 is significantly higher in poorer countries. According to Edmonds (2016), more than half of the variance in child labour across countries can be accounted for by differences in GDP per person.

This striking relationship, however, is not necessarily causal in the sense that countries would gain immediate economic growth by reduced child employment. Interactions between economic growth and child labour are far too complex to allow for such simple causal explanations. Regardless, the literature shows that **economic development can be impeded by intensive child labour**. Schooling and health may suffer from work—with long-lasting consequences for later adult life and employment that may harm a society's future economic prospects.

As Edmonds (2016) pointed out, there is compelling evidence that these disruptions persist through generations: former child workers become parents of future child labourers if precarious living standards do not change. Hence, **the economic**

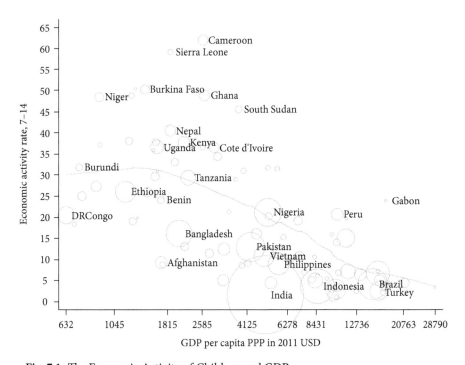

Fig. 7.1 The Economic Activity of Children and GDP

Note: Fraction of children who are economically active at the age 7–14 against GDP per person adjusted for purchasing power parity (2011 USD). Circle size proportional to a country's population under 15. Curve represents average child labour across countries' national income spectrum.
Source: Edmonds (2016), based on World Development Indicators

disadvantages of child labour, in terms of jeopardizing growth and better employment prospects, are perpetuated and may end in a vicious circle—all the more so if more children work, as this will reduce adult labour wages and thus increase the need for child employment.

If wages for low-skilled or unskilled work come under pressure along with intensive child labour, then a negative impact on economic growth also arises through another mechanism: an abundance of unskilled labour encourages inefficient production methods that are complementary to unskilled labour, while discouraging investment in human capital (for example skills) and the adoption of skill-orientated technologies. As a result, wages are further depressed, and the efficacy of skilled labour and capital is reduced. Economies will then lag further behind, and miss opportunities to grow and integrate into world economics.

At the same time, child employment is poor families' enforced reaction to poverty traps and a lack of economic prospects. Child employment—mostly in family-based agriculture—offers a chance to better withstand extreme poverty and economic shocks. According to the World Bank's World Development Indicators

(World Bank, n.d.), 65% of child labour takes place in agriculture, roughly 20% of child workers are engaged in manufacturing, and less than 15% work in the service sector.

It is important to understand that **initial steps towards growth and a better living could result in additional demand for child labour. This may occur if an increase in output prices leads families to increase adult labour and rely on their children working at home, or if increasing child labour wages stimulate additional child employment outside of the household.**

Furthermore, the effect of economic growth in terms of bringing additional assets into poor households should not be underestimated. Most child labour is unpaid work on the household level, but with an increasing availability of productive assets the likelihood of child labour in family-owned businesses increases also (Turk and Edmonds 2002). This happens up to a certain point when families' increased wealth allows them to reduce and then fully cease child labour. Recent research (see, for example, Basu, Das, and Dutta 2010) has emphasized that rising income, rising living standards, and a rising demand for goods of higher quality than households can produce themselves, reduce the incentives for child labour.

There is no doubt that economic growth offers poor societies better chances to cope with economic setbacks without relying on child labour. For instance, the existence of a larger manufacturing sector goes hand in hand with less child labour (see Figure 7.2).

Another interesting effect has been studied with respect to the mechanisms between urbanization and child labour (see, for example, Fafchamps and Shilpi 2005; Fafchamps and Wahba 2006). When household specialization increases with urban proximity, child labour in the household is reduced substantially, without being offset by a rise in children's work out of the home. Most importantly, **growth leads to policies that foster social safety nets, insurance, and credit markets— all reducing the pressure on child labour.** When more households climb the job quality ladder and specialize in production, unskilled child labour is no longer a useful tool—and educating the next generation becomes the more rational option.

Edmonds (2016) summed up research findings on the effect of child labour on the accumulation of human capital. Infrequent child employment serves as a means to cover school costs, whereas evidence from the vast majority of low-income countries shows that working children are more likely to achieve lower test scores at school or not attend school regularly due to overburdening or a lack of time. Some studies conclude that child workers complete up to one or two years less schooling than non-working children (see, for example, Psacharapoulos 1997; Ray 2002).

The consequences are obvious: **child labour results in substantially lower educational attainment and human capital formation, thus downgrading a society's future prospects.** These negative effects are more acute if educational losses are accompanied by health problems. Excessively early work experiences leave children

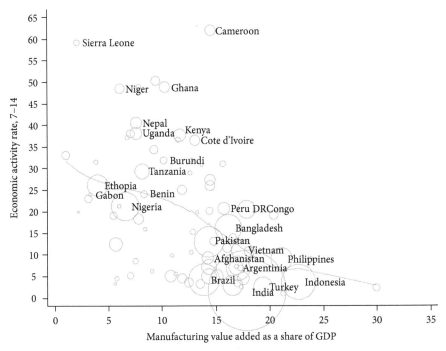

Fig. 7.2 The Economic Activity of Children and Value Added in Manufacturing

Notes: Fraction of children who are economically active at the age 7–14 against share of GDP contributed by manufacturing. Circle size proportional to a country's population under 15. Curve represents average child labour across countries' national income spectrum.
Source: Edmonds (2016), based on World Development Indicators.

more vulnerable: they may not get enough food, and exhausting or hazardous jobs may affect physical and mental health in the short or long term. In a report, Fallon and Tzannatos (1998) explain that these effects can harm children's psyche and future social adjustment, while Foster (1995) finds that child work can affect children's growth pattern.

Generally speaking, the world's poor families face more frequent shocks—driven by civil conflicts, economic setbacks, natural disasters, or health problems—than wealthier households. In this context, child labour is an element of families' strategies to self-insure against these transitory risks. Child labour supply as a component of insurance is not limited to rural environments (as studied, for example, by Beegle, Dehejia, and Gatti 2006)—similar mechanisms apply in urban areas where child employment may compensate for periods of adult unemployment in the absence of unemployment insurance, or other economic shocks. In the worst scenario, when urban households suffer from lasting adult unemployment, children may be completely and permanently withdrawn from school (see, for example, Duryea, Lam, and Levison 2007).

However, **research does not suggest that regulation aiming to ban child labour is an efficient way to reduce child employment, or that economic growth would lead to more effective enforcement of existing regulation policy.** On the contrary, recent research shows that imperfectly enforced child labour regulation (see Bharadwaj, Lakdawala, and Li 2020, a study of the Indian experience) may result in employers offsetting the risk of a fine by decreasing child wages—which in turn may increase child labour further.

Even with efficient enforcement, the negative implications of child labour will continue since regulation is usually based on the United Nations Convention on the Rights of the Child (UN-CRC) to avoid hazardous or harmful employment interfering with education. This definition leaves ample room for interpretation. Also, as Edmonds (2016, p. 21) argues, simply banning child labour would ignore the fact that most child labour is not voluntary but forced by families' extreme poverty. **'Punishing the poor for being poor' would be a short-sighted strategy with inevitable undesired consequences.**

Edmonds and Schady (2012) have shown that patterns of child labour may be overcome by rather simple policies. Avoiding child labour does not require extensive subsidy programmes. Even a limited—conditional—cash transfer not fully replacing child labour earnings but serving as a minimum insurance may have a very positive outcome. That is because **families seem willing to accept a reduction in household income, and use the transfer to secure schooling of their children** since adult income combined with the transfer enables them to meet subsistence needs and avoid illiquidity (for example, as a result of school fees).

In a Kathmandu case study (Edmonds and Shrestha, 2014), a roughly 20% replacement of child income with conditional cash transfers almost eliminated child labour—at least for the programme period. However, lasting impacts are not likely if these policies are run on a short-term basis only, while an expensive long-term transfer policy may be beyond many LICs.

Other potential constraints of cash transfer programmes have been highlighted only recently by a Lesotho case study (Pellerano, Porreca, and Rosati 2020). This analysis revealed that, while cash transfers may reduce child labour overall, the effect on the poorest households may fail to materialize. Below a minimum household income—or below a minimum transfer level tailored to the poorest—even an unconditional transfer does not seem to increase investment in children's education. These findings underline the need to carefully design such programmes—and the importance of strategies in promoting economic growth.

Economic growth raises the probability of social safety nets emerging and protecting the poorest households against income losses in the long term. If they do arise, these social assistance programmes may be an important ingredient of policies against child labour (see a case study on Indonesia in De Silva and Sumarto 2015). If they have no health insurance, then illness or disability of adult family members may force children into additional or even hazardous employment in an attempt to secure subsistence (see Dillon 2012). Providing health and accident insurance for adult family members may thus help reduce child labour incentives (see the findings in Landmann and Frölich 2015).

At the same time, economic development induces improvements in banking infrastructure, credit markets, and the spread of bank accounts, which may reduce demand for children's employment, even in the face of temporary economic shocks (see the Tanzanian example studied in Bandara, Dehejia, and Lavie-Rouse 2015). In general, low-income countries with a better-functioning finance sector seem to experience less child employment (see Dehejia and Gatti 2005). But there is also some evidence that microfinance projects that aim to help poor families avoid child labour may actually increase it, depending on the availability and type of adult employment opportunities (see Islam and Choe 2013).

Obviously, there is no silver bullet against the distribution of child labour since it can change substantially and quickly in response to different conditions. The effects of the COVID-19 pandemic are not yet clear but will presumably reinforce trends towards child labour instead of investment in their human capital. This would be a severe setback for international efforts to overcome child labour. Against this background, Edmonds (2016) highlighted the potential of strategies to raise households' valuations of child non-labour activities by encouraging positive actions. **Initiatives to improve access to schools, raise school quality, and reduce school fees, may efficiently raise the net return of alternative (non-labour) child time**—provided that families do not face lasting liquidity constraints and have access to at least a minimum of social insurance.

7.2 Better Measurement and Accounting for Gender Issues of Child Labour

Despite a continuously growing literature on child labour, its statistical measurement is often rather inaccurate in LICs, thus complicating policy design. Statistics usually rely on proxy reporting by adults, which may include some bias due to social and cultural values. Furthermore, data collection may not sufficiently take account of the seasonality of agricultural child employment, and hence misreport the actual labour time.

To explore these potential statistical limitations, GLM|LIC initiated a study on the variation in child labour statistics in Ethiopia (Galdo, Dammert, and Abebaw 2018). The research team designed a random survey covering 1,200 rural households fully dependent on growing coffee, and their farm and non-farm child labour activities during the thirty days before the survey. In one-third of participating households, children (6–14 years of age) were selected as respondents (treatment group) instead of the adult head of the family and their spouse (control group). To allow for seasonal divergence and fluctuating demand for child labour, the survey was conducted in three different seasons—before, during, and after harvest—between July 2015 and January 2017.

The main results of the study confirm a clear correlation between the intensity of child labour and the agricultural calendar:

1. **Reported child labour rates swung between 45% in the main rainy season and 76% in the harvest season,** with a strong under-reporting of girls' labour in families with children of both genders.

2. Apparently, **reporting of child employment was not only very sensitive to agricultural seasons but also to child gender,** gendered labour market segmentation, and the gender of the proxy respondent.

3. **If the survey respondent was the male head of household, girls' labour was significantly underreported** compared to the rates reported by girls themselves, especially in the main rainy season (9 percentage points lower) and the harvest season (8 percentage points lower). Boys' labour was meanwhile reported in line with self-reported rates across the seasons.

4. **Female spouses reported higher levels of girls' employment,** roughly corresponding to the self-reported rates of girls.

5. The differences between self- and proxy-reported child labour were not driven by the age of the child and their growing cognitive abilities; younger and older subsamples report almost identical levels of work on the family's farm.

6. **Across all seasons, boys were more active in child labour.** The boy–girl gap varied from 20 percentage points during the main rainy season to 5 percentage points in the harvest season.

These findings are highly relevant for future child labour measurement and a more careful accounting for seasonal variation in the demand for agricultural child labour. The timing of survey also plays a role. Regardless of the type of respondent, the proportion of children working in farming activities over thirty days prior to the questionnaire increased from 45% in the rainy season to 52% in the short rainy season, and to 76% in the harvesting season (see Figure 7.3). The figure also depicts important gender gaps in child labour participation with boys having higher participation rates than girls.

The findings also confirm that the deficiencies in female labour statistics in LICs (mainly due to male-dominated gender norms) extends to child labour as well. This may reflect a traditional segmentation of responsibilities and tasks between males and females in an agricultural environment, whereby younger children spend most of their time with women learning to help with household chores. As they grow older, children take on gendered tasks, with girls remaining more orientated towards household tasks. The study controls for different types of (male)

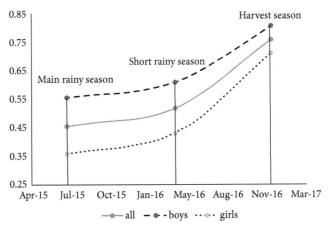

Fig. 7.3 Seasonality of Child Labour in Rural Ethiopia: Past Thirty Days in Farm Work
Source: Galdo, Dammert, and Abebaw (2018)

proxy respondents, revealing that the gap between child labour statements of girls and male adults decreases significantly when the male is more familiar with the girls' tasks (for example if a widower or the only decision-maker) or when no boys belong to the family.

From a policy perspective, **measurement of (girls') child labour could benefit from female household members playing a more active role in reporting on girls' working activities, instead of relying solely on the (male) head of household.** When designing social protection policies to address child labour, the seasonality determinants of child employment and family incomes are highly relevant.

7.3 Meeting the Youth Employment Challenge in Africa

As shown in section 7.2, child labour may diminish the next generations' schooling prospects, have lasting negative effects until and throughout adult age, and interfere with a society's chances for economic growth. Young people in low-income countries are thus not only suffering from a potential earlier 'career' as child workers, but also from the prevalent inefficiencies of educational systems and labour markets. The large cohort of young people entering Africa's labour force is better educated than all previous cohorts, while African economies have grown at significant rates in the recent past. However, jobs too often remain elusive in the formal wage sector, due to the limited success of African economies in transitioning from low-productivity agriculture to higher-productivity non-agricultural sectors.

A recent comprehensive analysis published by the International Labour Office (ILO) drew a mixed picture of youth employment in sub-Saharan Africa in the aftermath of the global financial crisis at the end of the 2000s (Elder and Koné 2014). While the region has been able to weather the crisis and continue on a path of increased economic growth and educational investment since the year 2000, youth employment prospects did not keep up with these overall positive trends.

Year after year, a better-educated cohort of young people enters the regional labour markets. The most likely future prospects they find are: unstable, vulnerable employment opportunities; rising unemployment risks with rising qualification levels resulting in employment far below qualification; and precarious self-employment or informal jobs. Reliable written contracts are the exception; some 40% of employed young people work on the basis of verbally agreed durations of less than one year. More than 50% are undereducated for their jobs, while around 80% are informally employed. Agriculture and services are the main sectors, with industry jobs scarce among the young (Elder and Koné 2014).

A lack of prospects for stable and satisfactory employment, despite better education, is one of two ticking time bombs in many low-income societies. The second time bomb results from a lost generation of youth who have no adequate access to education, and leave school at primary level or below. More than half of the youth population in sub-Saharan Africa belong to this disadvantaged group (Elder and Koné 2014), with hardly any chance to avoid becoming trapped in the poorest-quality employment. The COVID-19 crisis may even heighten social tensions and delay successful strategies towards better youth prospects in sub-Saharan Africa.

An extensive World Bank report (Filmer and Fox 2014) further illustrated the widening gap between prevalent low-productivity jobs and the rising aspirations of better-qualified young people in the region. To create inclusive growth, the report concluded that the challenge of sustainable youth employment in sub-Saharan Africa requires a comprehensive approach targeted at the poor and the young. Widespread constraints on productivity, business environment, and earnings growth, should be relieved by improving access to land, agricultural technologies, markets, and finance for young people.

7.3.1 Supporting the Informal Sector May Help to Boost Youth Employment Opportunities

A further study supported by GLM|LIC (Fox 2016) emphasized that such strategies will only succeed (if at all) as part of a broader strategy also targeting the large informal sector. Its diagnosis is not very encouraging at first sight: transforming traditional, inefficient labour market structures from low-productivity agriculture towards higher-productivity sectors has failed on a broad front.

However, economic growth rates would have given some scope for structural reforms in sub-Saharan Africa. Since the mid-1990s, the region's growth rates have repeatedly exceeded the level in East Asian low-income and lower-middle-income countries. Nonetheless, sub-Saharan Africa fell back significantly with respect to output transformation and the share of GDP of the industry sector and manufacturing. A large share of non-farm growth took place—and still takes place—in household enterprises, with self-employment thus generating only few regular wage jobs.

The youth employment challenge has a gender dimension that should not be underestimated. Many sub-Saharan African countries continue to have early marriage, early onset of childbearing, and high fertility rates—factors that limit educational and economic opportunities for women. As noted in Chapter 1, continued high fertility rates also play an important role in creating the young age structures and rapid growth of youth cohorts that exacerbate the youth employment challenge. Improving women's education and increasing economic opportunities for women is an important goal in its own right, and is also likely to reduce fertility and eventually reduce rapid growth of the youth labour force.

In a GLM|LIC study by Herrera, Sahn, and Villa (2019) studying the labour market segmentation in relation to teenage fertility in Madagascar, the authors find that the common intuition and results from previous studies on the relation between the informal sector and early childbirth also holds true. Their study design allowed for the measurement of the average likelihood of entering the informal sector depending on the age at the first birth. Their results showed that for every additional year delay in the age at first birth the likelihood of a young woman to work in the informal sector decreases by 7.2%. Correspondingly, and among many important conclusions, the authors were able to assert that the age at childbirth plays a crucial role in the human capital formation of young woman and thus their capacity to improve their conditions through formal and arguably more beneficial labour.

The rapid growth rate of sub-Saharan Africa's labour force, the result of continued high fertility rates, sets the region apart from LICs in Asia, where fertility decline has been faster. Overall, sub-Saharan Africa still faces rather low productivity in agriculture, and a lack of diversity in its non-agricultural (urban) employment structures, with only some 25% of all new jobs located in the formal non-farm wage sectors (see Figure 7.4).

As a result, good jobs for young people in African formal labour markets are scarce, thus consolidating the core role of informal youth employment, particularly for the less educated. The study argued that policies aiming to generate better prospects for the young generation need to refocus and strengthen the informal sector of non-farm self-employment—in both rural and urban areas—instead of trying to restrict it through initiatives of questionable value.

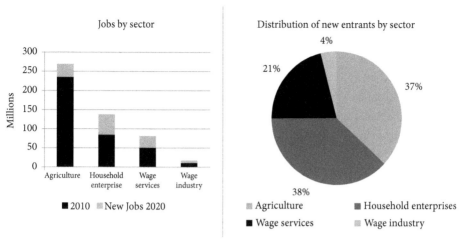

Fig. 7.4 Job Creation by Sector in sub-Saharan Africa, 2010–20
Note: Figures for 2020 projected.
Source: Fox (2016)

While efforts to industrialize, attract foreign investment, and create additional wage employment momentum should not be abandoned, it would be naïve to expect a substantial rise in formal jobs in the foreseeable future. From this perspective, enhancing the informal sector appears to be an obvious approach that goes to the very root of the problem without taking a defeatist viewpoint. If the informal sector is to keep its dominant role, then raising its productivity and job quality by supporting rural farms and household enterprises in rural as well as urban regions may offer a way to support the formal sector and structural transformation. Sub-Saharan Africa would thus follow the example of Asia and Latin America, where a growing sector of household enterprises initiated and stimulated structural progress.

In the context of sub-Saharan Africa, with its rapid population growth and available land resources, increasing agricultural productivity need not mean reducing jobs in the farm sector. **Supporting informal agricultural employment in household enterprises would instead help to overcome poverty, and make farms more market-orientated. It would also encourage youth labour market entrants to accept agriculture as a serious business for entrepreneurs** that will provide a living, and not feel trapped in their parents' self-employment conditions. In fact, turning young people towards agricultural labour markets will only work as part of a comprehensive strategy to develop the informal sector as a step towards inclusive growth.

As Fox (2016) illustrated, the scope for initiatives directly targeted at the youth is rather limited. Traditional programmes addressing general employability and vocational training of the youth have often had disappointing results relative to

Table 7.1 Distribution of Donor Projects to Support Youth Employment in Africa

Type of intervention	Frequency	%
SKILLS TRAINING	**366**	**77.5**
Vocational training	182	38.6
On-the-job training/apprenticeships	37	7.8
Life-skills trainings/second-chance education	291	61.7
Financial support	22	4.7
ENTREPRENEURSHIP PROMOTION	**281**	**59.5**
Training	241	51.1
Advising (mentoring, business development)	198	41.9
Providing access to microfinance	152	32.2
EMPLOYMENT SERVICES	**159**	**33.7**
Job-search assistance	105	22.2
Job counselling	87	18.4
Job placement	95	20.1
Financial assistance for job search	8	1.7
Sanctions for not complying with the intervention's rules	16	3.4
SUBSIDIZED EMPLOYMENT	**32**	**6.8**
Wage or hiring subsidies to firms to hire youth	8	1.7
Public works/employment guarantee/voluntary service programme	30	6.4
REFORMS (LABOUR MARKET)	**6**	**1.3**
N	**472**	**100.0**

Source: Fox (2016) based on data of the ILO's Youth Employment Inventory accessed in 2016.

their cost. Yet most public and private donor projects still target general employa-bility in the regular (urban) wage sector—risking counterproductive effects if they fail to meet their targets, given the lack of available jobs relative to the supply of young workers (see Table 7.1).

At the same time, most countries in sub-Saharan Africa do not have pro-grammes designed to stimulate the productivity and sustainability of household enterprises. A report by the Alliance for a Green Revolution in Africa (AGRA 2015) recommended national strategies including focused agricultural educa-tion, short business training, developing life skills and skills needed by the pri-vate sector, reforming land tenure systems, and grant financing for low-income youth.

Last, but not least, such strategies should integrate young people as 'change leaders'; for example, through introducing modern information and communication technologies in agricultural life. Filmer and Fox (2014) showed that **projects providing short business training and (microcredit) finance, thus facilitating new businesses in the private sector, may be useful tools for young people. Projects that upgrade household enterprises to small businesses through entrepreneurship training do not seem to be cost effective, however**; a lack of scale and sustainability due to high programme costs are strong constraints in sub-Saharan Africa.

In the case of youth labour supply exceeding demand, Fox (2016) argued in favour of programmes encouraging investment in labour-intensive enterprises, for example through improved management of existing infrastructure services, additional infrastructure investments, and lower levels of taxes and costs for business registration. These programmes should take an educational approach, to develop the business and financial skills, and networks, necessary to establish successfully in the informal sector, and provide thorough information about existing opportunities instead of raising expectations to unrealistic levels through long-term vocational training.

Such a strategy would apply to both rural and urban environments. In the urban context, frustration of the (better-educated) young people needs to be tackled in particular. Here the gap is the widest between the expanding educational opportunities and the limited returns to these human capital investments. There are limited opportunities for the majority of the better-educated urban youth to take up and keep a regular wage job in the near future. To defuse this time bomb, policies will need to develop and not hinder informal sector employment in urban societies, the study concludes convincingly.

Key Takeaways from this Chapter

- Child labour is both a consequence and a cause of poverty as it impedes human capital formation.
- Strict enforcement of a child labour ban would hurt the poorest.
- Lower schooling costs, better school quality, and conditional cash transfers can make education a more attractive and affordable alternative to child labour.
- Economic growth may initially increase the demand for child labour, but reduces it in the long term by fostering social safety nets, insurance, and credit markets.
- Social protection policies to address child labour must take the seasonality of child employment and family incomes into account.

- Assessing the true scope of child labour should rely more on women's reports as male household members tend to underreport girls' labour.
- Better educational and economic opportunities for young women lead to lower fertility, thereby also alleviating the youth employment challenge.
- Short business training and microcredit finance can help young people create new private-sector businesses and become 'change leaders'.
- Where job prospects in the formal sector do not keep pace with improved education and training, policies should develop rather than hinder informal sector employment.

References

AGRA (Alliance for a Green Revolution in Africa), 2015. African Agriculture Status Report 2015: Youth in Agriculture in Sub-Saharan Africa. Nairobi. Available from: https://www.tralac.org/images/docs/8202/aasr-2015-youth-in-agriculture-in-sub-saharan-africa.pdf

Bandara, A., Dehejia, R., and Lavie-Rouse, S., 2015. The Impact of Income and Non-Income Shocks on Child Labor: Evidence from a Panel Survey of Tanzania. *World Development*, 67: 218–237.

Basu, K., Das, S., and Dutta, B., 2010. Child Labor and Household Wealth: Theory and Empirical Evidence of an Inverted-U. *Journal of Development Economics*, 91: 8–14.

Beegle, K., Dehejia, R. H., and Gatti, R., 2006. Child Labor and Agricultural Shocks. *Journal of Development Economics*, 81: 80–96.

Bharadwaj, P., Lakdawala, L. K., and Li, N., 2020. Perverse Consequences of Well-Intentioned Regulation: Evidence from India's Child Labor Ban. *Journal of the European Economic Association*, 18: 1158–95.

Brown, D. K., Deardorff, A. V., and Stern, R. M., 2003. Child Labor: Theory, Evidence, and Policy. In K. Basu, H. Horn, L. Roman, and J. Shapiro (eds.), *International Labor Standards: History, Theory, and Policy Options*. Maldon, MA: Wiley, 194–247.

De Silva, I., and Sumarto, S., 2015. Dynamics of Growth, Poverty and Human Capital: Evidence from Indonesian Sub-National Data. *Journal of Economic Development*, 40: 1–33.

Dehejia, R. H., and Gatti, R., 2005. Child Labor: The Role of Financial Development and Income Variability across Countries. *Economic Development and Cultural Change*, 53: 913–32.

Dillon, A., 2012. Child Labour and Schooling Responses to Production and Health Shocks in Northern Mali. *Journal of African Economies*, 22: 276–99.

Duryea, S., Lam, D., and Levison, D., 2007. Effects of Economic Shocks on Children's Employment and Schooling in Brazil. *Journal of Development Economics*, 84: 188–214.

Edmonds, E. V., 2005. Does Child Labor Decline with Improving Economic Status? *Journal of Human Resources*, XL (1): 77–99.

Edmonds, E. V., 2006. Child Labor and Schooling Responses to Anticipated Income in South Africa. *Journal of Development Economics*, 81: 386–414.

Edmonds, E. V., 2014. Does Minimum Age of Employment Regulation Reduce Child Labor? IZA World of Labor 2014: 73 doi: 10.15185/izawol.73

Edmonds, E. V., 2016. Economic Growth and Child Labor in Low-Income Economies. GLM|LIC Synthesis Paper No. 3.

Edmonds, E. V., and Schady, N., 2012. Poverty Alleviation and Child Labor. *American Economic Journal: Economic Policy*, 4: 100–24.

Edmonds, E. V., and Shrestha, M., 2014. You Get What You Pay for: Schooling Incentives and Child Labor. *Journal of Development Economics*, 111: 196–211.

Elder, S., and Koné, K. S., 2014. Labour Market Transitions of Young Women and Men in Sub-Saharan Africa. Work4Youth Publication Series No. 9.

Fafchamps, M., and Shilpi, F., 2005. Cities and Specialisation: Evidence from South Asia. *The Economic Journal*, 115, 477–504.

Fafchamps, M., and Wahba, J., 2006. Child Labor, Urban Proximity, and Household Composition. *Journal of Development Economics* (special issue in honour of Pranab Bardhan) 79(2): 374.97.

Fallon, P., and Tzannatos, T., 1998. Child Labor: Issues and Directions for the World Bank. The World Bank, Washington D.C.

Filmer, D., and Fox, L., 2014. Youth Employment in Sub-Saharan Africa. Africa Development Forum; Washington, DC: World Bank and Agence Française de Développement. Available from: https://openknowledge.worldbank.org/handle/10986/16608.

Foster, A., 1995. Prices, Credit Markets and Child Growth in Low-Income Rural Areas. *Economic Journal*, 105(430): 551–70.

Fox, L., 2016. What Will It Take to Meet the Youth Employment Challenge in Sub-Saharan Africa? GLM|LIC Working Paper No. 10.

Galdo, J., Dammert, A. C., and Abebaw, D., 2018. Child Labor Measurement in Agricultural Households: Seasonality, Proxy Respondent and Gender Information Gaps in Ethiopia. GLM|LIC Working Paper No. 43.

Herrera, C., Sahn, D. E., and Villa, K. M., 2019. Teen Fertility and Female Employment Outcomes: Evidence from Madagascar. *Journal of African Economies*, 28(3): 277–303.

ILO, 2017. *Global Estimates of Child Labour – Results and Trends, 2012–2016*. Geneva: ILO.

Islam, A., and Choe, C., 2013. Child Labor and Schooling Responses to Access to Microcredit in Rural Bangladesh. *Economic Inquiry*, 51: 46–61.

Landmann, A., and Frölich, M., 2015. Can Health-Insurance Help Prevent Child Labor? An Impact Evaluation from Pakistan. *Journal of Health Economics*, 39: 51–9.

Pellerano, L., Porreca, E., and Rosati, F. C., 2020. Income Elasticity of Child Labor: Do Cash Transfers Have an Impact on the Poorest Children? *IZA Journal of Development and Migration*, 11(1).

Psacharopoulos, G., 1997. Child Labor versus Educational Attainment: Some Evidence from Latin America. *Journal of Population Economics*, 10: 377–86.

Ray, R., 2002. The Determinants of Child Labour and Child Schooling in Ghana. *Journal of African Economies*, 11: 561–90.

Turk, C., and Edmonds, E., 2002. Child Labor in Transition in Vietnam, Policy Research Working Papers. The World Bank.

World Bank, n.d. World Development Indicators Data Bank. Available from: https://databank.worldbank.org/source/world-development-indicators.

8

Gender Dimensions of Developing Labour Markets

Emerging labour markets in low-income countries are mostly characterized by rather high levels of discrimination against certain groups of workers. This has negative implications for the growth potential of these economies. Identifying mechanisms of discrimination and quantifying the lost economic potential caused by discrimination is an important step towards unleashing growth. While women are not the only group facing substantial disadvantages in the labour markets, they are certainly one of the groups most discriminated against, and hence most vulnerable to shocks.

Barriers to equal opportunities in early childhood development, schooling, higher education and vocational training, widespread gender oppression, and persistent role allocations to women, pave the way for—explicit and implicit—discrimination that still inhibits most parts of women's lives in low-income societies. Notwithstanding some progress that has been achieved more recently in educational attainment and in building public awareness that fairer opportunities are needed, releasing the potential of modern women in LICs will take targeted and sustainable action. This is all the more important since the COVID-19 pandemic, which will presumably bring heavy setbacks for women's progress towards equal opportunities, and might even reinforce traditional notions of gender roles that exclude women from regular labour market participation.

The GLM|LIC programme has paid special attention to gender issues since its beginning in 2011; by 2019 it had increased this focus, with the aim of guiding future gender and labour market policies to enhance equality of opportunity for women. This chapter summarizes the core findings of selected GLM|LIC publications alongside a brief review of recent relevant literature in the field.

8.1 Trends in Women's Employment, Gender Gaps in Wages, and Employment

'Women in developing countries are disempowered: high youth unemployment, early marriage and childbearing interact to limit their investments into human

Labour Markets in Low-Income Countries. David Lam and Ahmed Elsayed, Oxford University Press.
© David Lam and Ahmed Elsayed (2022). DOI: 10.1093/oso/9780192897107.003.0008

capital and enforce dependence on men' (Bandiera et al. 2018, p. 1). As a result, women still lag far behind in terms of educational attainment, formal labour force participation, and social and political representation. Trends are heavily affected by: how independent women's labour force participation is from household economic conditions; how jobs seen as appropriate for more-educated women are growing relative to the supply of more-educated women; and to what extent women are able to break down occupational barriers within the sectors where employed women predominantly work. Strategies for economic growth will certainly need to be accompanied by other policies to improve the situation of women in LICs.

An important contribution to this field of research was provided by Duflo (2012), in a review of the existing research on the link between economic development and the empowerment of women. The study suggests that the interrelationship is too weak to allow policy to simply focus on one or the other, based on the assumption that either (a) economic growth would be sufficient to foster equality or (b) tackling inequality would necessarily go hand in hand with positive effects on growth. As the study emphasizes, poverty remains a driver of inequality as it typically limits women to unpaid household work, reinforces stereotypes regarding the abilities of women, leaves them without any social security net—for example in the case of divorce—damages the education prospects of girls, and sustains high fertility.

This does of course mean that successful strategies against poverty will, in general, benefit women more than men (Duflo 2012, p. 1053) by giving women control over at least a minimum of resources, allowing investments in (financial and business) education, enabling female labour supply, and at least providing them with some basic social security. But the prevailing social and economic structures, traditions, beliefs, and caveats mean that sustained gender equality will not automatically result. At the same time, policies that aim to empower women may have indirect negative economic effects, for example on childcare time of working mothers or wage levels in the labour market, notwithstanding the positive effects in terms of creating more equal opportunities. Against this background, it seems somewhat naïve to forecast a virtuous cycle of development and empowerment, each stimulating the other to the benefit of an entire society. Instead, as Duflo (2012) convincingly argued, reaching equality goals in the long run will require long-lasting efforts to empower women, possibly at the cost of distortions that may accompany redistribution policies.

This is further emphasized by the findings of Bhalotra and Umana-Aponte (2010), who studied the dynamics and cyclicality of women's labour supply, which is related to smoothing household consumption in the face of income volatility. The study covered a large number of developing and transition countries over a time span of two decades. A major finding was a clear drop in female non-employment during recessions, with all developing regions showing an increase in self-employment and some (for example Asia and Latin America) revealing a parallel rise in paid women's employment.

For Africa, the study noted a decline of paid employment, which may be explained by a lack of work opportunities and the fact that households' income shocks are tied closely to rainfall variation. In summary, the authors find that insurance motives are a core driver of women's labour supply decisions.

8.1.1　Is the Female Labour Force on the Rise?

From a development policy perspective, it is important to learn more about the puzzling heterogeneity in regional trends of female labour force participation rates and its determinants. This is because the growth of women's labour market attachment has recently not been very large in developing regions, on average. Starting from this point, a cross-country survey supported by GLM|LIC analysed the interdependence of female labour force participation, economic growth, and (in-)equality outcomes (Klasen 2019) focusing on the heterogeneous trends that have been noted for different low-income regions. The author investigates the hypothesis that these startling differences in women's participation rates can be traced back to causal effects, in terms of societal development, gender norms and economic conditions—which would underline the need for empowerment strategies.

In fact, up until the global COVID-19 pandemic, economic development trends in low-income countries gave much hope for a global rise in female labour participation. Overall, educational attainment of women strongly expanded in most developing countries (see Figure 8.1), increasing female access to labour markets, while a substantial decline in fertility in most regions should have offered women additional options to spend time free from childcare responsibilities.

Along with rather steady economic growth rates since the mid-1990s, these trends should have resulted in a growing demand for, and supply of, female labour, given that male participation rates were already at a high level. However, this effect has only been achieved in limited parts of the developing world (see Figure 8.2), with the relatively positive trend in some countries' glossing over the general picture of a very moderate expansion of female labour force participation in recent years (Klasen 2019).

A look at the group aged 25–54, reveals that—apart from Latin America, the Caribbean, and sub-Saharan Africa—developing regions hardly experienced a significant rise in the female labour force participation rate. Overall, the gap between female and male participation rates remained remarkable. At the labour market

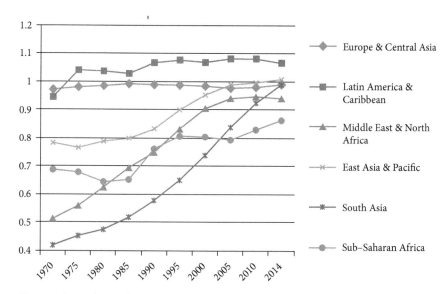

Fig. 8.1 Secondary Education Enrolment Rates: Female–Male Ratio, 1970–2014
Source: Klasen (2017), World Development Indicators

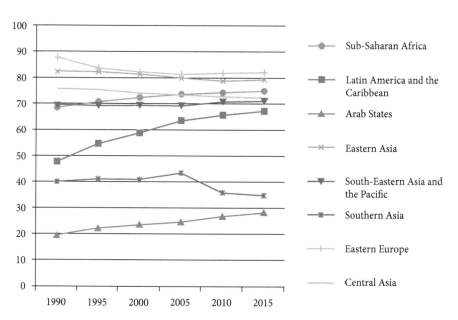

Fig. 8.2 Female Labour Force Participation Rates, Age 25–54
Note: The participation rate definition used here includes subsistence farming resulting in relatively high levels for sub-Saharan Africa.
Source: Klasen (2017), ILOSTAT

'prime age' of 25–54, male labour force participation rates were above 90% in all developing regions, yet for women it stagnated far below 40% in South Asia, the Middle East, and North Africa, while seeming to converge to roughly 70–80% in Eastern Asia, Latin America, the Caribbean, and sub-Saharan Africa.

The high absolute levels for these regions should be interpreted with care, though, as they include subsistence farming and other production for-own-use, which plays an important role mainly in sub-Saharan Africa. The participation rates thus represent a broader definition of labour to better cover widespread female labour in the subsistence economy. Even when taking these activities into account, the gap relative to male participation rates remained very large, which needs an explanation given trends in education and fertility that would have been expected to increase female labour force participation.

Strikingly, the massive decline of fertility rates in Middle East and North Africa (Arab states) did not lead to a significant rise in female labour force participation rates, although they were accompanied by a strong rise in the educational attainment of women. Even more striking is the example of South Asia (mainly India), with its falling participation rates despite clear improving trends in fertility and education. An instructive study by Klasen and Pieters (2015) provided detailed findings for the case of India, showing that even women with completed tertiary education barely exceeded the 30% level of participation, and that increases in female wages had little impact on participation rates.

Taken together, these trends rebut the traditional 'feminization U hypothesis', as Klasen (2019) pointed out. **The story behind the trends of female labour force participation appears to be much more complex than to assume any longer that, when moving from an agricultural to an industrial and services-orientated economy, participation of women will first fall and then increase significantly during the next development stages.**

Needless to say, shedding new light on this context is highly relevant with respect to formulating and promoting development policies. Most importantly, **without a rise in female labour force participation, many developing countries will miss the chance to earn at least some 'demographic dividend'.** Instead of utilizing the current, but temporary, high share of the working-age population resulting from declines in fertility rates (see Figure 8.3), they will then suffer from persistently high dependency rates due to too few women entering the labour markets. Accordingly, economic growth will be dampened with low savings and investment rates. These mechanisms again illustrate the importance of focusing on the labour force participation of women from the economic as well as equality perspective.

Klasen (2019) highlighted the relevance of historical gender norms and shock effects that are often underestimated with regard to the causes of different levels of female labour force participation and gender inequality. External shocks such

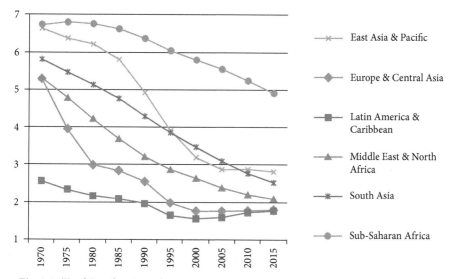

Fig. 8.3 Total Fertility Rates by Region, 1970–2015
Source: Klasen (2017), World Development Indicators

as war (rising female participation rates), civil riots (setback lasting longer for females), or societal transition—for example from socialism to market-orientated economies (falling participation rates of women)—may substantially affect how females act in the economy of different countries.

So-called 'deep drivers' may be rooted in the past yet still have strong effects on participation levels: the longer the history of an agriculturally dominated society, and the more intense its cultivation methods, the higher the demand for cheap family labour which gives way to patriarchal structures, and conventions limiting the role of women to raising children and working in-house (see Hansen, Jensen, and Skovsgaard 2015). The more an agricultural system depends on the plough and hard labour, the more male-orientated a society and its cultural norms have developed until now (see Alesina, Giuliano, and Nunn 2013). Scarcity of resources may act as another deep geo-historical driver of gender inequality in the labour market (see Hazarika, Jha, and Sarangi 2015), whereas the continuous availability of fresh water throughout the seasons and other climate benefits can be interpreted as a favourable baseline for better female opportunities (see Santos Silva et al. 2018).

Religion may be an important driver also, though it remains uncertain to what extent, as studies have shown a rather ambiguous picture (Klasen 2019). **In summary, these drivers may explain to a certain extent why female labour force participation remains relatively low, for example in South Asia, the Middle East, and North Africa. However, these barriers are not set in stone but may be influenced, weakened, and finally overcome by targeted, sustained policies.**

Trends in female labour force participation and their determinants are not easy to measure in low-income societies, and research has not yet provided ample evidence for all developing countries. Models need to include a set of variables, including wage income and other household income, age, education levels of working-age family members, the presence of young children or other dependents, and local labour market characteristics. Given the high prevalence of subsistence labour in rural areas, distinguishing women's contribution to family income may be very difficult.

Nonetheless, Klasen (2019) synthesized three rather clear findings and policy implications from the existing literature (see Table 8.1 for country results):

Education matters

A substantial share of low-educated women enter the labour market due to extreme household poverty, but they leave these often precarious jobs when the household income makes it affordable and corresponding social norms are in favour of women doing home and care work. Secondary education is often accompanied by low participation levels, whereas completed tertiary education results in high participation. Hence, policies to further expand women's education and equality of opportunities could stimulate female labour force participation, although they will not necessarily change societal views regarding it.

For several countries (for example India, Sri Lanka, or Jordan, see Klasen 2019), available studies show a rather U-shaped link between female education levels and the intensity of women's labour market activities. **While low education (no or few years of schooling) forces women into the labour market to avoid poverty, medium education levels seem to drive many of them out of this forced employment, resulting in lower employment but perhaps better welfare outcomes, thus the U-shape.** Women with tertiary education show high employment levels; social norms seem to no longer play a core role at this educational level.

This link between education and labour force participation provides one important explanation for the different trends of female participation rates across regions that vary in their educational progress. For instance, in East Asia and Latin America the expansion of education resulted in a strong rise in the share of women with university degrees, who mostly enter the labour market (see Gasparini and Marchionni 2015), while in some countries participation rates of women increased linearly along education levels (for example Brazil, South Africa, Vietnam, Bangladesh, see Rahman and Islam 2013; Klasen et al. 2020).

As noted by Klasen (2019), international initiatives for better secondary education of women, based for example on the United Nations Sustainable Development Goals, do not necessarily change families' views on the labour market activity of wives and daughters. Thus, they are not necessarily followed by a rising labour force participation of women in developing countries.

It should be taken into account that education investments are not only a matter of individual decisions but are closely related to existing policy programmes. When households follow incentives and respond to these initiatives, only a thorough evaluation of long-term effects will reveal whether attitudes and behaviour are changing sustainably. However, a better education of young women is able to generate returns that reach beyond direct labour market effects. As mentioned earlier, better education in general is accompanied by better health and better living conditions of dependent children. Educated women's role in promoting additional education efforts in their families should be valued highly (see Afridi et al. 2018). In that respect, future investments in women's education will certainly see indirect positive labour market effects as well.

It is not only education that matters with regard to stimulating female labour market proximity. Rising household income levels are another important cause of changes in female labour force participation, since a more stable income reduces the immediate pressure on women to work. Of course, this negative household income effect on labour market participation can also be observed in developed regions. But while it has become less relevant in most OECD countries, revealing a decoupling of female labour market attachment and household conditions, the effect remains strong in many developing countries or is falling rather slowly. Only few developing countries (for example, Brazil and South Africa, see Klasen 2019) have shown a stronger labour force attachment of women, with the family income effect disappearing completely over time.

Presumably, a further increase in female education levels in the developing world will help reduce the relevance of family income as a decisive factor in women's labour market proximity. **Nonetheless, women's labour market attachment will likely remain counter-cyclical at lower education levels—bad economic times aggravate household conditions and poverty risks, forcing women to enter the labour market.**

Another aspect should not be overlooked while research findings run contrary to mainstream thinking: the remarkable decline in low-income countries' fertility rates does not necessarily promote a rise in female labour market participation. In fact, an Indonesia case study by Priebe (2011) has emphasized that work decisions are driven by poverty rather than fertility. A decline in fertility may thus lead to lower participation rates, particularly of poor, lesser-educated women in rural environments. Overall, the decline of fertility seems to contribute less than expected to an increase in female labour market participation. Policy planning needs to take this into account.

Overcoming social norms against working women matters
Prevalent stigma are among the most relevant factors behind low or stagnating female labour market participation rates. While they seem to play a limited role for very poor households of the less educated, higher education levels of women

Table 8.1 Determinants of Female Labour Force Participation across Countries, 1990–2010

	Education U?	Head Education	Household Income	Children
India	Strong, more shallow over time	Strong negative effect	Strong negative effects, falling slightly over time	Moderate negative effect 0–4, no effect 5–9
Sri Lanka	Shallow U, insignificant over time	No effect	Strong negative effect, falling slightly over time	Strong negative effect 0–4, small effect 5–9
Bangladesh	No U, linear increase	Small negative effect	(Sizeable)*	Moderate negative effect 04
Jordan	Strong U, more shallow over time	No effect	Small stable negative effect	Moderate stable negative effect 04, 5–14
Vietnam	No U, linear increase	No effect	Moderate stable negative effect	Rising negative effect 0–4, no effect 5–14
Brazil	No U, linear increase	Sizeable falling negative effect, gone by 2009	Small negative, turning positive by 2013	Sizeable effect 0–4, small effect 5–14
Bolivia	No U, small linear increase	Small effect appearing after 2008	Moderate stable negative effect	Sizeable effect 0–4, no effect 5–14
South Africa	No U, linear increase	No effect	Small negative, insignificant by 2014	Sizeable effect 0–4, small effect 5–14

* The regression does not include household income but number of male earners and assets. Number of male earners has a sizeable negative effect, assets a small negative one.

Source: Klasen (2017)

and their husbands bring these norms into play significantly. Policymakers should be aware of the long process that will be needed to overcome these obstacles.

The nature and strength of social norms that prevent women from entering or re-entering the labour markets in low-income regions is as difficult to evaluate as it is to overcome through targeted policies. Societal barriers against female employment may apply in general or focus on market segments only, depending on regional conditions and traditions. The traditional role of women as secondary earners has been fostered by recent male wage growth, and is further cemented by tax provisions in many countries. This contributes to making social norms in favour of non-working women.

Klasen (2019) used the example of male education levels influencing the acceptance of working women in Asia to illustrate the complexity of correctly measuring and evaluating these effects. In India a rising level of male education has an obvious strong and lasting negative effect on women's participation rates, and seems to be the core factor behind the overall low rates among females (see Klasen and Pieters 2015; Afridi et al. 2016). In contrast, findings from Vietnam show that this negative effect may decline and almost vanish as an economy grows, while it has apparently had no effect in Sri Lanka (see Klasen 2019; Seneviratne 2019).

Notably, the sectoral distribution of working women differs by education level: it is significantly wider among lesser-educated women. This indicates that those who are more qualified may have more difficulty finding a job when labour markets in white-collar public services (70–80% of secondary-educated working women are segregated in this sector on average across countries) are competitive or not yet developed, since social norms mostly bar entrance to other sectors.

Employment of educated women in particular is often viewed as a 'failure' of the male household head to secure the living of his family. India is a country where these beliefs take full effect (see Klasen and Pieters 2015). If there are labour market bottlenecks, scarce jobs should be given to men—this is still a widespread opinion in the developing world, as documented in the World Value Survey (see World Bank 2011) affecting women's chances in the public sector.

By contrast, lower-educated women are represented in white collar services as well as domestic services and manufacturing—the survival needs of poorer households widely prevail over the social stigma against working women. Policies should open up public debate about existing stigmas, and learn from the example of regions such as the Middle East and South Asia where such discussion takes place.

Economic growth matters

Limited employment opportunities for educated women in many developing regions do not keep up with the rising potential of this group. New cohorts of working women are better educated than ever, which is an asset for LICs that should not be wasted. Constraining their employment to white-collar services in the public sectors leads to stagnating or even falling participation rates and a loss of human capital. To avoid this, employment opportunities need to be broadened.

The supply of educated women often surpasses the demand growth in white-collar sectors of LICs. At the same time, many developing societies experience a stronger growth rate of a better-educated female labour force in relation to the overall growth of the working-age population. This feature collides with the previously mentioned social stigma against working women, and leads to substantial economic inefficiencies. Economic growth cannot 'switch off' prevalent stigma but will contribute to better-functioning labour markets and a better allocation of human capital resources. While this will need long-term efforts, short- and mid-term strategies to enhance female labour market participation are also needed to help educated women find appropriate jobs.

Klasen (2019) proposed a twofold strategy for developing countries' governments, both needing affirmative action in favour of women:

1. **Growing sectors of the economy should be opened systematically for educated women.** Learning from East and South Asia, but also from the Middle East and North Africa, other countries could also utilize the widespread growth of their labour-intensive and export-orientated manufacturing sectors to increase employment of educated women.
2. **Make a virtue out of necessity and lift the glass ceiling in white-collar services like education, public service, and health that prevents educated women from entering higher and senior positions.** If the sector develops in this direction, segregation will not diminish but better job prospects for women will emerge, even in segments traditionally dominated by men (for example university professors, lawyers, medical doctors). In the recent past, Latin America has found some success on this road, whereas South Asia and the Middle East—along with the prevalent norms—have so far missed this opportunity. Both strategies should be accompanied by clear incentives for secondary earners' employment (for example tax reforms) and targeted programmes for women's empowerment.

8.1.2 Globalization and the Gender Gap

To achieve gender equality and empower all women and girls is Goal 5 of the United Nations Sustainable Development Goals (UN SDGs). Despite some positive trends, women still lag far behind men in important social and economic aspects, while some trends are even negative, as shown above. Most existing research has studied the topic from a country or cross-country perspective, in a closed-economy setting. Analyses that pay attention to the potential effects of globalization and international trade on economic and well-being outcomes for women in developing regions are still scarce.

A research project supported by GLM|LIC aims to contribute to this important field of research, by highlighting the effect of open markets on the probability of rising employment and wages of women, as well as the impact on fertility. The study by Do, Levchenko, and Raddatz (2016) started with the central hypothesis that, given the extremely variable shares of female workers in a country's industries, the effect of globalization on women will depend on whether trade openness results in a comparative advantage in sectors where women are strongly represented. If it does, then, women's wages and labour force participation rates should rise while fertility should fall in response to increased openness in trade. By contrast, trade and export focused on male-dominated sectors should have the opposite effect. In other words, globalization will not generate a clear single impact on the gender gap; instead its direction and magnitude will depend on a country's specific comparative advantage in international trade.

The study introduced a theoretical model and provided empirical evidence based on export data on the industry level for sixty-one manufacturing sectors in 145 developing and developed countries, over a period of fifty years. The data reveal stunning variation in the female worker share in developing countries, ranging from under 10% in some heavy industries to 60–70% in textile and apparel industries.

These data were combined with information on the countries' export shares to capture the degree of comparative advantage in female-intensive sectors, and to understand whether fertility reacts to these globalization effects. To rule out reverse causality (low-fertility countries exporting in female-dominated sectors for other reasons), the study controlled for exogenous geographical factors, the prevalence of child labour, educational patterns, and other factors.

Using this comprehensive approach, the analysis concluded that **countries with a trade focus on female-intensive sectors do indeed exhibit substantially lower fertility, by up to 20%** across countries. While this effect is significant, the same does not apply for female labour supply responses to trade openness. Instead, the authors' findings show that the positive labour market participation effect is mostly limited to countries with higher fertility rates and lower levels of income and female education. As falling fertility offers chances to invest time in education and occupations, the restrictions and societal barriers mentioned above come into effect once more.

One lesson from Do, Levchenko, and Raddatz (2016) should nonetheless be kept in mind by decision makers: **countries engaged in more technological— and thus more male-based—trade, should not rely on positive globalization outcomes to empower women. International trade is no remedy for policy inactivity in this respect,** as these countries will need initiatives on the issue in other fields to avoid overly slow progress in women's empowerment and thus a loss of the opportunity demographic changes and its dividends have brought about. **One** short- and mid-term option could be to better promote those sectors with a high share of female workers. Whereas in the long run, education efforts and affirmative policies should systematically open up the highly traded sectors for female employment.

8.2 The Influence of Social Transfers and Migrant Remittances on Women's Labour Supply

Given the low and stagnant labour force participation rates of women in many developing countries, the impact of social transfers to poor households on women's labour supply behaviour is a highly relevant field for policy and research. From a theoretical perspective (valid for developed societies as well), social transfers could either lower the probability of female employment by establishing an unconditional basic income, or stimulate labour supply, if correctly targeted and dimensioned so that risks and costs associated with work (for example childcare, schooling costs) are covered.

In most cases, nationwide anti-poverty and other social transfers in developing countries are not gender based. Hence, research that aims to inform policy in the field of women's empowerment needs to separate the specific outcomes of existing social transfer programmes on female labour supply, and to address the uneven gender distribution of care responsibilities within families that potentially prevent women from entering the labour force, even if social transfers would enable them to do so. This research is complex and only just starting with respect to developing countries. Programmes with a maternalistic orientation hence deserve the full attention of economic research.

For this reason, GLM|LIC supported a study on the impact of the social transfer system of Kyrgyzstan on women's labour supply (Barrientos and Kudebayeva 2018). Besides the pension, early retirement, and disability insurance systems and other standard social transfer provisions, which in general do not impact labour supply decisions of direct beneficiaries (but may influence the supply behaviour of—female—dependents or co-residents), the Kyrgyz set of additional social assistance mainly focuses on mothers. The so-called Monthly Benefit for Families in Poverty (MBPF) not only covers the distance between children's actual per capita income and a minimum income threshold set by the government; it also includes one-time maternity payments and additional monthly maternity benefits for eighteen months, thus targeting the poorest households in the country.

The transfer level accordingly depends on the number and age of children— that is, deciding to work may result in a substantial transfer reduction. The special significance of this programme stems not least from the fact that the Kyrgyz labour force working informally has risen sharply during the transition from socialism.

Informality rates are calculated to be above 50% in urban areas and beyond 90% in rural environments (data as of 2012 reported in Schwegler-Rohmeis, Mummert, and Jarck 2013). This further enhances the relevance of the MBPF and its focus on the poorest households. Though, relative to household incomes, mean transfer values do not seem large, with social transfers providing less than 20% of poor families' income in Kyrgyzstan.

Using data from the Life in Kyrgyzstan survey as well as cross-section data, the study found rather low labour force participation rates for working-age women, mostly under 50% in recent years (2010–13). According to the survey, housework and childcare were the core reasons for not being in the labour force. Against this background, the authors evaluated whether the receipt of social transfers affected the labour supply decisions of females in a positive or negative direction.

The results suggest that receiving social insurance or assistance transfers may matter for labour supply; among working age women it is associated with a lower probability of participating in the labour market, reduced working hours, and a marginally rising probability of giving birth to the next child earlier. Remarkably, these effects seem larger for insurance transfers than for additional social assistance like the MBPF. Causality remains unclear, however; negative responses to MBPF transfers in terms of labour supply could either be a direct reaction to the transfer or result from the targeting of the programme itself.

Besides highlighting the need to better adapt social security systems to the needs and changing conditions of transition economies, the findings rebut the assumption that social assistance cash transfers to poor families with children pose a high risk of causing low female labour force participation rates. However, to make the reverse argument would be wrong: **in the case of Kyrgyzstan at least, social assistance cash targeted at working-age women apparently fails to stimulate the employment of women in low-income households, but instead narrows birth spacing (the gap between pregnancies).**

These results are certainly disappointing, in the sense that even tailored social assistance programmes provide no guarantee of strengthening the position of women in the labour market. One possible explanation may be that policies in transition economies face specific challenges with respect to tailoring their social security systems to changed needs, and that a high level of economic uncertainty may particularly influence women's labour supply decisions when labour markets are partly still disrupted. The study by and large confirmed the existing literature's ambiguous findings on the effect of social assistance programmes on the labour market activities of adult women.

From a theoretical perspective, Doepke and Tertilt (2019) added an important argument that needs to be further studied: different concurrent policies targeted at women may have counteracting effects. For example, while targeting transfers explicitly at women may at first stage have a positive effect, this impact may be interfered with by other policies aiming at women's labour market attachment, in that for example a shrinking wage gap could limit or deter the effect of social transfers to women. Research in this direction certainly needs to be intensified.

That anti-poverty provisions may work more successfully under different conditions has been shown, for example, in Barrientos and Villa (2015). Here the authors examined the labour market outcomes of a conditional cash transfer programme targeted at families in poverty (Familias en Acción) in Colombia (2007–10) and identified significantly positive effects for women. Despite the overall marginal effect on the aggregate labour supply of males and females, analysing by gender suggests that the cash transfer positively affected formal women's employment and has a strong effect on the female-dominated households with single adults. Overall, households seemed to respond to anti-poverty transfers by reallocating the productive resources of the household, which may benefit women's longer-term employment prospects, in particular.

In the absence of functioning social insurance systems, migrant remittances may replace public transfers—and have similar effects on the likelihood of women in low-income countries staying employed or entering the labour force, since migration is usually male-dominated. Remittances may also complement social insurance benefits and thus reinforce their effects.

The existing literature on these effects largely suggests that women staying behind work less outside the household when they receive additional income via remittances. This enables them to reduce their own paid work or stay at home, which is even more likely when strict social norms are against women working. Many studies have found that women increase unpaid but income-generating work to substitute the migrant's work (for example maintaining farms and other household businesses) thus increasing their labour force participation. Other studies have revealed that incomes from remittances are directed to savings, consumption, or investments into the education of family members (see the brief literature survey provided by Kan and Aytimur (2019)).

8.2.1 The Impact of Migration on Women Staying Behind

The effects of migration and remittances on female labour force participation rates are particularly relevant in poor countries with a high share of labour emigrants and social norms affecting the labour market attachment of women staying behind. In a project supported by GLM|LIC, Kan and Aytimur (2019) provided a case study for Tajikistan where roughly 25% of all households are affected by emigration, while traditional societal structures and gender roles lead to rather low employment rates and education levels of females. The country is among the poorest worldwide with over 30% of its population living below the national poverty line, almost 75% living in rural areas with a significant lack of employment prospects, and a very high unemployment rate of about 30% (numbers for 2016,

Kan and Aytimur 2019). Migrant households belong to the poorest in the country, sending mostly low-skilled workers to Russia. Notably, roughly 25% of families staying behind do not receive any remittances (see OSCE 2012).

The study exploited a three-wave panel of representative household survey data for 2007, 2009, and 2011, and controlled for unobserved factors that could simultaneously affect women's decision to participate in the labour market, as well as for time-variant and time-invariant variables. Challenging the existing literature, Kan and Aytimur (2019) found no significant effect of migration and remittances on female labour force participation in the context of Tajikistan. According to the analysis, the country's characteristics neutralize the effects on consumption and labour participation of increased income (income effects) through remittances that have been identified by a large body of literature as the general cause of falling female participation rates in the context of migration. Although lacking prospects of paid employment, and with social norms mostly preventing women from entering the labour market or expanding any paid employment, remittance effects do not lead them to reduce their work hours.

Kan and Aytimur (2019) synthesized four main channels of muting or neutralizing the income effects of remittances that would usually decrease female labour force participation rates:

1. A shortage of household labour increases the 'shadow wage' of women working in the household.
2. A lack of employment opportunities outside the home combined with financial constraints forces women staying behind to work at home as a substitute for male migrants' work, as 'unpaid' workers.
3. High costs of migrating mean the poorest households need to work—at least in the early phase of migration—until they receive remittances.
4. The absence of any remittances increases the pressure on women to work.

While the income effect of remittances on women's labour force participation is apparently muted in the case of Tajikistan, the substitution of unpaid labour by paid labour (substitution effect) is also not straightforward, but is instead hampered by cultural norms and family structures. Furthermore and interestingly, households with farms as the main source of income increase female labour force participation independently of migrant status, by 10.8 work hours per week according to Kan and Aytimur (2019). This may be due to women being disproportionally relegated to farm work given widespread discrimination, role norms, and the better compatibility of agricultural household work with childcare (see Short et al. 2002).

In this respect the findings in Kan and Aytimur (2019) fit results from earlier studies, which at first sight provided an opposite assessment of the impact of male migration and remittances in low-income regions. For instance, Lokshin and Glin-skaya (2009) studied the effect of male migration on the employment patterns of women in Nepal, showing that female participation rates were partly negatively affected but that the overall picture remains ambiguous; depending on the house-hold characteristics and the degree of substitutability of male and female tasks before migration, the absence of the male migrant and remittances could either decrease or increase women's productive work in the household. While a decreas-ing effect is most likely for landless and urban households, those households that own land and farms showed a weaker participation effect that could even turn pos-itive given the complementarities between males' and females' work in agricultural businesses.

Taken together, these results should give reason to policymakers in LICs to carefully reconsider their approach towards the issue of remittances, and the role of women staying behind in the labour market, to avoid lasting negative out-comes on women's economic prospects and the well-being of their families. Due to migration being mainly male-dominated, inefficient labour markets, a lack of ap-propriate jobs for women, restricted occupational mobility across sectors, and the underlying social stigma, there is a high risk of further expelling female workers out of the labour market and thus into economic dependence.

Existing substitution effects also hint at the need to develop the wage labour market, allowing women to at least partly replace male labour in rural areas and use remittances to pay for education. Even in the event of a rising participation rate, undesired socio-economic effects may occur with regard to extended unpaid fam-ily work, as Kan and Aytimur (2019) rightly noted. These risks need to be tackled by policies aiming to avoid lasting negative well-being effects from male migration and to curb gender inequality.

8.3 Lessons from Training Programmes Targeted Towards Women

Gender inequality in low-income countries is a topic that requires assorted policy activities, given the complexity of discrimination, social stigmatization, and other barriers that cause women to lag behind men. **To shatter the 'unholy alliance' of educational deficits, restrictions barring access to labour markets, repressive social structures and norms in favour of economically inactive women, and sex-ual oppression, will take perseverance. The strong increase in youth population in many developing countries gives policymakers every reason to be concerned about this generation's prospects—and young women's opportunities in partic-ular**. Multifaceted action will be needed, and acceptance of substantial uncertainty about which measures will be sustainable in the end.

Gender-independent interventions at a very early stage of life may generate sub-stantial long-term benefits for women in their teen and adult years (see Anderson

2008). Targeted training programmes that address girls' schooling and life skills, women's vocational training, business-orientated skills, or financial constraints, seem to be a viable road towards an increase in female labour force attachment and more equal opportunities. Yet a growing literature in this field has provided mixed evidence on the effectiveness of these interventions. GLM|LIC research aims to enrich our view of which training strategies are the most promising.

A fundamental contribution to the economics of 'women's empowerment in action' has been provided by Bandiera et al. (2020). The study focused on a key aspect of female inequality: the vicious circle between high (and early) fertility of young women and persistent low labour force participation. Using the example of a training programme in Uganda (Empowerment and Livelihood for Adolescents— ELA), implemented by the non-government organization BRAC Uganda), that offers a combination of vocational and life skills to empower adolescent girls, the authors convincingly showed that such interventions may prove very efficient and cost effective under certain circumstances.

The ELA programme started in Bangladesh but has been transferred to a number of other LICs. In the case of Uganda, it operates in a country where 60% of the population are under 20 years old. It runs so-called 'development clubs' in local meeting places, led by selected female mentors close in age to the target group of girls aged 14–20 enrolled in school.

The clubs (more than 1,200) do not only offer training but also serve as a platform for recreational group activities, and a safe place for informal exchange. Participation in a two-year training period is voluntary. Qualified professionals engage in vocational training modules that react flexibly to local economic demand and the participants' level of education. Courses on income-generating activities in small own-businesses (for example tailoring, computing, agriculture, small trades) are accompanied by modules that provide financial literacy, budgeting, and accounting skills. The life skills courses are delivered by mentors or BRAC staff, and contain information on sexual health and family planning as well as negotiation and management skills, or basic legal knowledge on women's issues. In contrast to many existing training programmes, ELA operates outside of school, thus offering a more open learning environment. Furthermore, the programme has a comparatively long term of two years, instead of a few weeks or months (as in most comparable programmes).

Using randomized control trial methods, Bandiera et al. (2020) selected one hundred communities as treatment group that opened an ELA club in 2008, and fifty communities as controls without access to ELA training. Participating women were observed in two-year intervals over a period of four years, to capture the immediate course impact and longer-term effects. A first survey was conducted among almost 4,000 ELA participants and 2,000 individuals in the control groups at the beginning of the programme. The second survey showed a tracking rate of over 80%, while about 60% responded in the third survey after four years.

The ELA club participation rate until the end of the two-year training period was above 20% and did not drop afterwards, even in the absence of further training offers. About 50% attended at least one club meeting per week during the entire two-year period. More than half of all participants passed the vocational skills training, and 85% took part in the life skills courses. Half of the women attended both training modules, 33% participated in the life skills training only, while 1% took part in vocational training only. These numbers reveal the high acceptance of the programme among participating girls and women.

Against this promising background, the rather positive findings of Bandiera et al. (2020) do not come as a surprise, though the range of effects is impressive. Four years after the programme was initiated, participating female adolescents were 48% more likely to be economically active and generate income, mostly by engaging in self-employment. At the same time life skills training reduced teen pregnancies by 34% and early marriage or cohabitation by 62%.

Furthermore, the women widely reported as now aspiring to a clearly later age of marriage and first childbirth, while also reporting a strong decline in sex against their will. These results more than indicate that **extended, voluntary training in business and life skills may be very efficient in empowering women and creating lasting effects**. With regards to cost efficiency, the study calculates rather low programme per capita costs—for example, related to unconditional cash transfers—and notes the easy scalability of ELA.

The outcomes of the ELA programme in Uganda show that it is possible to transfer and amend existing programmes that have proven successful in different cultural and regional settings (South Asia vs. sub-Saharan Africa) into another environment. More importantly, they underline that **there are means to overcome the vicious circle of a lack of labour market opportunities leading to lower education efforts of young women and early family formation. Additional demand-orientated education and a new awareness of fertility decisions, enhanced by targeted education, may pave the way to improving the socio-economic prospects and self-confidence of a promising generation of young women**. However, there is still much room for research on the effects of such programmes on the attitudes of (young) men and the further weight and acceptance of social stigma against working women.

A recent GLM|LIC study is closely related to this instructive research. Brudevold-Newman et al. (2017) compared two approaches that aimed to increase entrepreneurship among young women at the age of 18–19 in Kenya's capital Nairobi through:

(1) an unconditional cash grant without any accompanying support.
(2) a short-term 'microfranchising' programme including business as well as basic life skills training, franchise-specific vocational training, start-up physical capital, and mentoring.

Given the high probability that only a minority of youth cohorts entering the labour force will find paid employment in sub-Saharan Africa, studies that provide such a kind of comparative analysis are highly welcome and illustrative. As the analysis shows, **both interventions resulted in significant short- and medium-term income effects, but this positive impact did not last longer than a year after the programme, dissipating in the second year after treatment.** This lack of lasting impacts on income suggests that **enhancing self-employment may not be a sustainable strategy for addressing young women's disadvantages and underemployment in the labour markets of developing countries.**

To evaluate the outcomes of the cash programme and the microfranchise training, the authors conducted a randomized controlled trial. Potential participants living in one of Nairobi's poorest neighbourhoods could apply for business training (the cash grant programme was not announced in advance) before being randomly assigned to one of the three groups (cash grant, microfranchise, and control). Two surveys of the participants were conducted—the first after seven to ten months and the second fourteen to twenty-two months after the end of the intervention.

Notably, over 40% of all participating young women were mothers already, with 16% married or cohabitating. The education level was low, with only about 40% having completed secondary education; roughly 35% had some earlier experience with vocational training. Over 54% of the sample had been involved in income-generating activities in the past, but only around 15% were generating income when both programmes started. On the other hand, the women spent a median twenty-one hours of unpaid housework at baseline. Only around 9% of the sample reported having a bank account.

The microfranchise treatment was designed by the International Rescue Committee (IRC) and jointly implemented with local organizations. Three main differences distinguish it from the ELA programme studied by Bandiera et al. (2020): it covered only a rather short period (ten weeks at most, with mentoring as a follow-up); it focused strictly on two specific franchise business models; and it contained a starter package of physical capital to start the microfranchise. Hence the two programmes followed completely different strategies.

In partnership with two Kenyan businesses, the franchise programme offered the participants the chance to self-employ either as a hairdresser or with a food cart franchise. After two weeks of general training courses, including modules on the franchise models, the participants were matched with their chosen franchise partner who took over to complete the training. If assigned to the hairdresser franchise, women completed further six weeks of classroom training and a two-week internship in a salon, and then received start-up kits.

Those women assigned to the food cart franchise only took part in a one-day event introducing the brand's products and preparation methods, before they were given a mobile cart, logo-branded equipment, and an initial stock of food.

Mentoring included visits to the business every few weeks, as well as help with financial management or contacting the franchise partners. The cash grant treatment was organized in a very simple way to contrast sharply with the 'competing' franchise treatment: randomly assigned women were informed that a one-off payment of 20,000 Kenyan shillings (239 USD at the exchange rate at that time) was unconditional and to be paid back independently from how the grant was used. In relation to the median savings of all participants of below 9 USD, this cash grant represented a very substantial boost to income.

The labour market outcomes of the cash transfer and microfranchise treatments can be summarized as follows. After seven to ten months, both programmes had a positive and significant effect on the likelihood of being self-employed, which increased by around 10 percentage points for the franchise and the grant treatments. The cash grant led to a 38% increase in aggregate work hours, whereas the franchise approach did not significantly affect the total number of hours worked. Self-employment hours were increased substantially by both treatments— an additional 4.1 hours per week in the franchise treatment and 7.6 in the grant treatment—while a parallel decline in hours of paid work was insignificant according to the study.

The increases in income from the treatments are quite impressive at first sight; they range from a 30% (1.6 USD per week) increase—compared to the mean income of the control group—for the franchise treatment to 56% (3.2 USD) for the grant treatment. These increases in income stem from the newly established self-employment and are not offset by any significant loss of income from paid work. The figures highlight the encouraging short-term effect of both treatments in enabling young women to engage in self-employment and benefit from large income increases.

However, the picture changes almost completely fourteen to twenty-two months after treatment. By the time of the final survey, the impacts on work hours and income gains had entirely disappeared for both treatments. At this time, neither the microfranchise approach nor the grant treatment can boast any positive labour supply effect relative to the control group. The training component of the franchise approach seemingly did not help to establish a sufficient degree of productivity to ensure profitable self-employment in the long run. What remained is a lasting effect on occupational choice, as both programmes resulted in a persistently higher likelihood of self-employment (around 12 percentage points compared to the control group).

These rather disappointing results raise the question of whether the programmes may have had longer-term impacts on other labour market outcomes with regards to, for example, expenditures, living conditions, time use, savings, household assets, self-confidence, and empowerment. The study's answer is as straightforward as it is disillusioning: there is hardly any evidence indicating the existence of any such long-term impacts. The income effect of the interventions disappears soon, and no permanent welfare effect replaces it later on. Even the assessment of the programme's cost efficiency does not brighten the picture.

Cash grants seem to be a more cost-efficient way of increasing entrepreneurship in the context of a large poverty-stricken urban area. The franchise model achieves lower temporary gains in income at higher costs, in comparison to the simple grant approach that at least appears to stimulate sustainable investments instead of consumption only. In summary, however, benefits of both treatments do not exceed the accompanying costs. **The absence of long-lasting impacts on income and labour supply suggests that self-employment may not be the solution to high underemployment of female youth in poor and competitive urban regions.**

Brudevold-Newman et al. (2017) confirmed findings of other studies in the field (see, for example, Haushofer and Shapiro 2016) that credit constraints should not be viewed as the main barrier to sustainable self-employment of women (and men) in low-income settings. Savings constraints show a stronger impact on the observed outcomes, which may be traced back to the limited access of the disadvantaged—poor women in particular—to savings technologies (see Dupas and Robinson 2013a, 2013b). Given that Brudevold-Newman et al. (2017) did not find any evidence that women used the cash grant for additional consumption or decreasing labour supply, cash transfer programmes may have indirect positive effects. Providing formal or informal safe methods to store money for later investment would be an important feature in the context of strengthening the economic position of women, and could thus justify limited one-off cash transfers to this highly vulnerable target group.

8.4 Women's Empowerment and Employment

Supported by GLM|LIC, Field et al. (2017) continued from this point with a comprehensive analysis of whether strengthening women's financial control and bargaining power, along with better targeting of benefits payments, could boost female labour supply in India by countering persistent social constraints. Given that India is among the countries with the lowest labour force participation rates of women worldwide (see Fletcher, Pande, and Moore 2018), research to further decode the barriers in place is much needed. The main result highlighted by the study is that linking low-skilled women's labour income to their own bank accounts, and providing basic financial training, may substantially increase female labour market activities.

The study starts by depicting female and male attitudes to women's work and mobility, revealing the extent of the barriers women face in numerous low-income countries—and notably in patriarchal societies as in India. Based on data from the

World Values Survey (2010–2014) and figures on female labour force participation reported by the International Labour Organization (ILO), the authors developed an index of support for female work among women and men. This index illustrates the persistence of social norms and their different global levels, where a higher value indicates more support for female labour (see Figure 8.4 and its notes for a detailed description of the index). Not surprisingly, participation rates of women are higher when both genders support an economically active role for women, while the gender gap in attitudes towards working women is highest where women hardly play an active role in the labour market—specifically in regions of the Middle East, in Pakistan, and in India.

Against this background, the analysis focuses on the federal Mahatma Gandhi National Rural Employment Guarantee Scheme (NREGS), a workfare programme that provides members of households in rural communities who work within the framework of the programme with a fixed minimum wage. Its level is below the income provided by cash-paid casual wage work, which is the most common labour besides unpaid household and agricultural activities for both genders in Indian rural regions. Though generally demand driven in the sense that individuals may apply and community authorities—'gram panchayat' (GP)—are obliged to find appropriate jobs for all of them, it is in practice widely supply-orientated with GPs planning work projects and looking for workers to take part in them—which does not necessarily cover all applicants. More than 55 million households in India are entitled by NREGS to take up minimum wage jobs for a maximum period of one hundred days per year (in practice covering some 80–95%). This makes NREGS one of the largest welfare programmes worldwide (see Subbarao et al. (2013) and Chapter 4 in this volume).

The programme has a rather clear gender component: it mandates equal wages, includes quotas for female participation (though over-reporting cannot be ruled out), and widens the job opportunities in rural communities, which is especially important for mobility-constrained women. Furthermore, the programme has been modified in terms of its wage payment procedures. Originally starting with cash payments, it began electronic payments to bank accounts in 2008, followed by a government decision in late 2012 to refrain from payments to one account for all working household members and instead prescribe individual accounts in an attempt to foster women's empowerment. Implementation of the latter strategy has been sluggish, though, and shows extreme regional differences, with the average share of wages paid to female-owned accounts ranging far beyond the 100% goal (see Field et al. 2017 for further details).

As shown by two earlier studies, the Indian public works programme has indeed managed to generate important effects from a gender perspective: NREGS design apparently managed to raise female participation rates and wages at a level that significantly increased total rates (see Azam 2012). Afridi, Mukhopadhyay,

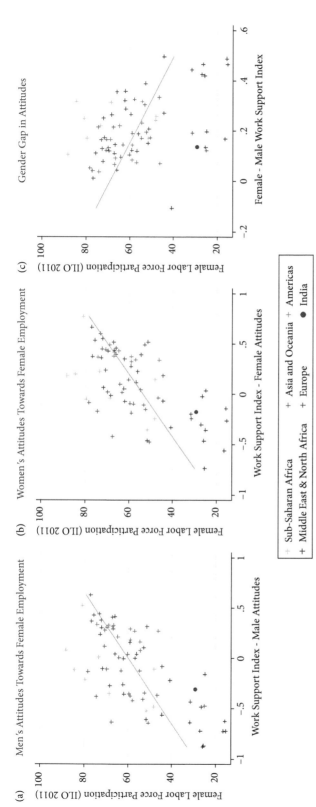

Fig. 8.4 Male and Female Attitudes towards Working Women and the Relation to Female Participation Rates

Notes: This work support index, developed by Field et al. (2017), uses data from 2010–14 World Values Surveys. The index aggregates a dummy variable equal to one if the respondent agrees that men should have more rights to jobs than women when jobs are scarce, a dummy variable equal to one if the respondent agrees that men make better political leaders than women, a dummy variable equal to one if the respondent agrees that men make better business executives than women, and a dummy variable equal to one if the respondent agrees that being a housewife is just as fulfilling as working for pay. These variables are standardized (pooling across countries and years) and then averaged by country. The index is then multiplied by −1; higher values correspond to more support for female work. Country-wide calculated averages by gender are correlated with data from the ILO's estimate of female labour force participation among women aged 15–64 in 2011.

Source: Field et al. (2017)

and Sahoo (2016) complemented this finding by showing a positive correlation of increased female NREGS participation and children's education outcomes.

To enrich this strand of the literature, Field et al. (2017) partnered with the northern Indian state of Madhya Pradesh and one main banking institution to further modify the standard provisions of NREGS in a large-scale experiment using RCT methods. Two regional particularities gave a broad scope for experimental design: the share of wages paid to women's bank accounts only reached 30% according to official statistics, while ongoing state-wide initiatives were about to expand the network of closely available banking kiosks offering cost-free accounts and secure authorization via fingerprint.

The experiment took place in 2014 and 2015 among households that had formerly worked for NREGS. A sample of 197 localities with functional local banking kiosks was randomly divided into control and treatment groups of 5,800 couples with no pre-existing female bank account. Actively participating women were on average 40 years old with only low education; roughly 90% reported illiteracy. The surveyed husbands reported four years of schooling on average, while 57% reported being literate. The study team first informed eligible women about the option of opening a free bank account, and in a second step helped with the bank account opening process at the local kiosk.

The treatment strategy included four interventions plus untreated controls:

1. 'Accounts Basic'. Participating women were advised and helped to open a new bank account at their community banking kiosk.
2. 'Accounts Plus'. After opening an individual bank account, eligible women participated in a short information session to learn more about the local bank, the functioning of their accounts, and the advantages of safe banking and savings.
3. 'Accounts Basic Linking'. The GPs in this treatment group were asked to update their NREGS data and redirect wage payments to women's new individual bank accounts, giving them direct access to the money they earned.
4. 'Accounts Plus Linking'. Women received the same basic financial information as 'Accounts Plus', while NREGS wages were paid into their new individual bank accounts.

This experimental design made it possible to distinguish between the effect of increasing women's access to banking and the effect of increasing control over their wages, while all household resources remained unchanged. Implementation of the treatments was later followed by a survey of all participating women, and their husbands, on the effects of the different treatments.

Building on this survey and an elaborated model of labour supply with social constraints, the study revealed remarkable findings:

1. Most importantly, **the combined treatment of bank account, linked to wage payment, along with basic financial information (Accounts Plus Linking), affected private sector employment in a remarkably positive way**. Six months after the intervention, female labour force participation was 12 percentage points higher while annual earnings in this sector increased 24%. Women reported roughly 60% higher bank balances. Since private sector wages are traditionally paid in cash, this trend cannot be explained by the introduction of bank accounts. Instead, control over earned income seemed to significantly increase bargaining power for the most vulnerable and dependent women. **In fact, the income gains were mostly seen for the women furthest away from the labour force and with husbands strongly opposed to their wives working**. Seemingly they find a way to stand up against social stigma and dependency if allowed some fundamental financial self-control.

2. **The Accounts Plus Linking treatment had a large positive effect on the take-up of additional NREGS minimum wage work. Fifteen months after the start of the intervention, participating women were 34% more likely to be engaged in the federal programme** compared to those women who received the bank account without the additional information package. At the same time, the average amount of NREGS payments received into the bank accounts during these fifteen months was relatively large (roughly 25% of their annual non-NREGS income sources) which rules out the possibility that women were enrolled in the programme only on a minor level. This finding further supports the hypothesis that participating women gained self-confidence.

3. These effects also translated into other improvements. **Surveyed women in this treatment group were more likely to be economically active outside the household** and make household purchases with their own money. They also reported higher levels of mobility compared to the control group, while there is no evidence that male economic activities declined. This impact does not seem to simply be due to men finding it increasingly difficult to take control of female earnings.

4. **Out of four treatments, only the most intensive was effective. Although offering bank accounts almost doubled the share of participating women with such accounts, this alone did not work**. Providing information courses but abandoning direct wage payments to women's accounts had no observable impact on female employment or earnings whatsoever. Likewise, directing wages to bank accounts without enabling low-educated women to understand, trust, and use them properly, proved a wrong strategy. To change behaviour, financial resources need to be put into the hands of women along with some financial literacy. Notably, the saving option of an own bank account was hardly activated by any programme participant, once

more showing that the ability to control own earned income is what matters most.

5. Conversely, this means that **norms preventing women from working, and thus keeping them at home, will continue in the absence of female financial empowerment and independence in male-dominated societies.**

6. The strongest effects were seen for women who had not previously been engaged in NREGS work, and those with husbands strictly opposed to women working. This contradicts traditional economic thinking that households' labour force participation decisions only react to wage levels and leisure preferences.

It should be noted that these results are rather short-term—the last survey so far was roughly half a year after the completion of the intervention. According to the study, however, administrative data from the workfare programme and the banking partners suggest the effects were sustainable. In summary, the findings illustrate that **social norms discouraging female economic activities may be overcome when women gain bargaining power based on some financial literacy and autonomy from men, and when active labour market policies have a gender focus.** That this approach is apparently successful even in an extremely male-focused society like India is a rather promising outcome of this GLM|LIC study. Future research should add evidence on the effects on altering household bargaining power and work attitudes. It remains to be seen (and studied) whether policies that encourage female labour force participation can offer a means to not only influence but also directly alter social barriers that constrain women on the road to greater equality.

In this respect, a recent study by Almås et al. (2018) deserves special mention as it adds interesting results from a laboratory experiment. To capture the intensity of women's willingness to receive cash transfers instead of their spouses, the participants in the experiment could take their own decision whether to receive a full cash payment to be transferred to their husbands or to accept a lower amount in order to receive payment themselves. By varying the cash reduction in case the women preferred to have control over the money, and by offering a rise of the cash if paid to men, to control for behavioural change, the study revealed women's trade-off between household income and empowerment.

According to the results (given for Macedonia), disadvantaged women on average showed a clear willingness to accept a loss of household money to gain more financial—and thus bargaining—power. This willingness was lower, though, if the women had already been part of a public transfer programme offering them a cash grant conditional on secondary school attendance of their children. These experimental findings provide an important supplement to survey- and randomized trial-based studies and clearly indicate that financial control is a crucial means of empowering women in the developing world.

It should be noted, though, that effective empowerment will also require concerted action in many other fields. **Hardly any aspect of development policy is as multifaceted, and to a certain extent so hard to predict, as the improvement of female living and economic conditions. Depending on the country context, to further empower women in developing countries may need action on a very basic level.**

8.4.1 Social Norms even Affect Women's Mobility

Social norms do not only directly prevent labour market entrance for many women, but also restrict women's mobility in many regions. In South Asian countries such as India or Pakistan, serious safety concerns add to the prevalence of these norms, preventing independent female mobility outside the household and use of public transport in urban areas. This reinforces the dependence on male assistance, even for active women whose ability to attend their jobs or training facilities is not in their own hands. Policies need to counteract this issue efficiently, since mobility is a decisive prerequisite to join the labour and education markets, and thus escape a trap of poverty, dependence, and incapacitation.

In fact, gendered transport has become a policy issue in countries such as Pakistan (see UN Women Pakistan 2018) and India (see Women in Cities International 2011 on the Delhi Gender Inclusive Cities Programme), as well as in international development aid debate (see for example Kunieda and Gauthier 2007). Various projects at the local level aim to address this issue in these countries. Thorough research on existing interventions and their impact on women's equal opportunities is still lacking, though.

Does the road to empowerment need the scaling up of public transport initiatives tailored to women's needs? To find an answer to this question an ongoing research project supported by GLM|LIC explores the impact of transportation initiatives for women in Pakistan (see Sajjad et al. 2018 for early results). A randomized control trial will allow an evaluation of the impact of different transport-to-work modes on female employment and earnings outcomes and inform a cost–benefit analysis of alternative transport options.

According to a demand assessment survey, women in Lahore, the second largest city in Pakistan, are 30% more likely in principle to use public transportation than men, since social norms exclude independent use of motorbikes or bicycles. Of female respondents, 25% stated that access to safe and reliable transport would increase their chances in the labour market. At the same time, while 70% of male survey respondents reported actually discouraging female family members from using public transport, almost 90% claimed they would approve of female household members using women-only transport (see Figure 8.5).

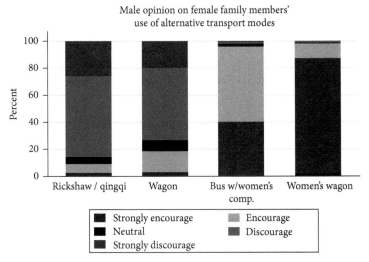

Fig. 8.5 Male Opinion on Female Family Members' Use of Alternative Transport Modes in Pakistan

Note: Authors' calculations based on a demand assessment survey of 1,000 households in Lahore, Pakistan.
Source: Sajjad et al. (2018)

Despite policy efforts in Lahore (and other urban areas) to facilitate women's travel—for example by 'pink buses' or separate vehicle compartments for women—access is still rather limited, as are financial and infrastructure resources. Thus, the underlying problems of inefficient scheduling and exposure of women to harassment prevail. These massive constraints may result in women giving up job opportunities or even leaving the labour force. Surveys show women have a strong interest in improved public transportation and expect to be better protected in terms of shorter, predictable wait times and the avoidance of overcrowded vehicles through either tighter schedule or women-only public transport (see UN Women Pakistan 2018).

Another GLM|LIC project provides evidence on the extent to which travel that requires a woman to move outside her village could hamper her ability for skill acquisition (Cheema et al. 2020). In the context of an RCT conducted with a large and highly subsidized skills development programme in rural Pakistan, the researchers show that setting up a training centre in woman's village makes her two to three times more likely to enrol and complete a skills development course compared to women who have to travel an average distance of just a few kilometres.

Strikingly, the authors document that half of the access difference between in-village and out-of-village is generated simply by crossing the village boundary. This strong boundary effect cannot be reconciled with any standard economic or time opportunity costs, as there is no official village border one has to wait to cross, nor any toll paid at entry or exit, suggesting that it is likely due to non-economic/social costs women encounter when temporarily leaving their village.

Cheema et al. (2020) exogenously vary the amount of stipend to quantify monetary terms for both the boundary and per-kilometre travelled effects. They compare the increase in take-up rates induced by additional stipend with the distance penalties and provide an equivalence between the penalties and the stipend. Using these estimates, the study finds that one would need to receive a monthly stipend equivalent to about half of monthly household expenditure to merely overcome the boundary effect.

Before the start of the programme, Cheema et al. (2020) used focus groups to identify the following key household concerns regarding attending courses outside their villages: limited information, household and community-level barriers, a nd perceived safety concerns. This enabled them to investigate the role of these concerns using additional design variations: (1) more intense course dis-semination to address informational gaps and trainee/household concerns, (2) community engagement to discuss societal concerns, and (3) group transport to address perceived safety and security. The authors find little impact of the first two interventions but a strong effect of offering group transport: half to two-thirds of the boundary effect can be compensated for by offering women group transport from their own village to the training centre outside of their village.

Cheema et al. (2020) further show the boundary effect is due to social percep-tions that constrain women's agency and mobility: it is lower for women who enjoy more influence over domestic affairs, have fewer dependents, higher social status, and are from more ethnically diverse communities. This suggests that the access barrier is less likely due to real economic or even (real) safety considerations, but instead arises from women's lack of agency within their households and concerns about perceived 'status loss' because of their leaving and potentially being exposed to outside influences.

The findings of Cheema et al. (2020) suggest that while changing conserva-tive norms could take time, working within these norms by allaying the concerns behind them may offer a promising and constructive initial direction towards improving women's access to services. In subsequent work, the authors plan to investigate whether doing so ultimately changes these norms in the longer term. Further G^{2}LM|LIC research will scrutinize the impact of tailored transporta-tion on women's empowerment. Nonetheless, transport separation should be viewed as an intermediate 'solution' only. Gendered transport will hardly offer a long-term perspective as it reinforces stigmatization effects. In the long term, governments need to focus even more on creating awareness and updating social norms, along with extending public transport, to tackle gender inequality in mobility.

Overall, policies aiming to empower women will certainly need a shift of paradigms, from a deficits-based to a rights-based approach, but this will be a long-term endeavour needing strong societal support. Moving the role of women and other disadvantaged groups from that of supplicants to drivers of more equal opportunities will also require better political representation.

Key Takeaways from this Chapter

- High youth unemployment, early marriage, and childbearing limit women's human capital investments and reinforce dependence on men.
- Policies to empower women create more equal opportunities but may also have indirect negative economic effects, for example on wage levels and childcare time.
- Due in part to historical gender norms, female labour market participation does not necessarily increase with lower fertility and improved education.
- While low education forces women into the labour market to avoid poverty, medium education makes home and care work more affordable.
- Government policies should systematically open growing sectors of the economy to educated women and lift the glass ceiling in white-collar services.
- Countries with a trade focus on male-dominated sectors especially need affirmative policies and should not rely on positive globalization outcomes to empower women.
- Rising income of poor households through social transfers or migrant remittances does not seem to substantially affect female labour supply.
- Voluntary training in business and life skills can be a cost-efficient way to enhance women's economic activity.
- Programmes to promote self-employment have failed to improve women's income and labour supply in the long term.
- Gaining bargaining power based on some financial literacy and more autonomy from men can help women overcome social norms discouraging their economic activity.

References

Afridi, F., Dinkelman, T., and Mahajan, K., 2018. Why Are Fewer Married Women Joining the Work Force in Rural India? A Decomposition Analysis over Two Decades. *Journal of Population Economics*, 31: 783–818.

Afridi, F., Mukhopadhyay, A., and Sahoo, S., 2016. Female Labor Force Participation and Child Education in India: Evidence from the National Rural Employment Guarantee Scheme. *IZA Journal of Labor and Development*, 5(7).

Alesina, A., Giuliano, P., and Nunn, N., 2013. On the Origins of Gender Roles: Women and the Plough. *Quarterly Journal of Economics*, 128: 469–530.

Almås, I., Armand, A., Attanasio, O., and Carneiro, P., 2018. Measuring and Changing Control: Women's Empowerment and Targeted Transfers. *Economic Journal*, 128(612): 609–39.

Anderson. M., 2008. Multiple Inference and Gender Differences in the Effects of Early Intervention: A Reevaluation of the Abecedarian, Perry Preschool, and Early Training Projects. *Journal of the American Statistical Association*, 103(484): 1481–95.

Azam, M., 2012. The Impact of Indian Job Guarantee Scheme on Labor Market Outcomes: Evidence from a Natural Experiment. IZA Discussion Paper No. 6548.

Bandiera, O., Buehren, N., Burgess, R., Goldstein, M., Gulesci, S., Rasul, I., and Sulaiman, M., 2018. Women's Empowerment in Action: Evidence from a Randomized Control Trial in Africa. CEPR Discussion Paper No. 13386.

Bandiera, O., Buehren, N., Burgess, R., Goldstein, M., Gulesci, S., Rasul, I., and Sulaiman, M., 2020. Women's Empowerment in Action: Evidence from a Randomized Control Trial in Africa. *American Economic Journal: Applied Economics*, 12: 210–59.

Barrientos, A., and Kudebayeva, A., 2018. Social Transfers and Women's Labour Supply in Kyrgyzstan. GLM|LIC Working Paper No. 41.

Barrientos, A., and Villa, J. M., 2015. Antipoverty Transfers and Labour Market Outcomes: Regression Discontinuity Design Findings. *The Journal of Development Studies*, 51: 1224–40.

Bhalotra, S., and Umaña-Aponte, M., 2010. The Dynamics of Women's Labour Supply in Developing Countries. IZA Discussion Paper No. 4879.

Brudevold-Newman, A., Honorati, M., Jakiela, P., and Ozier, O., 2017. A Firm of One's Own: Experimental Evidence on Credit Constraints and Occupational Choice. GLM|LIC Working Paper No. 33.

Cheema, A., Khwaja, A. I., Naseer, M. F., and Shapiro, J. N., 2020. Glass Walls: Experimental Evidence on Access Constraints Faced by Women. Working Paper. Available from: https://scholar.princeton.edu/sites/default/files/jns/files/ckns_glass_walls_2020-10-08.pdf.

Do, Q.-T., Levchenko, A. A., and Raddatz, C., 2016. Comparative Advantage, International Trade, and Fertility. *Journal of Development Economics*, 119: 48–66.

Doepke, M., and Tertilt, M., 2019. Does Female Empowerment Promote Economic Development? *Journal of Economic Growth*, 24: 309–43.

Duflo, E., 2012. Women Empowerment and Economic Development. *Journal of Economic Literature*, 50(4): 1051–79.

Dupas, P., and Robinson, J., 2013a. Savings Constraints and Microenterprise Development: Evidence from a Field Experiment in Kenya. *American Economic Journal: Applied Economics*, 5: 163–92.

Dupas, P., and Robinson, J., 2013b. Why Don't the Poor Save More? Evidence from Health Savings Experiments. *American Economic Review*, 103: 1138–71.

Field, E., Pande, R., Rigol, N., Schaner, S., and Moore, C. T., 2017. On Her Account: Can Strengthening Women's Financial Control Boost Female Labor Supply? GLM|LIC Working Paper No. 32.

Fletcher, E. K., Pande, R., and Moore, C. T., 2018. Women and Work in India: Descriptive Evidence and a Review of Potential Policies. Harvard Kennedy School Faculty Research Working Paper No. RWP 18-004.

Gasparini, L., and Marchionni, M., 2015. Bridging Gender Gaps? The Rise and Deceleration of Female Labor Force Participation in Latin America: An Overview. CEDLAS Working Paper No. 0185.

Hansen, C. W., Jensen, P. S., and Skovsgaard, C. V., 2015. Modern Gender Roles and Agricultural History: The Neolithic Inheritance. *Journal of Economic Growth*, 20(4): 365–404.

Haushofer, J., and Shapiro, J., 2016. The Short-Term Impact of Unconditional Cash Transfers to the Poor: Experimental Evidence from Kenya. *Quarterly Journal of Economics*, 131: 1973–2042.

Hazarika, G., Jha, C., and Sarangi, S., 2015. The Role of Historical Resource Scarcity in Modern Gender Inequality. LSU Department of Economics Working Paper No. 2015-06.

Kan, S., and Aytimur, R. E., 2019. Labor Force Participation of Women Left behind in Tajikistan. *Oxford Development Studies*, 47: 1–28.

Klasen, S., 2017. What Explains Uneven Female Labor Force Participation Levels and Trends in Developing Countries? GLM|LIC Synthesis Paper No. 7.

Klasen, S., 2019. What Explains Uneven Female Labor Force Participation Levels and Trends in Developing Countries? *World Bank Research Observer*, 34: 161–97.

Klasen, S., and Pieters, J., 2015. What Explains the Stagnation of Female Labor Force Participation in Urban India? *World Bank Economic Review*, 29: 449–78.

Klasen, S., Tu Thi, N., Pieters, J., and Silva Santos, M., 2020. What Drives Female Labor Force Participation? Comparable Micro-Level Evidence from Eight Developing and Emerging Economies. *Journal of Development Studies*, 57(3): 417–42.

Kunieda, M., and Gauthier, A., 2007. Gender and Urban Transport: Fashionable and Affordable. Eschborn: Deutsche Gesellschaft für technische Zusammenarbeit.

Lokshin, M., and Glinskaya, E., 2009. The Effect of Male Migration on Employment Patterns of Women in Nepal. *World Bank Economic Review*, 23: 481–507.

OSCE (Organization for Security and Co-operation in Europe), 2012. Tajikistan, Social and Economic Inclusion of Women from Migrant Households: Assessment Report. Warsaw.

Priebe, J., 2011. Child Costs and the Causal Effect of Fertility on Female Labor Supply: An Investigation for Indonesia 1993–2008. Proceedings of the German Development Economics Conference, Berlin.

Rahman, R. I., and Islam, R., 2013. Female Labour Force Participation in Bangladesh: Trends, Drivers and Barriers. ILO Asia Pacific Working Paper. Available from: https://www.ilo.org/wcmsp5/groups/public/—asia/—ro-bangkok/—sro-new_delhi/documents/publication/wcms_250112.pdf.

Sajjad, F., Anjum, G. A., Field, E., and Vyborny, K., 2018. Overcoming Barriers to Women's Mobility: Improving Women's Access to Public Transport in Pakistan. GLM|LIC Policy Brief No. 24.

Santos Silva, M., Alexander, A. C., Klasen, S., Welzel, C., 2017. The Roots of Female Emancipation: From Perennial Cool Water via pre-Industrial Late Marriages to Postindustrial Gender Equality. University of Göttingen Courant Research Center Discussion Paper No. 241.

Schwegler-Rohmeis, W., Mummert, A., and Jarck, K., 2013. Labour Market and Employment Policy in the Kyrgyz Republic: Identifying Constraints and Options for Employment Development. Eschborn/Bishkek: Deutsche Gesellschaft für Internationale Zusammenarbeit.

Seneviratne, P., 2019. Married Women's Labor Supply and Economic Development: Evidence from Sri Lankan Household Data. *Review of Development Economics*, 23(2): 975–99.

Short, S. E., Chen, F., Entwisle, B., and Fengying, Z., 2002. Maternal Work and Child Care in China: A Multi-Method Analysis. *Population and Development Review*, 28: 31–57.

Subbarao, K., del Ninno, C., Andrews, C., and Rodríguez-Alas, C., 2013. Public Works as a Safety Net: Design, Evidence, and Implementation. Washington, DC: World Bank. Available from: https://openknowledge.worldbank.org/bitstream/handle/10986/11882/9780821389683.pdf?sequence=2&isAllowed=y.

UN Women Pakistan, 2018: Women's Safety Audit in Public Transport in Lahore. Lahore: Women Development Department, UN Women Pakistan, and Aurat Publication Information Service Foundation. Available from: https://asiapacific. unwomen.org/-/media/field%20office%20eseasia/docs/publications/2018/05/pk-women-safety%20audit-report.pdf?la=en&vs=5414.

Women in Cities International, 2011. Tackling Gender Exclusion: Experiences from the Gender Inclusive Cities Programme. Montréal. Available from: http://www.safedelhi.in/tackling-gender-exclusion-experiences-gender-inclusive-cities-programme.html-0.

World Bank, 2011. World Development Report 2012: Gender Equality and Development. Washington, DC.

9

Lessons about Labour Market Programmes and Policies

The research described in the previous chapters provides a number of lessons about what kinds of labour market programmes and policies can make a difference in low-income countries. Some of these lessons are about the difficulties that many well-intentioned programmes face when they are implemented. Vocational training programmes, for example, one of the most widely implemented labour market interventions, have a disappointing record when subjected to rigorous evaluation. Public Works Programmes (PWPs) have also had mixed results when rigorously evaluated. Other lessons are more positive, however. Some of the modifications and additions to traditional programmes that have been tested in GLM|LIC projects have had encouraging results. A number of the key lessons for programmes and policies, both positive and negative, are summarized in this chapter, which concludes with an outlook on some new GLM|LIC projects that have not been included in this book.

9.1 Skills Training Programmes

As discussed in Chapter 3, vocational training programmes and others designed to build job and entrepreneurial skills are among the most widely used labour market initiatives by governments and non-governmental organizations. They have also been among the most extensively evaluated labour market programmes, although many training programmes continue to run without rigorous evaluation. GLM|LIC's research projects have produced some important new lessons about training programmes, with both positive and negative results.

Two GLM|LIC projects in West Africa, one in Liberia (Blattman, Jamison, and Sheridan 2017) and one in Togo (Campos et al. 2017, 2018, 2020), both added important new evidence regarding the effectiveness of 'mindset training'. The Liberia project provided evidence that cognitive behaviour therapy addressing anger, impulsivity, depression, and other behaviours can help reduce anti-social and risky behaviours among a group of former street youth, ex-criminals, and ex-combatants. The project also showed a positive impact of combining CBT with

Labour Markets in Low-Income Countries. David Lam and Ahmed Elsayed, Oxford University Press.
© David Lam and Ahmed Elsayed (2022). DOI: 10.1093/oso/9780192897107.003.0009

unconditional cash grants, with the cash tending to reinforce, stabilize, and prolong the effects of CBT. The Togo project showed that personal initiative training focused on teaching skills such as self-starting, innovation, goal-setting, planning, and feedback cycles had significant effects on outcomes such as innovation and capital investment, with the entrepreneurs who received the training having 30% higher profits than a control group of entrepreneurs who received more traditional business training. The personal initiative training, which cost about 750 USD per participant, paid for itself within one year, given the increase in profits. The results of these two GLM|LIC projects suggest that training using techniques from behavioural psychology may be important additions to traditional skills training programmes.

Two GLM|LIC projects in the ready-made garment industry in Bangladesh looked at different approaches to skills training, with quite different outcomes and diverse lessons learned. A project on professional training for line managers (Macchiavello, Rabbani, and Woodruff 2015) had disappointing results, with low take-up rates that appeared to be due to the production pressures within the firms. The project demonstrates the challenges of trying to introduce within-firm training of production managers in a fast-paced competitive industry like the garment industry. Firms are reluctant to give critical line managers the time needed for training (which was only six days in this particular programme).

A project focused on training new entry-level garment workers (Shonchoy, Raihan, and Fujii 2017) had more positive results, with some lessons that reinforce those in other GLM|LIC projects. The project, based in a poor northern region of Bangladesh, found that training alone did not have substantial impact on the employment outcomes of programme participants, reinforcing the disappointing results found in many other skill training programmes. However, when the training was combined with a stipend to cover travel costs and foregone income, along with a paid internship in a factory, the programme had a substantial impact on employment. Six months after the programme, those with full treatment had employment rates of 67%, compared to 6% in the control group, with employment in the RMG industry accounting for almost all of the employment in the treated group. One lesson of these two skill training programmes in the garment industry is that targeting is important. Targeting unemployed residents of poor communities to give them new job opportunities was much more effective than targeting firms for a programme to train line managers. Another important lesson is that skill training alone may not have a significant impact on employment if it is not combined with direct assistance in finding jobs.

A GLM|LIC project with important lessons resulting from disappointing results was a programme designed to give entrepreneurial training to young women in the slums of Nairobi (Brudevold-Newman et al. 2017). As discussed in Chapter 8, the project tested the impact of a microfranchising programme designed by the International Rescue Committee. It also included an arm that received an unconditional cash grant. While both the microfranchising programme and the cash grant led to improvements in women's work and income in the first seven to ten months, there was no evidence of positive effects when the women were recontacted fourteen to twenty-two months after treatment. Women in both the microfranchising programme and the cash grant treatment continued to be more likely than the control group to be in self-employment, but this did not lead to higher incomes. One key lesson from this project may be that encouraging young women into self-employment may not be best for them in the long run, when compared to pursuing additional education or searching for jobs as employees rather than entrepreneurs. This project, like a number of GLM|LIC projects, also demonstrated the importance of long-term follow-up in programme evaluations. While short-term results looked encouraging, longer-term follow-up indicated that the impact had dissipated over time, with little evidence of long-term payoff to the participants in the programme.

9.2   Information, Matching, and Labour Market Clearing

As discussed in Chapter 2, many programmes have been developed to improve the efficiency of labour markets by reducing information barriers and helping firms and workers find each other. Several GLM|LIC projects have produced important lessons about what kinds of interventions can work to make labour markets work better.

A GLM|LIC project on job searching in Ethiopia found positive effects of low-cost programmes designed to help reduce search costs and improve matching, including a skills certification programme and transportation vouchers (Abebe et al. 2017, 2020). Although the programmes did not lead to increases in the probability of participants being employed, they did lead to increases in the probability that participants secured a stable permanent job or a job with a written contract. Importantly, the beneficial effects of the programmes were strongest for more disadvantaged groups, suggesting that the initiatives were helping to overcome the challenges faced by poor workers in financing job search. Taking advantage of the long-term follow-up used in many GLM|LIC projects, this project found that there continued to be significant positive effects of the skills certification workshop after four years, with participants in the programme having higher earnings, longer-lasting jobs, and jobs more closely matched to their skills, in comparison to the control group. The long-term increase in earnings exceeded the cost of the treatment. The effects of the transportation vouchers, on the other hand, dissipated over time, with no significant effects observable after four years.

Evidence for a positive role of programmes designed to improve labour market clearing was also provided by a GLM|LIC programme on job matching in Uganda (Bassi and Nansamba 2020). As discussed in Chapter 2, the programme included a matching component which gave randomly selected candidates job interviews with a firm, and a signalling component that provided certification of candidates' soft skills. The signalling component did not affect overall employment, but it did increase positive assortative matching in the job market, with higher-ability managers being more likely to hire workers who were certified to have high levels of soft skills. This led to an increase of 11% in the average earnings of those in the certification treatment relative to the control group. With a low cost of 19 USD per worker, the intervention was very cost effective. The certification did not benefit everyone, however, with those who had low scores tending to opt out of the matching component of the programme once they learned their scores.

Overall, it appears that these types of Active labour market policies can improve the kinds of jobs that job seekers are able to get, an important improvement in labour market outcomes. At the same time, these projects reinforced evidence from other studies that it is difficult to increase overall employment with these kinds of programmes.

Another worker–firm information asymmetry that may affect worker productivity is information about the relationship between wage differentials and productivity differentials. A GLM|LIC project on the impact of wage dispersion in rural India (Breza, Kaur, and Shamdasani 2018) found that workers responded negatively to higher wage dispersion in their work group when that wage dispersion could not be matched to observable productivity differentials. As discussed in Chapter 2, the project found that workers' productivity and attendance declined when they perceived that their pay was less than that of their peers. The policy implication is that firms should consider the impact of their wage structure and its transparency on productivity and absenteeism.

9.3 The Importance of Access and Mobility Constraints

Another important labour market friction comes in the form of limitations on mobility and access. Several GLM|LIC projects point to potential payoffs to programmes and policies that help address problems of access and mobility in labour markets. As noted above, the project providing transport vouchers in Ethiopia's capital Addis Ababa found that the vouchers improved the job search outcomes of recipients in the short term, although the impact dissipated over time.

In addition to transportation costs, other factors, including social norms, may create barriers to mobility, especially for women. As discussed in Chapter 8, a GLM|LIC project in rural Pakistan (Cheema et al. 2020) found that women were much more likely to take advantage of a training programme within their village than a programme outside its borders, even if the distance to the next village was only a few kilometres. The results indicated that crossing the village boundary was a critical barrier to women's participation. By varying the stipends given to women to participate in the training, the research team estimated that a monthly stipend equivalent to about half of monthly expenditures was required to overcome the boundary effect, netting out actual transport costs. This provides an important lesson about the extent to which social norms impose barriers on women's access to training and employment, and also reinforces the importance of taking such barriers into account in the design of training programmes.

Barriers to women's access to training and employment are not limited to rural areas. A GLM|LIC project in the city of Lahore in Pakistan (Sajjad et al. 2018) looks at the extent to which women are more likely to travel to work when they are provided with safe and reliable women-only transport. As discussed in Chapter 8, a demand assessment survey in the project found that women are 30% more likely than men to be dependent on public transport, the result of social norms discouraging use of motorbikes or bicycles, and that 25% of female respondents said they would be more likely to be active in the labour market if they had access to safe and reliable transportation.

9.4 Public Works Programmes

Another labour market intervention used heavily by governments around the world is Public Works Programmes. GLM|LIC projects produced some important lessons about these programmes. One of the most important lessons is that, like skills training programmes, PWPs do not always work. As discussed in Chapter 4, a GLM|LIC project analysing the Malawi Social Action Fund (MASAF) (Beegle, Galasso, and Goldberg 2017) found that the programme was not successful in meeting its goal of improving food security in the lean season, in spite of substantial investment in this large PWP. It appears that the programme's relatively low wage level and limited number of days of work provided to participants may have resulted in earnings being insufficient to have measurable impacts on food consumption. The results are a cautionary tale to those designing PWPs and point to the importance of rigorous programme evaluation.

A GLM|LIC project analysing India's famous Mahatma Gandhi National Rural Employment Guarantee Scheme (NREGS), the largest PWP in the world, provides lessons about ways in which adjustments to the implementation of PWPs can increase their effectiveness (Field et al. 2017). As discussed in Chapter 8, the research team partnered with the state of Madhya Pradesh to randomly introduce interventions into the way payments were made to women working in the NREGS programme. The interventions included helping women open bank accounts, providing basic financial literacy about the accounts, and direct linking of NREGS wages into their accounts. The project found that women's labour force participation was 12 percentage points higher when they received the combination of a bank account, financial information, and direct wage deposits. The results provide important lessons about the impact of women's financial empowerment on their labour force participation. Just as norms regarding women's physical mobility have been shown to limit their economic activity in both rural and urban Pakistan, norms that limit women's control over their earnings also appear to be playing a role in reducing women's labour force activity in South Asia.

9.5 Improving Rural Labour Markets

Since most workers in low-income countries continue to live in rural areas and work in agriculture, improvements in labour market outcomes require attention to the functioning of rural labour markets. Economists have long observed a wide range of imperfections and distortions in rural labour markets in LICs. Several GLM|LIC projects point to potential ways to improve the functioning of these markets and improve the lives of rural residents.

Development economists have become increasingly aware of the challenges posed by the seasonal harvest cycle in Africa. Farm households find it extremely difficult to maintain their consumption levels during the lean season preceding the harvest. This leads to food insecurity and potentially inefficient use of labour as households seek wage income from working off-farm rather than investing time in their own crop production.

A number of GLM|LIC projects have provided important new insights about this major policy challenge. The project analysing the MASAF, discussed above, had a strong focus on the problem of seasonal smoothing. The project introduced several variations in the timing of offering public works jobs as a way to help households smooth consumption and avoid food insecurity. As noted, the programme was unable to significantly reduce seasonal hunger or raise household incomes, perhaps because it did not provide a large enough increase in income. This has been an important new piece of evidence demonstrating just how challenging the seasonal smoothing problem is in poor rural areas.

A GLM|LIC project in Zambia provided some of the most important findings in this literature to date (Fink, Jack, and Masiye 2017, 2020). As discussed in Chapter 4, the project was designed to test whether credit constraints are responsible for the misallocation of labour from on-farm to off-farm work (*ganyu* labour) in the lean season. The results indicated a high demand for loans to help smooth consumption, a signal that some kind of market failure is preventing access to credit. Households with access to loans through the intervention increased their total farm output, increased labour used on the household's own farm, and reduced food insecurity. The results suggest that credit constraints do play an important role in the consumption volatility and related adjustments in household labour supply over the harvest cycle and point to potential interventions that may lead to improved ability to smooth consumption and more efficient allocation of labour.

Another project with important lessons about the seasonal harvest cycle and the labour market is an innovative programme in Rwanda using mobile phone records (Blumenstock and Donaldson 2017; Blumenstock 2018; Blumenstock, Chi, and Tan 2019). As discussed in Chapter 5, this project is important for its method-ological contributions as well as its policy implications, demonstrating how data science techniques can be used to convert millions of mobile phone records into valuable information about internal migration patterns and social networks. Com-bining the mobile phone data with data on weather, prices, and yields, the study shows that labour migration in Rwanda is highly responsive to seasonal variation in labour demand across regions. While many aspects of agricultural markets in Africa seem to be characterized by market distortions and ineffective market clear-ing, this novel evidence from Rwanda suggests that the short-term agricultural labour market is characterized by a high level of responsiveness and fluidity—factors that may be influenced by the availability of the very mobile phones that are providing these data.

At the same, time, other GLM|LIC projects point to significant imperfections in rural labour markets. As discussed in Chapter 4, a GLM|LIC project in Malawi identified substantial inefficiencies in the allocation of labour in agriculture in Malawi (Brummund and Merfeld 2016). The results showed that the returns to an extra hour worked are greater in non-farm activities than farm activities—an indication the households could increase their income if they shifted labour from farm to non-farm activity.

This evidence of inefficient allocation of labour in rural Africa is consistent with the results of another GLM|LIC project that analysed longitudinal household survey data from Ethiopia, Uganda, Tanzania, and Malawi (Dillon, Brummund, and Mwabu 2017, 2019). As discussed in Chapter 4, the project found evidence of inefficient labour allocations resulting from both too much labour and too lit-tle labour being used on farms, as evidenced by gaps between the productivity of farm and non-farm labour. In many regions there appears to be an excess sup-ply of labour, an indication of constrained labour demand. In Ethiopia, however, there is evidence of binding labour supply constraints, the result of financial mar-ket imperfections rather than a shortage of workers. One lesson is that rural labour markets continue to work imperfectly in rural Africa, with the result that labour is often misallocated as labour shortages and labour surpluses are created over the harvest cycle.

Child labour can be another manifestation of inefficient labour markets in ru-ral areas in low-income countries. As discussed in Chapter 7, there continue to be relatively high rates in a number of LICs, with levels of child labour falling sharply as GDP rises and economies shift their reliance away from agriculture. With high rates of return to schooling, and with negative effects of child labour on schooling outcomes, having children working rather than attending school tends to reduce economic growth. A GLM|LIC project in Ethiopia (Galdo, Dammert, and Abebaw 2018) found large increases in the use of child labour in the harvest season, a reflection of the seasonal labour shortages indicated in the other projects cited above.

The project also found evidence that the work activity of girls was often underreported, especially when males were doing the reporting. Another GLM|LIC project found evidence of other serious reporting issues in farm household labour data. A study in rural Tanzania investigated the extent to which reports of labour inputs on the farm are affected by the method of data collection (Arthi et al. 2017, 2018). As discussed in Chapter 4, the study compared standard recall questions, in which households are asked to recall labour inputs over the entire agricultural season, with a weekly face-to-face visit and a weekly phone interview. The results suggested that the amount of farm labour being used is often over-reported in standard recall interviews. This has important policy implications, since it implies that labour productivity in rural Africa may tend to be underestimated. These two projects point to the importance of collecting accurate data on time use and economic activity in the survey data that is essential for evidence-based policymaking.

9.6 The Importance of Rigorous Long-Term Evaluation

GLM|LIC set a high standard for rigorous evaluation of the programmes that were being analysed. Many governments, international agencies, and non-governmental organizations have come to see the importance of careful programme evaluation, and it is increasingly being built into the design of new programmes. The GLM|LIC projects that had disappointing results were in many ways as important as the projects that had more encouraging results. Not all labour market programmes are going to work, no matter how well motivated, how well designed, or how convinced the designers are of their value. The only way to find out what works and what does not is to subject programmes to rigorous evaluation. In many cases, this means using the kind of RCTs that were at the heart of many GLM|LIC projects.

An important feature of many of the GLM|LIC projects discussed in this book was the use of long-term follow-up studies that tracked results well beyond the end of the programme. This book has included a number of important cases in which the short-term impact of projects looked quite positive, only to find that the impact had disappeared when programme participants were followed up later. In other cases, the positive impact of the programmes was much longer-lasting, with the long-term follow-up providing valuable information about which interventions had the biggest impact. An important lesson of these GLM|LIC projects is that the best programme evaluations should run well past the end of the programmes, with long-term follow-up included from the outset in the design of programme evaluations.

9.7 Ongoing G²LM|LIC Research

This book covered only the first three phases of the GLM|LIC initiative. In 2018, the programme funded a fourth round of projects that are not presented in this book, with most of these projects still works in progress. The phase covers a wide range of topics and research ideas. The following subsections offer an insight into some of these projects.

9.7.1 Advancing Data Capacity for Policy Innovation

G²LM|LIC is funding the first wave of the Sudan Labour Market Panel Survey (SLMPS), the initial wave of a nationally representative longitudinal study of about 5,000 Sudanese households designed to improve data capacity for policy innovation and labour market growth in Sudan. The focus of the survey is to understand key relationships between labour market processes and outcomes and other dimensions of human development such as education, training, family formation and fertility, internal and international migration, gender equality and women's empowerment, enterprise development, housing acquisition, equality of opportunity, and intergenerational mobility. SLMPS is being conducted by the Economic Research Forum (ERF), in collaboration the Sudan Central Bureau of Statistics and the Ministry of Labour and Administrative Reform. ERF has made substantial investments in collecting Labour Market Panel Surveys (LMPS) in Egypt, Jordan, and Tunisia, and in making these data sets publicly available to researchers through the ERF open-access micro-data initiative (OAMDI) portal. The LMPS surveys are regarded as the most comprehensive publicly accessible and nationally representative micro-data source for understanding economic activity and human development in the three countries. A report published by the United Nations Development Project (UNDP) and International Labour Organisation in 2014 showed that among employed persons in Sudan, male or female, the vast majority are in vulnerable employment. Further, by average measures of lower-middle-income countries, Sudan is about 7 percentage points below average for female labour force participation and over 15 percentage points below average for female unemployment rates. The SLMPS project is designed to support policymakers in Sudan who require rich and reliable data to develop innovative policy solutions for resolving the nation's dilemmas of labour market stagnancy and gendered disparities in labour market outcomes.

9.7.2 Tackling Information Frictions through a Job Search Platform

Labour markets in LICs experience many frictions that impair efficient firm–worker matching, harming both workers and firms and potentially reducing employment. This project is conducting a series of interventions to alleviate search and matching frictions in the labour market in and around Lahore, Pakistan. The project builds on the GLM|LIC study on transport and labour markets in Lahore discussed in Chapter 8. In that project, the team successfully developed an innovative job search platform (Job Talash) to measure job search and labour supply. Job Talash generates rich, high-frequency data on both the supply and demand sides of the labour market. The new $G^2LM|LIC$ project uses Job Talash to randomly vary the frictions facing firms and job seekers and quantify the importance of these frictions. Specifically, the project uses a number of approaches:

(1) It assesses job seekers' skills and randomly varies the information firms observe to understand demand for specific skills.

(2) It randomly varies the probability of auditing job seekers' self-reported qualifications and whether firms know this probability in order to understand job seekers' incentives to misreport skills and how firms respond to the risk of misreporting.

(3) It randomizes the information job seekers observe about job and firm characteristics, such as wages and the gender composition of the workforce to understand labour supply responses to job prospects.

(4) It randomly varies the information workseekers have about firms' preferences over job seeker attributes to understand how sensitive workers' decisions to invest in short-term training and internships are to perceived demand for these attributes.

(5) It contrasts centralized firm–worker matching that provides explicit recommendations about matches to decentralized matching that facilitates communication between firms and workers but does not make recommendations.

The project measures the effects of alleviating information frictions on job search, job offers, employment, wages, turnover, and productivity.

9.7.3 Training, Financing, and Matching between Workers and Firms

This new $G^2LM|LIC$ project uses a cluster randomized control trial to test the role of credit constraint and information and local labour market friction on firm growth in the informal sector in Bangladesh. One arm of the intervention examines the impact of combining access to financial capital and business training, while another arm analyses the interaction with access to skilled workforce on firm growth. The project compares firms that are randomly selected across different treatments. The research will provide evidence on the relative importance of access to financial capital and entrepreneurship training, and local labour market friction. The project also evaluates workers' outcomes in the local labour market using the saturation of trained entrepreneurs in each market to estimate the effect on labour demand when the quality of labour supply is higher. The research team is collaborating with the non-profit organization BRAC to implement the RCT through one of its existing programmes in the light engineering (LE) sector of Bangladesh. The LE sector plays a vital role in employment generation and socio-economic development in Bangladesh. The findings will provide policy input for job training programmes and policies related to the development of small and micro enterprise.

9.7.4 Impacts of Microfranchising on Young Women's Occupational Choices

This project builds on an earlier GLM|LIC project, discussed in Chapter 8, which evaluated a multifaceted active labour market programme intended to encourage entrepreneurship—a microfranchising initiative that offered young women in some of Nairobi's poorest neighbourhoods a combination of vocational and life skills training, together with start-up capital and ongoing business mentoring. The project estimated the impacts of the microfranchising intervention through a randomized trial, comparing those assigned to the programme to both a pure control group and a third group that was offered an unrestricted cash grant, but no other training or support. Both the microfranchising programme and the cash grant shift women into entrepreneurship, increasing the proportion who are self-employed by approximately 10 percentage points. These occupational choice effects are very persistent: the estimated impact after eighteen months is no smaller than the impact observed after nine months. In the short term, both the microfranchising and grant treatments also increase income substantially; however, the impacts on income disappear in the second year after the programme as the women in the comparison group find jobs and 'catch up' to the treatment groups. The new G²LM|LIC project is conducting a long-term follow-up of the women in the study. Through this follow-up, the researchers hope to provide answers to three research questions: (1) Are the impacts on occupational choice persistent over the long-term? (2) If so, do incomes in the control group continue to grow faster than incomes in the treatment groups? Does treatment lead to significantly lower income in the long-term? (3) If so, why do women remain in self-employment?

9.7.5 Urban Density, Slum Redevelopment, and Labour Markets

Many of the world's poorest people live and work in dense informal settlements in Africa's growing megacities. The existence of these communities has important implications for the workings of labour markets. Urban labour markets provide access to formal jobs without long commutes, access to customers and markets, and access to social networks that support labour markets, particularly in informal economies. Each additional person who lives in the city centre not only gains from these urban labour markets but also contributes to these agglomeration economies, imposing positive externalities on others. But increasing density in informal settlements can also have negative externalities in terms of congestion, health, and poor infrastructure, which could limit the potential of cities to create high-productivity formal jobs. Estimating the scope and scale of these externalities is an empirical challenge. The government of Addis Ababa recently announced plans to redevelop large central areas of the Ethiopian megacity, which will lead to the relocation of 20,000 households out of informal settlements. This presents a unique opportunity to learn. Building on a sample of 30,000 geo-referenced surveys conducted in Addis before the announcement, the G^{2}LM|LIC project is estimating both the direct effect of being relocated out of a dense city centre, as well as the externalities of the relocations, on labour markets in the surrounding areas. The project draws on a variety of empirical techniques from labour and urban economics to estimate how these spillover effects extend over space. In doing so, the project will develop new methods for studying both treatment effects and externalities in dense urban labour markets, where they are not defined by geographically distinct clusters.

9.7.6 Entrepreneurship Education and Teacher Training

This G^{2}LM|LIC project examines how teacher training and support affects the delivery of Rwanda's revised secondary school entrepreneurship curriculum, introduced in 2016. For this purpose, a subset of schools was randomly selected for two years of intensive teacher training on the curriculum. A control group receives the curriculum only. The study measures the intervention's impact on student academic and economic outcomes. Baseline and two midline surveys have demonstrated compliance of the implementation and most importantly showed appreciable outcomes (for example, students in the treatment schools know more about entrepreneurship topics, budgeting skills, and product making—soap, envelopes—in comparison to their counterfactuals in control schools). An endline survey will measure outcomes three years after the project began. The results will inform government efforts to implement curriculum reforms in secondary schools across in Rwanda, but also in Africa in general.

9.7.7 Overcoming Constraints to Female Labour Force Entry

Using a randomized control trial this $G^2LM|LIC$ project will test the impact of motivational videos and information in overcoming constraints to female labour force entry. It focuses on female students enrolled in women-only colleges in urban Lahore, Pakistan. The project is motivated by a dearth of work on alleviating psychological constraints to female labour force participation and by its strong relevance in the Pakistani context. Existing literature has shown positive impacts of aspirational stories from peer groups on a wide range of behaviour, but there is no prior work that tests the effect of raising aspirations on labour force participation. Pakistan suffers from a chronically low female labour force participation rate despite very high enrolment of females at the graduate and undergraduate level and availability of a large number of jobs in general and for females in particular. The RCT involves three treatment arms: female students in the first treatment arm are shown a documentary of educated women who are employed and satisfied with their jobs; the second treatment involves a video and a facilitated exercise that provides information on job applications and existing job search sources; and those in the third treatment arm are shown both the motivational and information video. The project includes a placebo control group (comprised of female students from non-treated colleges) and a spillover control group (comprised of female students from treated colleges). The project tests the impact of the interventions on a series of input and effort outcomes such as whether the female creates a CV, applies for a job, reports a subjective improvement in aspirations, self-belief, and sense of control, as well as general effort exerted by the female to secure a job.

9.7.8 Women's Earnings, Household Division of Labour, and Women's Welfare Outcomes

With rising female educational achievements and labour force participation, Ghanaian women contribute significant resources to their households. According to economic models, as women increase their participation and earnings in the labour market, there should be a decrease in the amount of domestic work that they do. The issue of the division of domestic work has significant implications for women's welfare. Women who shoulder a large amount of childcare and domestic responsibilities often scale down their employment intensity, engage in less-challenging jobs and usually on a part-time basis. This implies that women continue to compete unequally with men in the labour market. Indeed, in Ghana, despite a 70% employment to population ratio among women, over half of these women are own-account workers, while almost a third are contributing family workers. The aim of the new $G^2LM|LIC$ project is to examine whether greater earnings by Ghanaian women is associated with increased household bargaining power, resulting in a changed division of housework between a woman and her husband. A more egalitarian division of domestic and childcare responsibilities between a couple may be indicative of women's greater bargaining and decision-making power in the household. Where increased earnings indeed lead to higher bargaining power by women within the household and a greater say in decisions relating to her reproductive health, women's health and welfare could be improved.

9.7.9 Seasonal Migration and Agricultural Labour Markets

As discussed in Chapter 4, in rural agrarian economies the period between planting and harvest is most often a lean season when labour demand and wages fall, and the price of staples rise. The landless poor reliant on agricultural work on others' farms are especially hard hit, and many millions of labourers and their families worldwide suffer from seasonal hunger. This problem is acute in rural South Asia, where the majority of the world's poor live, and where the majority of those poor are landless. A series of studies has generated strong evidence that in northern Bangladesh subsidies to encourage seasonal migration to more vibrant labour markets during this lean period successfully reduce seasonal hunger for migrants, are five to ten times as effective as traditional food aid programmes and have positive or null effects on other important outcomes. A new $G^2LM|LIC$ project expands this line of inquiry to rural Nepal, where the rural poor suffer from similar seasonal deprivation. The potential gains from migration are even larger in Nepal, because Nepalese workers have access to urban labour markets in India. A replication of the Bangladeshi programme in Nepal will have immediate policy impact because several donors and implementers who have supported a policy scale-up of the Bangladesh programme to reach hundreds of thousands of households stand ready to expand such a programme in Nepal if research results warrant it. The project also studies the effects of large-scale emigration on both labour demand and labour supply, helping to answer fundamental questions about rural–urban migration and structural transformation.

This brief insight into forthcoming $G^2LM|LIC$ research once more underscores the potential of development economics to provide useful lessons for policymakers and help low-income societies in the world's poorest regions to achieve welfare gains.

References

Abebe, G., Caria, S., Fafchamps, M., Falco, P., Franklin, S., and Quinn, S., 2017. Anonymity or Distance? Job Search and Labour Market Exclusion in a Growing African City. GLM|LIC Working Paper No. 34.

Abebe, G., Caria, S., Fafchamps, M., Falco, P., Franklin, S., and Quinn, S., 2020. Anonymity or Distance? Job Search and Labour Market Exclusion in a Growing African City. *The Review of Economic Studies*.

Arthi, V., Beegle, K., De Weerdt, J., and Palacios-López, A., 2017. Not Your Average Job: Measuring Farm Labor in Tanzania. GLM|LIC Policy Brief No. 6.

Arthi, V., Beegle, K., De Weerdt, J., and Palacios-López, A., 2018. Not Your Average Job: Measuring Farm Labor in Tanzania. *Journal of Development Economics*, 130: 160–72.

Bassi, V., and Nansamba A., 2020. Screening and Signaling Non-Cognitive Skills: Experimental Evidence from Uganda. USC-INET Research Paper No. 19–08.

Beegle, K., Galasso, E., and Goldberg, J., 2017. Direct and Indirect Effects of Malawi's Public Works Program on Food Security. *Journal of Development Economics*, 128: 1–23.

Blattman, C., Jamison, J. C., and Sheridan, M., 2017. Reducing Crime and Violence: Experimental Evidence from Cognitive Behavioral Therapy in Liberia. *American Economic Review*, 107: 1165–1206.

Blumenstock, J. E., 2018. Estimating Economic Characteristics with Phone Data. *AEA Papers and Proceedings*, 108: 72–6.

Blumenstock, J., and Donaldson, D., 2017. Using Mobile Phone Records to Estimate the Effect of Local Labor Demand Shocks on Internal Migration and Local Wages. GLM|LIC Policy Brief No. 11.

Blumenstock, J. E., Chi, G., and Tan, X., 2019. Migration and the Value of Social Networks. CEPR Discussion Paper No. 13611.

Breza, E., Kaur, S., and Shamdasani, Y., 2018. The Morale Effects of Pay Inequality. *The Quarterly Journal of Economics*, 133(2): 611–63.

Brudevold-Newman, A., Honorati, M., Jakiela, P., and Ozier, O., 2017. A Firm of One's Own: Experimental Evidence on Credit Constraints and Occupational Choice. GLM|LIC Working Paper No. 33.

Brummund, P., and Merfeld, J. D., 2016. Allocative Efficiency of Non-Farm Enterprises in Agricultural Households: Evidence from Malawi. GLM|LIC Working Paper No. 33.

Campos, F., Frese, M., Goldstein, M., Iacovone, L., Johnson, H. C., McKenzie, D., and Mensmann, M., 2017. Teaching Personal Initiative Beats Traditional Training in Boosting Small Business in West Africa. *Science*, 357(6357): 1287–90.

Campos, F., Frese, M., Goldstein, M., Iacovone, L., Johnson, H. C., McKenzie, D., and Mensmann, M., 2018. Is Personal Initiative Training a Substitute or Complement to the Existing Human Capital of Women? Results from a Randomized Trial in Togo. *American Economic Association Papers and Proceedings*, 108: 256–61.

Campos, F., Frese, M., Goldstein, M., Iacovone, L., Johnson, H. C., McKenzie, D., and Mensmann, M., 2020. Personal Initiative Training Leads to Remarkable Growth of Women-Owned Small Businesses in Togo. $G^2LM|LIC$ Policy Brief No. 32.

Cheema, A., Khwaja, A. I., Naseer, M. F., and Shapiro, J. N., 2020. Glass Walls: Experimental Evidence on Access Constraints Faced by Women. Working Paper. Available from: https://scholar.princeton.edu/sites/default/files/jns/files/ckns_glass_walls_2020-10-08.pdf.

Dillon, B., Brummund, P., and Mwabu, G., 2017. How Complete Are Labor Markets in East Africa? Evidence from Panel Data in Four Countries. GLM|LIC Working Paper No. 31.

Dillon, B., Brummund, P., and Mwabu, G. 2019. Asymmetric Non-Separation and Rural Labor Markets. *Journal of Development Economics*, 139: 78–96.

Field, E., Pande, R., Rigol, N., Schaner, S., and Moore, C. T., 2017. On Her Account: Can Strengthening Women's Financial Control Boost Female Labor Supply? GLM|LIC Working Paper No. 32.

Fink, G., Jack, K., and Masiye, F., 2017. The Impact of Seasonal Food and Cash Loans on Small-Scale Farmers in Zambia. GLM|LIC Policy Brief No. 3.

Fink, G., Jack, B. K., and Masiye, F., 2020. Seasonal Liquidity, Rural Labor Markets and Agricultural Production. *American Economic Review*, 110(11): 3351–92.

Galdo, J., Dammert, A. C., and Abebaw, D., 2018. Child Labor Measurement in Agricultural Households: Seasonality, Proxy Respondent and Gender Information Gaps in Ethiopia. GLM|LIC Working Paper No. 43.

Macchiavello, R., Rabbani, A., and Woodruff, C., 2015. The Market for Training Services: A Demand Experiment with Bangladeshi Garment Factories. *American Economic Review*, 105: 300–4.

Sajjad, F., Anjum, G. A., Field, E., and Vyborn K., 2018. Overcoming Barriers to Women's Mobility: Improving Women's Access to Public Transport in Pakistan. GLM|LIC Policy Brief No. 24.

Shonchoy, A. S., Raihan, S., and Fujii, T., 2017. Reducing Extreme Poverty through Skill Training for Industry Job Placement. GLM|LIC Policy Brief No 9.

Index

Note: Tables and figures are indicated by an italic *t* and *f* following the page number.